Nine American Film Critics

EDWARD MURRAY

James Agee
Robert Warshow
Andrew Sarris
Parker Tyler
John Simon
Pauline Kael
Stanley Kauffmann
Vernon Young
Dwight Macdonald

NINE AMERICAN FILM CRITICS

NINE AMERICAN
FILM CRITICS

A STUDY OF THEORY
AND PRACTICE

EDWARD MURRAY

Frederick Ungar Publishing Co.
New York

For my daughter, Jeanette

CONTENTS

My dear anonymous letter writers, if you think it so easy to be a critic, so difficult to be a poet or a painter or film experimenter, may I suggest you try both? You may discover why there are so few critics, so many poets.

PAULINE KAEL

INTRODUCTION

The subject matter of this book is the work of nine representative American film critics. As its subtitle indicates, it is concerned with both theory (critical theory, film theory, aesthetic theory) and practice (applied criticism, methodology, specific evaluations). My primary aim is to define, wherever possible, the general principles guiding each critic; to observe how those principles function in terms of practical criticism; and to evaluate the strengths and weaknesses of each critic in the light of his own, as well as other, criteria.

Except for several essays by Dwight Macdonald, all the work considered in this study was written after 1940. This fact does not mean that American film criticism before the Second World War is barren of interest. People like Vachel Lindsay, Robert E. Sherwood, Harry Alan Potamkin, James Shelley Hamilton, Gilbert Seldes, Lincoln Kirstein, William Troy, Hilda Doolittle, Louise Bogan, Edmund Wilson, Otis Ferguson, Paul Goodman, Clifton Fadiman, and Mark Van Doren—all of whom wrote film criticism at one time or another—are scarcely nonentities. Nevertheless, important changes have occurred in the last thirty years, particularly in the last fifteen years, to justify the concentration in this book on later critics, some of whom have acquired near-celebrity status. Before James Agee no American film critic was respected *as a film critic*. The reason for this is simple: film was not, until the late fifties, widely respected as one of the arts in America. Significantly enough, Agee's criticism was not collected in book form until 1958, three years after his death. By that time, what Macdonald refers to as the later, or renaissance, sound period in film history had already begun.

Actually, that renaissance could be said to have started, at least in Italy, in 1945, the year of Roberto Rossellini's *Open City*. Neorealist films of the forties like *Paisan*, *Shoeshine*, and *The Bicycle Thief* caught the attention of the world. It was not until the fifties, however, that a real upsurge of talent ushered in what can rightly be called a cinematic renaissance. Federico Fellini, Akira Kurosawa, Ingmar Bergman, Michelangelo Antonioni, François Truffaut, Alain Resnais, Jean-Luc Godard—all made their international reputations in the fifties and after; even established directors like Alfred Hitchcock and Luis Buñuel seemed to enjoy a creative rebirth during this period. Although not necessarily superior to the films of D. W. Griffith, Sergei Eisenstein, V. I. Pudovkin, F. W. Murnau, and Jean Renoir, the work of the renaissance figures does tend to be more sophisticated and complex, both in form and content.

In meeting the challenge of contemporary films, critics have developed a more sophisticated and more complex approach to their subject matter. The average reviewer of the past could satisfy his readers with a recounting of a film's plot and an unsupported "I liked it" or "I didn't like it" evaluation. This approach is still in use, (sometimes even by the critics examined in this book), but the practice has become increasingly untenable. The audience for motion pictures is more educated now than in the past. It has been estimated that prior to grammar school a young person spends 3,500 hours before the television screen, and that by the time he graduates from high school a typical teenager has seen 500 movies. Film is studied at the elementary, intermediate, and college level. From personal experience in teaching film I would say that though the level of cinematic literacy of young people is not quite as high as some media enthusiasts would have us believe, it is nevertheless significantly higher than in the past. Consequently, more and more is expected of the film critic.

Although not a formal history, this book is to a large extent a record of how well American film critics have responded to the renaissance. I say "to a large extent" because a number of the critics dealt with here have also been concerned with reevaluating both the classics of the silent period and the Hollywood sound films of the thirties and forties.

Some readers, I expect, will resist a book dedicated to criticism of criticism—thus unwittingly indulging in criticism of criticism of criticism. However, as Stanley Kauffmann makes clear in his anthology *American Film Criticism*, there is really nothing new about criticism of criticism, the practice having been introduced in this country at least as early as 1909. Far from impairing the mature viewer's response to film, an increased knowledge of the medium should enhance his enjoyment.

Nearly a hundred years ago, in "The Art of Fiction," Henry James defended the "loss of innocence" surrounding the novel as follows: "Art lives upon discussion, upon experiment, upon curiosity, upon variety of attempt, upon the exchange of views and the comparison of standpoints; and there is a presumption that those times when no one has anything particular to say about it, and has no reason to give for practice or preference, though they may be times of honor, are not times of development—are times, possibly, even a little of dullness. The successful application of any art is a delightful spectacle, but the theory too is interesting; and though there is a great deal of the latter without the former, I suspect there has never been a genuine success that has not had a latent core of conviction. Discussion, suggestion, formulation, these things are fertilizing when they are frank and sincere." James's words can be applied to the present subject: Film "lives upon discussion"; and in that discussion critical theory and practice—and the criticism of that theory and practice—have a vital and constructive role to play.

It is my hope that this book will help the reader to see what contemporary American film criticism has been and, more important, what it might become; and that it will also sharpen his perception and deepen his appreciation of the film medium itself.

CHAPTER ONE

James Agee, "Amateur Critic"

There are a good many people who honestly enjoy movies, know the difference between good work and bad, and care a great deal about the difference.
—JAMES AGEE

1

James Agee, who died in 1955 at the age of forty-six, was the first American film critic to aquire a reputation. A versatile artist, Agee published during his lifetime a volume of poems, *Permit Me Voyage* (1934); a documentary study of sharecroppers in the South, *Let Us Now Praise Famous Men* (1941); and a novel, *The Morning Watch* (1951). Agee's posthumous publications include: *A Death in the Family* (1957), a novel which won the Pulitzer Prize; *Agee on Film: Reviews and Comments* (1958); *Agee on Film: Five Film Scripts* (1960); *The Collected Poems* (1968); and *The Collected Short Prose of James Agee* (1969).

From 1941 to 1948 Agee was the movie critic for *Time*, and from 1942 to 1948 he also wrote criticism for *The Nation*. *Agee on Film: Reviews and Comments* contains selections from *Time*, all of the work from *The Nation*, two articles from *Life*, one from *Sight and Sound*, and one from *The Partisan Review*. The anonymous editor of the collection wisely allowed the pieces from *The Nation* to make up 300 of the roughly 400 pages, since, with few exceptions, the *Time* reviews are poor by comparison. As Dwight Macdonald, Agee's friend and fellow critic, puts it

5

(exaggerating only slightly), the work from *The Nation* is "superior in every way: is more serious and more witty; more sensible and more imaginative; more free and more disciplined. The stuff he ground out for the *Time* mill . . . is clever hack work, rhetorically shrill but muted as to his own thought: a gaudy, tightly confining uniform like a bandleader's whose jaunty vulgarity even Agee, with all his squirmings, couldn't make fit" (*Dwight Macdonald on Movies*).

When Agee took over his post at *The Nation*, he began by describing to readers his "condition as a would-be critic":

> I suspect that I am, far more than not, in your own situation: deeply interested in moving pictures, considerably experienced from childhood on in watching them and thinking and talking about them, and totally, or almost totally, without experience or even much second-hand knowledge of how they are made. If I am broadly right in this assumption, we start on the same ground, and under the same handicaps, and I qualify to be here, if at all, only by two means. It is my business to conduct one end of a conversation, as an amateur critic among amateur critics. And I will be of use and of interest only in so far as my amateur judgment is sound, stimulating or illuminating.

Agee then went on to add that being an "amateur" had certain advantages, in that it allowed him to focus on the quality of the film itself and not on the complex difficulties—technical and financial—which beset the film-maker and which might distract the professional critic from his proper function, namely, to render judgment on the finished product. "As an amateur, then," Agee concluded, "I must as well as I can simultaneously recognize my own ignorance and feel no apology for what my eyes tell me as I watch any given screen, where the proof is caught irrelevant to excuse, and available in proportion to the eye which sees it, and the mind which uses it."

If Agee reviewed a film which excited him in some way— either because of what the director had achieved or, with more awareness, might have achieved—he would describe its action, explain its technique, comment on its form. As a rule, however, Agee did not speak in analytical terms at his end of the "conversation," in spite of his statement, written on the occasion cited above, that the critic's job is "the analysis of a film." Sometimes Agee wrote, in part, as an historical critic (see his essay on Griffith); at other times he wrote as a sociological critic (as, to a large extent, in his discussion of Chaplin's *Monsieur Verdoux*). Always, he approached the screen in a highly personal, subjective way ("Since nothing is more repugnant to me than the pseudo-religious, I went to *The Song of Bernadette* gritting my teeth against my advance loathing"). For the most part, Agee's approach can be described as *impressionistic* ("Watching *The White Cliffs of Dover* is like drinking cup after cup of tepid orange pekoe at a rained-out garden party staged by some deep-provincial local of the English-speaking Union"); *moral* ("The elementary beginning of true reason, that is, of reason which involves not merely the forebrain but the entire being," he notes in beginning a review of *Shoeshine*, "resides, I should think, in the ability to recognize oneself, and others, primarily as human beings, and to recognize the ultimate absoluteness of responsibility of each human being"); and *evaluative* ("The best picture I saw this year was *The Gold Rush*" . . . "*The Postman Always Rings Twice* is mainly a terrible misfortune from start to finish" . . . *Tender Comrade* "is one of the god-damnedest things ever seen").

The closest Agee ever came to putting his theory of film into one sentence appears in a review, mainly negative, of Clarence Brown's *National Velvet*: "The makers of the film had an all but ideal movie: a nominally very simple story, expressing itself abundantly in visual and active terms, which inclosed and might have illuminated almost endless recessions and inter-reverberations of emotion and meaning into religious and sexual psychology and into naturalistic legend." If the words "sensitive" and "humane" appear repeatedly in descriptions of Agee as a critic, the words "realism" and "poetry" show up again and again in Agee's own writing. Since commentators have frequently misunderstood and oversimplified the meaning of these key terms, they are worth examining in detail.

2

Agee felt that the basic fault of "nearly all the good writing of this century" derived from the conflict between "artifice and nature." And that Agee favored "nature"—or "realism"—is manifest. But what, exactly, did he intend by such terms? Sometimes "realism"—"the essence of most good cinema"—seems to mean "unaltered." Hence Agee's persistent fondness for newsreels and documentaries about the war, which, even at "their weakest," have "things to show which no nonrecord war films, not even the greatest that might be made, could ever hope to show." Agee's bias in favor of "realism" shows in his criticism of acting. André Malraux's film *Man's Hope*, for example, "merely emphasizes, even more sharply than most of its kind, the superiority of amateurs over professionals for a large and crucially hopeful part of achievement and possibility in films." Agee's fondness for "realism" also explains, in part, his appreciation of Hitchcock (*Shadow of a Doubt* gives "some real attention to what places and people really look like") and his relative lack of appreciation for the "black-chenille-and-rhinestones manner" of Welles (*"Voice in the Wind* . . . is being advertised as 'a strange new kind of moving picture,' and that makes me realize, as the excitement over the 'originality' of *Citizen Kane* used to, that already I belong to a grizzling generation").

Now, if this were all Agee meant by "realism"—that is, factual authenticity, nonprofessional acting, location shooting, a plain cinematic style—then he could easily be dismissed as a shallow, naive critic. "Realism," however, has another meaning in Agee's thought. Macdonald quotes from a 1927 letter in which Agee tells him: "the screen needn't stop at realism. The moving camera can catch the beauty of swaying, blending lights and shadows, and by its own movement impart to it as definite a rhythm as poetry or music ever had." These remarks suggest that "realism" and "poetry" belong in separate categories. One gets a more ambiguous impression in reading Agee's comments on Griffith: "He was capable of realism that has never been beaten and he might, if he had been able to appreciate his powers as a realist, have found therein his growth and salvation. But he seems to have been a realist only by accident, hit-and-run; essentially, he was a poet. He doesn't appear ever to have realized one of the richest promises that movies hold, as the perfect medium for realism raised to the level of high poetry."

Agee's last sentence might be interpreted to mean either that "realism" can move beyond itself into "poetry," or that there is a "high" form of "realism" which is also "high poetry." The latter meaning of "realism" is developed in Agee's review of *Farrebique*, a French film about a year in the life of a farm family: director Georges Rouquier "realizes that, scrupulously handled, the camera can do what nothing else in the world can do: can record unaltered reality; and can be made also to perceive, record, and communicate, in full unaltered power, the peculiar kinds of poetic vitality which blaze in every real thing and which are in great degree, inevitably and properly, lost to every other kind of artist except the camera artist . . . [Rouquier] is infinitely more than a mere documentor . . . his poetic intelligence is profound, pure, and rigorous."

Although Agee seems to favor, in his early reviews, the documentary over the fiction film, he arrives at an opposite position in his discussion of Roberto Rossellini's *Open City* and Pat Jackson's *The Raider*: "The films I most eagerly look forward to will not be documentaries but works of pure fiction, played against, and into, and in collaboration with unrehearsed and uninvented reality." His bias for "uninvented reality" leads Agee to remark in a review of *To Have and Have Not* that the "better film . . . gets along on a mere thin excuse for a story." But he also observes, as previously noted, that the "ideal movie" tells a *"nominally* very simple story" (italics mine). Agee doesn't praise *Farrebique*, as Pauline Kael would have it in *Going Steady*, just because it is "simple," "direct," and "unaffected." It is the *combination* of surface and depth, "plainness" and "device," which interests him. Behind the apparent ("nominal") simplicity of *Farrebique* lies "poetry" . . . But what, in the context of a motion picture, does "poetry" mean? An answer to that question emerges only after a close reading of numerous Agee reviews.

Agee lauds the structure of *Man's Hope* because Malraux does not keep his film "tidily to one nicely shaped and euphonious event at a time," and because he lets "things and movements into his frame which have nothing to do with the central action or which enhance it only queerly and surprisingly." De Sica's *Shoeshine* is praised because "everyone [in it] bulges with a depth and complexity of realness that is immeasurably beyond the hope of mere naturalism; because everybody is perceived as a complete human being, one feels at every moment that almost anything could happen, and that the reasons why any given thing happens are exceedingly complex and constantly shifting their weight." The naturalistic reproduction of city streets in *A Tree Grows in Brooklyn* is a "dead" approach "compared with . . . the enormous advantages of submerging your actors in the real thing, full of its irreducible present tense and its unpredictable proliferations of energy and beauty." As Agee's comments on *The Fugitive* make clear, he was not a simple-minded realist who rejected symbolism and allegory; he expected metaphors and patterns of meaning, however, to "bloom from and exalt reality," not to be "imposed on and denature reality." Jean Vigo's *Zéro de Conduite*—which Agee calls "one of the few great movie poems" —is praised because its director "gets deeper inside his characters than most people have tried to on film, is not worried about transitions between objective, subjective, fantastic, and subconscious reality, and mixes as many styles and camera tricks, as abruptly, as he sees fit . . . I assume that he intended . . . to insist that these several levels of reality are equal in value, and interpenetrative; and I would accept this aesthetically for its enrichment of poetic perception, metaphor, and device, even if I rejected it intellectually."

(One of Agee's recurrent complaints is that most film-makers confine their approach to the objective world, a strategy which theorists too often correlate with "realism." *The Story of G.I. Joe* is criticized by Agee because it fails to give any sense of combat as it is experienced from the individual's point of view. *The Lost Weekend* is faulted because neither the camera nor the sound track are taken "inside the mind." But Hitchcock is praised because—rare among living directors—he uses, and uses expertly, the subjective camera. It is interesting to note that Agee's script for *The Bride Comes to Yellow Sky* calls for a shot from the viewpoint of the drunken Scratchy Wilson; and that in his *Noa Noa* script, Agee moves the action in and out of Gauguin's mind, dissolving space and time through wish-fulfillment, daydreams, and sleeping dreams. In 1943 Agee could say: "Color is very nice for costume pieces and musical comedies, and has a great aesthetic future in films, but it still gets fatally in the way of any serious imitation of reality." But a year later, in a review of *With the Marines at Tarawa*, he remarks: "It interests me that color, so harmless to musical fantasies and so generally fatal to films which deal, even nominally, with peacetime realism, adds a lot to the power and immediacy of these war scenes." *Noa Noa* ends with Gauguin gradually losing his sight. Like the rest of the script, the objective scenes leading up to the conclusion are in color; but in order to signal the protagonist's increasing visual disturbance—and in order to make the viewer share more closely in the painter's agony—Agee calls for subjective shots: "tormenting waverings between full color, part-color, and black-and-white.")

"Realism," then, appears to have had two meanings for Agee; accordingly, the films he describes as "realistic" fall into two classes. In one class—a lower class—are the works of the "mere documentor" and works of "mere naturalism." Generally, Agee seems to prefer this form of "realism" to self-consciously "arty" pictures. He could say, however, that "unlike many films of high quality," John Huston's *The Treasure of the Sierra Madre* "does not wear its art on its sleeve"; so "artifice" did not necessarily prevent a film from achieving a "high quality." All the same, "the difficult question of the proper and the incestuous relationship, in any work of art or entertainment, between nature and artifice" (see his discussion of *The Ox-Bow Incident*) created "a troubling of intuition" in him. It is precisely Agee's intuitive, impressionistic approach which makes it so difficult to know what, on some occasions, he is talking about. "Artifice" seems to be a quality that is imposed on "nature" or "reality"—it is showy, pretentious, fake. "Art" (the highest art, at any rate) rises above not only artifice but also above naturalism and the documentary, without thereby ceasing to be "realistic." This second class of "realism" equals a form of "high poetry." The film-maker here will use "devices" (metaphor, symbolism, allegory), but he will use them in a "natural" way, so that art conceals art, so that meaning appears to spring "naturally" from the objects photographed. "Poetry" on the screen results from the film-maker's revelation of the "vital essence" residing in "every real thing." In terms of film structure, characterization, and theme, "poetry" seems to mean "energy," "multiplicity," "depth," "indeterminacy," "fullness of being," and "complexity." Ironically, although Agee was forever speaking of "realism," there is a counter word that could be used to describe certain features of his film aesthetic. That word is, of course, "romantic."

3

In a review of Carl Dreyer's *Day of Wrath*, Agee observes: "there is only one rule for movies that I finally care about: that the film interest the eyes, and do its job through the eyes. Few movie-makers do that, few even of those who are generally well-esteemed." Not surprisingly, Agee's insistence on the primacy of the eye in the film experience is linked to the values of "realism": for (as he points out in a passage on *Tennessee Johnson*) it is the film-maker's task to record "living—rather than imitative—visual, aural, and psychological authenticity, and the paralyzing electric energy of the present tense." There was room in Agee's aesthetic for the montage construction of Eisenstein, the moving camera of Murnau, and the stationary photography of Chaplin.

If at times Agee seems to overrate the silent film ("To put it unkindly," he remarks in "Comedy's Greatest Era," "the only thing wrong with screen comedy today is that it takes place on a screen which talks"); and if he frequently seems to undervalue the contribution sound has made to the medium (he says in a review of *Prelude to War* that the "greatest service" words can do for the screen is "withdrawal"), the explanation is simple: he believed that American films of the thirties and forties tended to be "word-dominated." Discussing *Monsieur Verdoux*, he asserts that "virtually nothing has been done with sound" since its coming, and that contemporary directors (presumably American *and* European) are still using techniques worked out by the great Russian and German innovators of the silent film era. Evidently Agee felt that there was a place for speech in film, but that the right relation between image and word had not yet been developed. It doesn't appear, then, that Agee wanted characters in films to stop talking—he just didn't want them to talk so much. Nonetheless, Agee overstates the case against the sound film of the thirties and forties. One thinks of American gangster movies like *Little Caesar*, *Public Enemy*, and *Scarface*—wherein dialogue is deftly integrated with the visual action—and of pictures by René Clair and Hitchcock, both of whom, oddly enough, Agee admired, and both of whom used the sound track imaginatively.

With his background in literature, and with his understanding of film, Agee should have been an excellent critic of adaptations. Actually, his work in this area remains uneven—partly, but only partly—because of the split in his duties between *Time* and *The Nation*. Take, for example, his two reviews of Laurence Olivier's *Henry V*.

Agee knew, as he points out in a passage on Griffith, "that while a theater audience listened a movie audience watched"; consequently, he had to approach a film version of any Shakespeare play with skepticism. His piece in *The Nation* begins on a negative note. Olivier's film is not a masterpiece: "it is a re-creation of an old dramatic poem, not the creation of a new one." Furthermore, *Henry V* is not the best play Shakespeare ever wrote, though it remains the one most adaptable to the screen. "No attempt is made to develop a movie style which might in poetic energy and originality work as a cinematic counterpart to the verse," he continues. "The idea is, rather, to make everything on the screen and sound track serve the verse, as clearly and well and unobtrusively as possible. Within this relatively modest and, I think, very wise and admirable intention, moreover, the success is not complete." Agee then goes on to specify what he finds wrong with the film: the first half of the structure is "almost as fitful and choppy as the play"; some of the comedy in the original has not worn well; and then there is the clash—how could Agee ignore it?—between nature and artifice. The trouble Agee had with this problem is very much in evidence here. First he says: "I very greatly like the anti-naturalistic, two-and-a-half-dimensional effect that is got by obtunding shallow perspectives in painted drops"; but then he immediately adds: "The night sequence in the English camp might, I think, have been still better if it had taken more of its country-night poetic atmosphere straight from nature, and had wholly avoided the smell and look of a good, semi-naturalistic studio set." He further argues that "sharp naturalism" would have made the battle scene more "poetic." *Henry V* on film has beauty and charm; however, it remains a photographed stage play—skillfully done, but derivative. In time, Agee ventures, he might come to think even less highly of the adaptation.

Six months later, writing again in *The Nation*, Agee remarks in passing that Olivier would have been better advised to forget about a film version of Shakespeare and to aim instead at "great movie poetry, deliberately or intuitively undertaken from scratch, without benefit of hindrance of a classic."

In view of these remarks, it comes as a shock to read the opening sentence of Agee's piece on *Henry V* in *Time*: "The movies have produced one of their rare great works of art!" Nearly seven pages are devoted to lavish praise of Olivier's production, which more than once is credited with having "improved" on Shakespeare. "Almost continuously," Agee says of the film, "it invests the art of Shakespeare—and the art of cinema as well—with a new spaciousness, a new nobility, a new radiance." Even the anti-naturalistic approach is cited with unreserved approval; indeed, the "result is a new cinema style." Only once does Agee sound faintly like the critic who wrote the review in *The Nation*: "*Henry V* is one of the great experiences in the history of motion pictures. It is not, to be sure, the greatest," he adds; "the creation of new dramatic poetry is more important than the re-creation of old." Then the rhapsody begins again: "But *Henry V* is a major achievement—this perfect marriage of great dramatic poetry with the greatest contemporary medium for expressing it." And so on.

Agee's review of *Hamlet* in *Time* (he did not review the film in

the ethics seems beefy, over-comfortable, love-your-fellow-mannish, and in general rather uninteresting."

Agee's emphasis on the value of "sincerity" was tied to his belief in the importance of "love." A "movie, like any other work of art, must be made for love," he insists. *Sunset Boulevard* misses greatness because of its "coldness." In his discussion of *The Raider*, he observes: "Few Americans either behind or in front of our cameras give evidence of any recognition or respect for themselves or one another as human beings." Chaplin is supreme among film comedians because "he worked most deeply and most shrewdly within a realization of what a human being is, and is up against." In his review of *Shoeshine*, Agee calls the attitude of mind and heart in De Sica's film "humanistic"—which is, of course, the very word to describe Agee's own philosophy.

But "sincerity" and "love," Agee knew, were not enough. Griffith was "all heart," and this sometimes led him into "ruinous excesses"; however, the man who directed *The Birth of a Nation* and *Intolerance* also possessed "talent or genius as an inventor and artist." Lloyd Bacon's *Sunday Dinner for a Soldier* fails in spite of the fact that "most of the people who worked on the show appear to have loved it, believed in it, and had great hopes for its originality and worthiness." All the same, "sincerity" and "love" added to talent can take a film-maker farther along the road to artistic success than talent alone—as was the case, Agee believed, with *Shoeshine* and *To Live in Peace*, both of which "essentially were made from the heart, and so touched the heart."

It is easy to dismiss Agee's remarks on "sincerity" as further evidence of his "romantic" aesthetic. Pure analytical critics believe that only the work of art is important; the feelings, emotions, and motives of the artist remain irrelevant. The critical act of judging a film, they argue, should not be confused with the art of making a film. In their well-known essay, "The Intentional Fallacy," W. K. Wimsatt, Jr. and M. C. Beardsley remark: "It would be convenient if the passwords of the intentional school, 'sincerity,' 'fidelity,' 'spontaneity,' 'authenticity,' 'genuineness,' 'originality,' could be equated with terms of analysis such as 'integrity,' 'relevance,' 'unity,' 'function'; with 'maturity,' 'subtlety,' and 'adequacy,' and other more precise axiological terms—in

short, if 'expression' always meant aesthetic communication. But
this is not so."

The argument just quoted is not unassailable. Why, for instance, is "subtlety" an axiological term but not "originality"? Furthermore, some theorists would argue that "sincerity" refers not
only to the relationship between the artist's intentions and the
completed work of art, but also to the relationship of parts within
the work itself. In the latter sense, "sincerity" means the avoidance of effects which contradict the specific conventions established by the work (like the shots of the "phonily gnarled lynch-
ing tree" in *The Ox-Bow Incident,* a film in which, according to
Agee, "artifice and nature got jammed"); "sincerity" means the
avoidance of rewards to virtue and punishments to vice when the
"world" created by the film artist fails to vindicate such poetic
justice (an avoidance, for example, of what Agee calls "sugar-tit
treatments of death and its consequences"); "sincerity" means
the avoidance of actions which are unconvincing in their motivation—such as melodramatic action—and the avoidance of actions
which beg for unearned emotions—such as sentimental action
(Agee observes, in a piece on Preston Sturges, that the good film
"never fakes or dodges a motive, a character, an emotion, or an
idea").

Is Agee lacking in "objectivity" as a critic when he praises
"love" and espouses "humanism"? It would probably be futile to
argue the positive value of these factors with one who thinks it
irrelevant to evaluation whether the people on the screen—as
well as the people watching it—are treated with love and respect
(though not necessarily uncritically), or with hatred and contempt. Are the beliefs of the artist, as they are embodied in his
art, unimportant to the critical act? "Imagine a beautifully written tragedy with a convinced Nazi SS man as hero, his tragic
error consisting of a temporary, and fatal, toying with bourgeois
democratic ideals," Wayne C. Booth writes in *The Rhetoric of
Fiction.* "Is there any one of us, regardless of our commitment to
objectivity, who could seriously claim that agreement or disagreement with the author's ideas in such a work would have
nothing to do with our accepting or rejecting his art?" Booth

poses here one of the most difficult problems with which a critic must contend.

If a film was implicitly "humanistic"—that is, if the story unfolded with "sincerity," "love," and "respect for man"—Agee's aesthetic response could be favorable, even though the film's explicit theme ran counter to his own philosophical assumptions. Consider his review of *Man's Hope*. "Nonpolitical or essentially 'humanistic' movie artists have made many unbeatable comedies and quite a few good dramas," he observes; "but with exceptions so rare I can scarcely think of them, the only movies whose temper could possibly be described as heroic, or tragic, or both, have been made by leftists." In an earlier piece, written on April 28, 1945, Agee described himself as being "fairly close to political agnosticism." And still earlier, in a review of *Wilson*, he reported: "I believe that political ideas at their most mature and serious are still childish and frivolous as compared with those ideas or conceptions which attempt to work in, to perceive, and to illuminate, the bottoms of the souls of human beings." In his piece on *Man's Hope* he goes on to say that, though he trusts "only the individualist in art" and tends to "dismiss all political and propagandist art," he nevertheless finds Malraux's picture "a great leftist film." Agee praises the use of nonprofessionals as actors, the depiction of "men in courage and sorrow," the form of the work, and its cinematic "poetry" . . . He does not analyze the political content of *Man's Hope*.

Similarly, Agee calls Rossellini's *Open City* the best picture of 1946, in spite of the fact that "the film is among other things communist propaganda." He justifies this evaluation of a highly political film by maintaining that one need not agree with all the ideas expressed in a movie in order to appreciate its artistry. Many critics would concur. However, Agee's enthusiastic approval of the Rossellini film seems rather at odds with the low opinion he expresses elsewhere of even "mature" political ideas. Not that he doesn't have reservations about the film. "*Open City* lacks the depth of characterization, thought, and feeling which might have made it a definitively great film"; but on the whole the picture to him seems admirable. Of the seven paragraphs devoted to *Open City,* one paragraph of analysis is given over to the political theme of Rossellini's film. Agee refuses to face squarely the question of how a picture can at once be art and communist propaganda.

Ideas—including political ideas which the critic finds distasteful—remain part of the total screen experience, and they should be analyzed together with every other filmic element. A critic who ignores *what* a film "says" is as much open to the charge of evasion as a critic who avoids discussion of *how* the film "says" it. Macdonald points out that Agee, in his review of *Monsieur Verdoux,* is "defensive and often equivocal" on Chaplin's film *qua* film but "enthusiastic when he analyzes, as he does at length and with subtlety, its social and political meanings—or what he says they are . . ." Whereas Agee tells the reader much about the form of *Man's Hope* but leaves too much unsaid about Malraux's ideas, he fails to justify *Monsieur Verdoux* as art and prefers instead to argue its thought.

In his reviews of *Farrebique, Zéro de Conduite,* and *Sunset Boulevard,* Agee strikes a balance between analysis of form and analysis of content. He rarely had enough space, however, to do a satisfactory critique in depth. Most of his reviews of bad movies are justifiably short; but most of his assessments of important films are also brief, and sometimes—as the essays on *Man's Hope, Open City,* and *Monsieur Verdoux* show—they are lacking in critical perspective. Still, Agee was conscious of his bias in one direction or another (whether it was *for* "realism" and *against* "all political and propagandist art," or *for* "sincerity" and "love" and *against* "the puff-paste, onanistic, heartless quality of most" films), and he generally warned the reader of his partial, subjective approach.

Since Agee was appreciative of aesthetic values, his impressionistic method is not as offensive or blameworthy as it would be if practiced by a true "amateur critic" (that is to say, by a buff). Agee rarely confused the film itself with his psychological experience of it. No doubt he prepared a review by examining the formal details of a picture, though he generally neglected to include the analysis in his essay—perhaps because he was afraid of boring the average reader, who is almost always more concerned with what a movie is "about" than the way that "about" is communicated. Although not often enough as analytical as Kauffmann, Young, and Macdonald at their best, Agee made up for his lack through the quality of his mind, the refinement of his sensibility, the humaneness of his responses, and his wide knowledge of films. And there is no question that Agee's personal approach made for an engaging unpretentiousness.

Although Agee's response to the screen was clearly subjective, his taste was more catholic than some commentators would have us believe. As I have tried to show, Agee was opposed to allegory only if it was imposed on the subject matter of a film instead of growing out of it. He could say: "It would be nice to see some screen 'fantasy' if it were done by anyone with half a heart, mind, and hand for it. But when the studios try to make it, duck and stay hid until the mood has passed." He admitted to enjoying *Casablanca*—which is a melodrama—but unlike some critics, he did not mistake that delightful picture for great art. He could also say: "There is no reason, after all, why a movie musical should not be as good as any other sort of movie." He esteemed the work of John Huston, presumably for its "realism" (lower class); yet he found Huston "narrow, both in subject matter and technique," again presumably because the work failed to reach that level of "realism" (upper class) which is equivalent to "poetry." He consistently treated Hitchcock with respect; and he defended the master's search for a new style, even though the American films of the forties were generally not as impressive as the English suspense pictures of the thirties. (Agee, who praised *Notorious*, had stopped reviewing films when *Strangers on a Train* and *Rear Window* appeared; *Vertigo, Psycho,* and *The Birds* were made after his death.)

Finally, Agee could write. The only other critic who can make the reader "see" a film as vividly as Agee is Vernon Young—a point which can be verified by opening to almost any page of *Agee on Film*. But Agee is equally good at making the reader *comprehend* a film. His expository style remains clear, direct, exact, graceful, resonant, humorous, serious—in a word, *varied*.

5

No other American film critic has received more praise from his fellow critics than Agee. Arthur Knight says: "He was the best movie critic this country has ever had." "Agee's work, in its intensity of personal feeling, is the best criticism offered to the movies in this country," observes Arlene Croce. "Wherever his eye detected the slightest trace of good intentions or cinematic style, he exhumed the worthy passage and flourished it like a trophy [; but in] Agee's view, a bad film, whether it issued from wartime perversity or peacetime flatulence, was more than a violation of the public trust; it was a criminal abuse of a noble, and ennobling, art form." "The greatness of critics like Bazin in France and Agee in America," Kael remarks in *I Lost It at the Movies*, "may have something to do with their using their full range of intelligence and intuition rather than relying on formulas." The title of Simon's essay in *Acid Test*—"Let Us Now Praise James Agee"—speaks for itself; in *Private Screenings* Simon extolls Agee's "passionate scrupulousness" and "constantly self-searching enthusiasm," and in *Movies Into Film* he cites "humanity," "sensitivity," "scrupulousness," "literary gifts," and "multiplicity of interests" as reasons for Agee's critical stature. Bosley Crowther observes: "Agee's distinction as a critic was his exceptional sensitivity to the intimate nature of cinema expression and his ability to put his feelings into vivid, terse, and witty words."

Agee considered film "the greatest art medium" of the twentieth century. Unlike some early movie reviewers—who were hired to amuse readers with their patronizing attitude toward the screen—Agee loved and respected pictures. He considered "entertainment and artistry . . . inseparable and virtually synonymous"; he believed that a good film worked through the eyes to "awaken curiosity and intelligence"—both of which are "essential to good entertainment . . . [and] good art." He felt that, in any given year, the average film could hold its own with the average novel or play. Nevertheless, he realized that the forties was not one of the better decades of film production. He saw a growing sophistication in technique but little concomitant growth in maturity of theme. There were moments when he felt pessimistic about the future of pictures: commercialism, TV, compromise, problems of financing and distribution (yes, Agee even began to consider such mundane subjects, contrary to what he says in his opening piece for *The Nation*)—all threatened to kill off the film before it fully realized its potentialities.

No stranger to bad luck throughout his life, Agee died just before the arrival of Fellini, Bergman, Antonioni, Kurosawa, Godard, and Truffaut.

CHAPTER TWO

Robert Warshow and
Sociological Criticism

. . . how vulgar art and belief can be when measured against the purity of a real event.
—ROBERT WARSHOW

1

When Robert Warshow died in 1955, at the age of thirty-seven, he left unfinished a book of film criticism which he had only just begun to write. Published in 1962 *The Immediate Experience* included an "Author's Preface"—originally the Statement of Project submitted with an application for a Guggenheim Fellowship in 1954—outlining the aims of his proposed study; a never-completed essay entitled "Re-Viewing the Russian Movies," which was apparently intended for the book; and eighteen other essays, eleven of them on the movies, which had been published between 1946 and 1955 in *Partisan Review, American Mercury,* and *Commentary* (for which Warshow had worked as an editor). Although Warshow had hoped to develop a critical method which would take him beyond the sociological approach to film, the evidence of *The Immediate Experience*—including "Re-Viewing the Russian Movies"—makes it clear that his continuing main interest was in the social, political, moral, and cultural implications of the screen. His two most famous pieces—"The Gangster as Tragic Hero" and "Movie Chronicle: the Westerner"—also show him to be a practitioner of genre criticism.

The sociological criticism of film comes out of the same tradition as the sociological criticism of literature. Scholars have traced the sources for the approach to Giambattista Vico's *New Science* (1725), Madame de Stael's *Literature in Its Relation to Social Institutions* (1800), Sainte-Beuve's *Port-Royal* (1840), and the scientific social theories of Auguste Comte. The more immediate sources of sociological criticism, however, are the writings of Hippolyte Taine, Karl Marx, Friedrich Engels, and Matthew Arnold. With Taine the sociological critic assumes that national character, the period, and the environment influence the arts; with Marx and Engels the sociological critic believes that art is ultimately determined by the economic conditions of man's existence; with Arnold the sociological critic argues that art and society shape each other, and that artists should deal with serious moral subjects. The sociological critic of the twentieth century is chiefly concerned with the interaction of art and life, an interaction which he describes in terms largely derived from the social sciences and psychology.

For Warshow the problem of the American film was an aspect of a larger problem—namely, the problem of American popular culture, which had been brought about by industrial capitalism. Before 1929, Warshow argues in "The Legacy of the Thirties," the role of the intellectual involved a search for truth and justice; after 1929, the intellectual became "corrupted" by his affiliation —direct or indirect—with the communist movement. It was a decade of "organized mass disingenuousness, when every act and every idea had behind it some 'larger consideration' which destroyed its honesty and meaning." Popular culture absorbed a large part of the intelligentsia, thus drawing "its ideological support from the most advanced sectors of society." Standards were lowered Warshow complains: *The Grapes of Wrath, Confessions of a Nazi Spy,* and "Ballad for Americans" became great works of art. In short, truth was replaced by propaganda, justice by expediency.

How can the intellectual criticize popular culture when he is a part of popular culture, when even his vocabulary is the product of popular culture? "The most important effect of the intellectual life of the thirties and the culture that grew out of it," Warshow writes, "has been to distort and eventually to destroy the emotional and moral content of experience, putting in its place a system of conventionalized 'responses.'" According to Warshow, mass culture alienates the individual from himself. But serious art, though it too distances the individual from his experience, allows him to meditate on the meaning of his life; it thus increases self-knowledge and leads to greater personal happiness.

The problem facing the film critic, then, remains an enormous one—since mass culture is ubiquitous and serious art rare—yet it remains a problem that must be solved.

2

In his "Author's Preface," Warshow observes that film criticism has been largely of two kinds: aesthetic and sociological.

Aesthetic criticism emphasizes "the formal qualities of the medium and the self-consciousness of the film artist. Such criticism is likely to base itself on some fairly clear concept of the 'cinematic' and to use this as a standard of judgment. Depending on the critic's predilections, he may think of the 'cinematic' as residing primarily in visual patterns (a view which leads toward abstract films) or as residing primarily in the medium's power of 'truthful' representation (a view which leads toward documentary films)," Warshow writes. "In either case, it is typical of this criticism to place great stress on matters of technique, to minimize the importance of film actors in favor of directors (who are regarded as the artists of the medium), and, very often, to deplore the introduction of sound, and especially of dialogue, as having impaired the purity of the medium." As examples of aesthetic criticism, Warshow cites Rudolf Arnheim's *Film as Art* and Sergei Eisenstein's *Film Form* and *Film Sense*.

Sociological criticism "either minimizes the aesthetic problem or ignores it altogether, treating the films . . . as indexes to mass psychology or, sometimes, the 'folk spirit,'" Warshow observes. "Criticism of this sort ranges from the discovery of direct correspondences between the movies and life . . . to the complex and 'deep' interpretations of psychoanalysis." Warshow adds: "Ideas of film aesthetics need not be excluded, but they are subordinate to the primary aim of sociological analyses. Thus, the sociological critic who is alive to the aesthetics of the movies will not make the mistake of assuming that the effect of a film can be conveyed by recounting its plot, or that the repetition of a theme is necessarily a measure of its importance, but he will still be concerned with those elements which he believes to be affecting or expressing 'the audience' rather than with what he himself responds to." This is an important point, one which Warshow will return to shortly, inasmuch as it is the point from which he plans to shape a new critical method. He continues: "Sometimes, indeed, the sociological critic may try to resolve this difficulty—if he feels it as a difficulty—by a kind of forced identification with 'the audience'; sociology and aesthetics then become one, 'mass psychology' is likely to become 'myth,' and aesthetic value is likely to be identified with 'mythic' intensity. The detached (if not necessarily objective) tone of social science is more typical, however, and if there are value judgments, they usually refer not to the films in themselves but to the social facts which the films are believed to reflect." Warshow mentions Siegfried Kracauer's *From Caligari to Hitler*, and *Movies: A Psychological Study* by Nathan Leites and Martha Wolfenstein as examples of sociological criticism.

Both these methods, according to Warshow, have made valuable contributions to film criticism; however, both "have tended to slight the fundamental *fact* of the movies, a fact at once aesthetic and sociological but also something more. This is the actual, immediate experience of seeing and responding to the movies as most of us see them and respond to them . . . The sociological critic says to us, in effect: It is not *I* who goes to see the movies; it is the audience. The aesthetic critic says: It is no! the *movies* I go to see; it is art." Note the opposition Warshow sets up between "movies" and "art." Persuaded that few films are worthy of being classified in the latter category, Warshow had hoped that his work would "make some contribution to the 'legitimization' of the movies." In short, he sought to understand his relationship to popular culture (the "world of culture that came into being in the thirties"), as well as his relationship to all those bad movies which only on rare occasions had bored him. "A man watches a movie," he says, "and the critic must acknowledge that he is that man . . . [I]t must be that I go to the movies for the same reason that the 'others' go: because I require the absorbing immediacy of the screen; because in some way I take all that nonsense seriously." He thinks that the "special power" of the movies "has something to do with their being a kind of 'pure' culture, a little like fishing or . . . drinking or playing baseball—a cultural fact, that is, which has not yet fallen altogether under the discipline of art." And then—most revealingly—he adds: "I have not brought Henry James to the movies or the movies to Henry James, but I hope I have shown that the man who goes to the movies is the same man who reads James."

Warshow's desire to combine aesthetic and sociological criticism is, of course, just what is needed. And nobody will deny that the critic cannot, finally, escape acknowledging that his judgments are, no matter how objective he tries to be, to some extent subjective. But it is clear that Warshow had a tendency to regard serious films ("art") as merely pretentious ("when I have been bored, it has usually been at a 'good' movie"). As Agee points out, the average film is no better or no worse than the average novel or play. Does the existence of Mickey Spillane mean that the novel must be "legitimized," even though Turgenev and Dostoevsky and Tolstoy have also written novels? The critic who reads Henry James and watches *Citizen Kane* is indeed the same man; but why can't that man bring James to *Kane*, and *Kane* to James? Why should Warshow have taken "all that nonsense" in Bogart movies "seriously," if he really believed that is *was* "nonsense"? The "special power" of pure entertainment pictures may be equated with the "special power" of baseball; surely, however, the "special power" of *Forbidden Games*, say, or *The Bicycle Thief* remains of a different—higher—order. Actually, Warshow seems not to have had too much respect for art. His remark (to take just one example for the moment) that the "special power" of the screen might be traced to the fact that pictures have "not yet fallen altogether under the discipline of art" suggests that art

threatens the enjoyment of trash. No doubt Warshow would
have resisted such an interpretation; nonetheless, the implication
remains.

3

In "The Anatomy of Falsehood," Warshow discusses *The Best
Years of Our Lives*. The film purports to be a serious and truthful
study of American society; the optimistic ideas presented in the
picture, however, fail to square with reality, in spite of the care
with which the camera has photographed the surface of experience. The biggest falsehood in the movie "is a denial of the
reality of politics, if politics means the existence of real incom-
patibilities of interest and real *social* problems not susceptible of
individual solution." In "Father and Son—and the FBI," Warshow attacks *My Son John*, a wretched film which scarcely deserves the nearly nine pages devoted to it. The picture makes
clear, Warshow argues, that there is a "wrong way, a dangerous
way, to be anti-communist." Instead of characters, *My Son John*
gives us cartoon figures; the communist son of the title is no more
"monstrous" than his father, "a pillar of the American Legion"
who represents not intelligent anti-communism but mere stupid-
ity. *My Son John* is another false picture of life, and, in the
bargain, an attack on intellectuals.

Paisan is praised because its "images of danger, suffering, and
death . . . remain in one's consciousness with the particularity of
real experience." But Rossellini's "rejection of ideas is also a rejection of principles. Rossellini has no intellectual defenses, and
when he attempts to go beyond the passive representation of
experience, he falls at once into the grossest sentimentality and
falsehood." In "The Movie Camera and the American," Warshow
discusses *Death of a Salesman*, both as a play and as a film.
According to Warshow, Miller's play is bad—still another false
picture of American life; the adaptation, however, is even worse:
too talky, too stagy. Samuel Goldwyn's *I Want You* "is in many
ways better and more serious than *Death of a Salesman*." Even
Carl Dreyer is not spared. By excluding the "historical" and

"dramatic" at the beginning of *Day of Wrath*, Dreyer "deprives events of the quality of reality." The film-maker's "love for the purely visual" conflicts with "the tendencies of a medium that is not only visual but also dramatic." Dreyer appears to be guilty of "aestheticism": "The historical past, being real, embodies a multitude of possibilities; the aesthetic past is created by eliminating all possibilities but one."

It is difficult not to conclude that any film or play that doesn't present a view of life in conformity with Warshow's is "false to reality." This bias is not apparent in the critic's discussion of bad movies like *My Son John*, or of overrated ones like *The Best Years of Our Lives*; but it does become evident in his essays on good films like *Day of Wrath* and *Paisan*, and on a good play like *Death of a Salesman*. (Warshow is right about the film version of Miller's play; it *is* bad.) Dreyer, according to Warshow, fails to "explain" witchcraft; and "the question of its reality" cannot be avoided: a "psychological answer is impossible," the "supernatural answer" which Dreyer chooses is unacceptable (that is, to Warshow). Hence what the critic misses in *Day of Wrath*—and what he means by the "dramatic" as opposed to the purely "visual"—is some form of "social realism."

Not only is Warshow's view of "reality" a limited one, since his thinking remains hobbled by sociological preconceptions, but his view of film as an art form is also surprisingly naive. In "The Movie Camera and the American," for example, he argues that Willy Loman's memories "were awkward enough on the stage but at least belonged to an accepted framework of theatrical convention; the film manages the transitions from the real to the hallucinatory more smoothly, but these sequences still wrench it out of shape: the very fluidity of the medium favors simpler and more direct exposition (even the accepted use of the 'flashback' —Willy's hallucinations do not quite belong to that convention— is almost never accomplished without a kind of purely technical sentimentality)." True, there are no "flashbacks" in *Death of a Salesman*; but the shifts in viewpoint are treated as though they *were* flashbacks. No wonder the movie version of the play handled the transitions smoothly; after all, the "theatrical convention" Warshow speaks of was influenced by the screen. (By the way, Warshow doesn't tell us what "shape" the memory-sequences are supposed to "wrench" *Death of a Salesman* out of.) What would Warshow have thought of *Wild Strawberries* or *Hiroshima Mon Amour?* For that matter, what did he think of *Citizen Kane?* These films can hardly be said to favor simple and direct exposition. And what does Warshow intend by "purely technical sentimentality"? "In the screen's absolute clarity," he argues in his piece on *Day of Wrath*, "where all objects are brought close and defined unambiguously, the 'reality' of an event can be made to inhere simply in its visible presence." It is fitting for Warshow to put quotation marks around "reality"; but one can only smile at his assertion that on the screen all objects are "defined unambiguously."

When Warshow approves of a film's "social realism," he usually gives the picture a passing grade. Nearly thirty-two pages in *The Immediate Experience* are given over to Chaplin. In the early movies the Tramp and society clashed "but neither side was impelled to draw any conclusions from this. The absurdity of the Tramp's behavior consisted in its irrelevance to the preoccupations of the society; the viciousness of the society consisted in its failure to make any provision for the Tramp, in its complete indifference to his fate." The depression changed this situation: society came to regard the individual as a tool and a threat; the individual had to declare himself "for or against" society. *Modern Times* shows the change. The factory exploits the Tramp, who now appears even smaller, more helpless than before. In *The Great Dictator* "the whole mechanism of society is brought to bear against the Tramp in a deliberate effort to make him suffer and, ultimately, to kill him." The Tramp is no longer adequate to the thematic burden Chaplin puts upon him; society must be destroyed, but the Tramp cannot manage this revolution by himself.

"With Verdoux," writes Warshow, "the opposition between the individual and society has lost its old simplicity." Now the two have "in a sense become co-extensive . . . it is man himself who is corrupt, both as individual and as society." *Monsieur Verdoux* "must be approached with a willingness to understand and enjoy it as a shifting pattern of ambiguity and irony, made up of all the complexities and contradictions not only of our society but of Chaplin's own mind and the mind of the spectator."

All Warshow can find to say about the film's visual quality, or its existence as a work of art, is that Chaplin "always does whatever is needed in the most direct way possible" (and this remark appears in parenthesis!); and that there "is a great deal of talk, and a number of critics have found it objectionable, either because it bored them or because they saw it as a violation of the rather artificial principle that a movie must rely only on the camera. I do not wish to claim that Verdoux's expositions of his ideas are among the best things in the movie, but I found them full of interest in themselves and extremely important in developing the total effect of the movie's involved irony." Warshow likes the ideas in *Monsieur Verdoux*; consequently, the film gives a "true" picture of life. (In his essay on *My Son John*, Warshow observes: "in a movie it is not the intrinsic worth of an idea that counts, but the power with which it is made into an image; in the movie theater, we think with our eyes.")

Warshow also likes *Limelight*. He says: "now that Chaplin has broken the silence, I confess I do not find these platitudes of his quite so distressing or inappropriate as, perhaps, I ought to"; "I have no convincing argument to advance against those who see *Limelight* as no more than a crude structure of self-pity and banal 'philosophy' interspersed here and there with glimpses of a past greatness. But the crudities of a great artist always have an extra dimension. . . . One way or another, the movies are always forcing us outside the boundaries of art; this is one source of their special power." To which one must reply: True, the movies force us "outside the boundaries of art"; a film should be evaluated, however, largely by standards of excellence derived from the nature of the medium itself, not entirely on the basis of its agreement with the critic's view of "social reality."

"They broke their eggs, and they made their omelette"—this sentence sums up Warshow's personal response to the classic Soviet cinema. Seeing the Russian Revolution as an "enormous historical failure," he could not evaluate *Potemkin*, say, or *The End of St. Petersburg* by artistic criteria. The "enthusiasms" of the films made him think of "the whole wearisome joke of human aspiration and wickedness." Aesthetically, the films were "as successful as ever"; but they represented "a triumph of art over humanity. It made me, for a while, quite sick of the art of the cinema, and sick also of the people who sat with me in the audience, *mes semblables,* whom I suspected of being either cinema enthusiasts or communists—and I wasn't always sure which was worse," As in his piece on *Day of Wrath,* Warshow favors the "historical past" over the "aesthetic past": "how vulgar art and belief can be," he observes, "when measured against the purity of a real event. There are innumerable examples of such vulgarity in the Russian cinema, moments when the director, taken up with his role as an artist who controls and interprets— few artists have put a higher value on that role than the early Soviet film directors—forgets what is really at stake and commits an offense against humanity."

In *Signs and Meaning in the Cinema,* Peter Wollen comments on Warshow's attitude towards the Russian silent-film masters as follows: "It is strange to see how the philistinism of the Stalinist regime in the 1930's finds its belated double in the United States of the Cold War two decades later."

4

When Warshow turns to genre criticism, as he does in "The Gangster as Tragic Hero" and "The Westerner," his bent is still largely a sociological one.

In the first essay, written in 1948, Warshow relates the prevalence of gangster pictures to a reaction against the official "cheerful view of life" in American society. Since the philosophy of optimism fools no one, the counter philosophy of failure asserts itself on the screen. The gangster is a creature of the city: "he is what we want to be and what we are afraid we may become"; for "we are always conscious that the whole meaning of [his] career is a drive for success: the typical gangster film presents a steady upward progress followed by a very precipitate fall." The audience and the genre have "an agreed conception of human life: that man is a being with the possibilities of success or failure." This principle grows out of the experience of city life: "one must emerge from the crowd or else one is nothing." But the moral of the gangster film is that "there is really only one possibility—failure. The final meaning of the city is anonymity and death." Two opposed social ideas conflict in the genre: the drive for success and the desire not to be alone. "And yet the very conditions of success make it impossible not to be alone," Warshow argues, "for success is always the establishment of an *individual* pre-eminence . . . The gangster's whole life is an effort to assert himself as an individual, to draw himself out of the crowd, and he always dies *because* he is an individual." Warshow concludes: "In the deeper layers of the modern consciousness, *all* means are unlawful, every attempt to succeed is an act of aggression, leaving one alone and guilty and defenseless among enemies: one is *punished* for success . . . The effect of the gangster film is to embody this dilemma in the person of the gangster and resolve it by his death." In short, the mode provides us with a vicarious therapeutic release: "for the moment, we can acquiesce in our failure, we can choose to fail."

In "The Westerner," written in 1954, Warshow describes the characteristics of the cowboy picture, and contrasts the genre with the gangster movie. Americans pretend to be offended by violence but the screen refutes such hypocrisy. "The gangster movie . . . belongs to [a] cultural 'underground' which sets forth the attractions of violence in the face of all our higher social attitudes," writes Warshow. "It is a more 'modern' genre than the Western, perhaps even more profound, because it confronts industrial society on its own ground—the city . . . But it is antisocial, resting on fantasies of irresponsible freedom. If we are brought finally to acquiesce in the denial of these fantasies, it is only because they have been shown to be dangerous, not because they have given way to a better vision of behavior." The Western film presents this "better vision," curiously enough, in spite of its violence. "But the drama is one of self-restraint: the moment of violence must come in its own time and according to its special laws, or else it is valueless," Warshow says. "There is little cruelty in Western movies, and little sentimentality; our eyes are not focused on the sufferings of the defeated but on the deportment of the hero. Really, it is not violence at all which is the 'point' of the Western movie, but a certain image of man, a style, which expresses itself most clearly in violence." We don't actually believe in the cowboy hero; but he serves a valuable function, anyway. "He is there to remind us of the possibility of style in an age which has put on itself the burden of pretending that style has no meaning, and, in the midst of our anxieties over the problem of violence, to suggest that even in killing or being killed we are not freed from the necessity of establishing satisfactory modes of behavior." Finally, the Western offers "us the pleasures of a complete and self-contained drama—and one which still effortlessly crosses the boundaries which divide our culture—in a time when other, more consciously serious art forms are increasingly complex, uncertain, and ill-defined."

Although Warshow gives some attention to the formal properties of the gangster picture and the Western, he is primarily interested in the sociological significance of each mode. Indeed, one finds his usual low opinion of the "merely" artistic. Discussing the *mise en scène* in *The Gunfighter*, for instance, Warshow remarks: "This 'authenticity' . . . is only aesthetic; the chief fact about nineteenth-century photographs [which the *mise en scène* here reminds him of] . . . is how stonily they refuse to yield up the truth." Warshow gives few examples in support of his thesis. In "The Gangster as Tragic Hero," *Scarface* and *Little Caesar* are the only films cited as belonging to the genre; *Kiss of Death* is mentioned (in a footnote) but dismissed as "unsuccessful," because it attempts "to bring the gangster film into line with the prevailing optimism and social constructiveness of our culture." *The Virginian* seems to be the model for the "true" Western. Pictures featuring William S. Hart, Tom Mix, Gene Autry, and Roy Rogers fall short of the archetype; *The Ox-Bow Incident*, *The Gunfighter*, and *High Noon* are "anti-Westerns," inasmuch as they violate the purity of the form, its mythic element, by a modern—and hence "false"—"social realism." *Stagecoach*, *My Darling Clementine*, and *Shane* are rejected because of their "aestheticizing tendency," because they carry the mythic element too far ("This is to yield entirely to [the form's] static quality as legend and to the 'cinematic' temptations of its landscape, the hcrses, the quiet men.") The gangster movie, we are told, "no longer exists in its 'classical' form"; and apparently, neither does the Western.

Warshow's error is a familiar one. Like the literary critic who accepts Aristotle's view of "tragedy," and who then measures all other plays against Sophocles's masterpiece, Warshow idealizes *The Virginian* (as Aristotle idealized *Oedipus*), and ends up dismissing just about every cowboy picture made since 1929. Whenever a critic says that this play is not a "true tragedy," or that film is not a "true Western" or a "true gangster" picture, we have a right to inquire whether the critic's definition of the genre is in need of repair. By regarding gangster pictures and Westerns as largely sociological documents, Warshow allows little room in his theory for the uses to which the genre might be put by individual directors.

5

Because the motion picture can depict physical reality and social experience so powerfully, it has always attracted its share of sociological critics.

No film is an island, entirely self-contained. Works of art are made by men for other men within a specific economic, social, and historical environment. The sociological critic—who brings a valuable moral intensity to film study, since he believes that movies have consequences outside themselves—can help us to see what the film is, or, at least, part of what it is. In the case of older pictures, he can recover for us the social conditions of the time; where later films are concerned, he can show us how they relate to widespread currents and tensions in our common milieu. Furthermore, sociological criticism can often throw the theme of a picture into illuminating perspective . . . Nonetheless, although aesthetic criticism needs to be tempered with humanism, the film itself must be judged chiefly by artistic standards.

Warshow tends not to give the film as film, or film as art, its due. And traditionally, this error has characterized sociological criticism, which frequently lapses into sociology and political science, and on occasion into Marxist propaganda. But it need not be so. The sociological approach can make a real contribution to film criticism. To do so, however, its practitioners must show more respect for art than they customarily evince. As Jean Anouilh has put it: "Life is very nice, but it lacks form. It's the aim of art to give it some."

CHAPTER THREE

Andrew Sarris and Auteur *Criticism*

Auteur *criticism is a reaction against sociological criticism that enthroned the what against the how.*
—ANDREW SARRIS

1

In his foreword to *Confessions of a Cultist* (1970), Andrew Sarris gazes back on the past and observes: "I was the beneficiary as well as the victim of the intellectual vacuum that occurred in movie reviewing with the death of Agee in 1955." The first issue of *Film Culture* came out that year. And Sarris—who had been studying film in an evening course at Columbia ("between meandering through graduate English and malingering in Teachers College")—got his start as a reviewer and editor without pay. He was nearly twenty-seven. Speaking of the *Film Culture* group, Sarris reflects: "I suppose we represented a new breed of film critic. The cultural rationale for our worthier predecessors—Agee, Ferguson, Levin, Murphy, Sherwood, *et al.* —was that they were too good to be reviewing movies. We, on the contrary, were not considered much good for anything else." What Sarris lacked in prestige, however, he made up for in a passionate devotion to film. "Whereas the late James Agee discovered cinema through his love for movies," he observes, "too many of his self-proclaimed successors chose to abuse movies in the name of *Kultur*." Critics appeared to be of two kinds: "journalistic reviewers who would be equally happy in the real estate

38

departments of their publications"; and "high-brow humanists" who admired *From Caligari to Hitler,* "because they, like [Siegfried] Kracauer, [were] more interested in Hitler than *Caligari.*" However, in his preface to *The American Cinema* (1968), Sarris concedes that the sociological critics brought a valuable professional discipline to film-study.

"American criticism, like American cinema, is eminently pragmatic and anti-theoretical," Sarris observes in *The Film* (1968). "Almost from the beginning, the cinema was saddled with transcendent moral obligations that converted critiques into sermons." Too much American film criticism has ignored technical and aesthetic concerns in favor of thematic values; as a result, most theories of film have come from Europe, where the medium was always taken much more seriously than in America. Consequently, Sarris sees film aesthetics dominated by two quasi-mystical European concepts: montage and *mise en scène.*

"Normally," Sarris writes, "montage is merely a fancy synonym for editing or cutting, but Eisenstein gave montage a mystique by linking it to the philosophical processes of dialectical materialism. As Eisenstein conceived of film-making, images equalled ideas, and the collision of two dynamically opposed images created a new idea." There are few subjects, Sarris believes, which lend themselves to the continual fast cutting of *Ten Days That Shook the World:* "For better or worse, the great majority of movies developed a dramatic style of expression to enhance audience identification with star personalities." Sarris can appreciate the montage technique of Resnais in *Hiroshima Mon Amour* and *Last Year at Marienbad;* but he can also argue that the best moments in *The Birth of a Nation* occur when Lillian Gish and Henry B. Walthall reveal the "visual subtleties of screen acting" in front of a "static, unblinking camera." According to Sarris, montage tends to subordinate ideas to rhythm and to overemphasize the value of editing. He agrees with Godard: a film is the product of both the camera and the cutting room.

Mise en scène, the mystique developed by André Bazin, Alexander Astruc, and Robert Leenhardt, stresses pictorial values instead of the rhythmic flow of images. Through the use of long takes and deep-focus shooting in which characters are kept in the same frame—instead of being shown alternately through cutting —the film-maker creates a world that is psychologically and spatially coherent. "Above all," Sarris writes, "*mise en scène* emphasizes the content of a frame rather than the relationship of one frame to the next . . . Ultimately, the people who believe in *mise en scène* believe in a cinema that records something that already exists. Direction is then not the completely creative act implied by montage, but rather a contemplative act that reveals the director's emotional attitude toward his material." Sarris remarks that *Open City* shows "reality in all its ambiguity through Rossellini's unblinking camera"; and that neo-realism, in Bazin's view, "marked a return to Lumière." Yet he also goes on to observe that the term *mise en scène* comes from the theater, and that the concept also "defends the theatricality of the cinema." Sarris makes no attempt to reconcile these statements. "*Mise en scène*, like montage, has been carried to extremes," he concludes. "If montage implies the fragmentation of the world, *mise en scène* implies the unity of the world. By the same token, extreme uses of montage are too jazzy for the meanings they seek to express, extreme emphases on *mise en scène* result in sheer boredom."

The European concept of the film which has had the greatest influence on Sarris, however, is the *auteur* theory.

2

The term *politique des auteurs* (literally "the policy of authors") comes from an essay entitled "*Une certaine tendance du cinéma français*" was François Truffaut which appeared in the *Cahiers du Cinéma* of January 1954. In his article Truffaut attacks some highly praised French films because, in his view, they are writer's pictures. The true *auteur* of a film should be the director; but for that to be possible, Truffaut argues, the director has to be actively involved in the scripting of the film.

Politique des auteurs subsequently took on at least two meanings: one, "to be for some directors and against others" (as Sarris puts it); two, to value the personality of directors, especially Hollywood directors, because they have to overcome more obstacles (assigned scripts, studio bosses, the vanity of stars, and so on) than their European counterparts. Thus, directors like René Clément, Marcel Carné, Claude Autant-Lara, and René Clair were downgraded in favor of Jean Renoir, Robert Bresson, and Jean Cocteau at home and Alfred Hitchcock, Fritz Lang, Howard Hawks, and John Ford abroad.

"I will give the *Cahiers* critics full credit for the original formulation of an idea that has reshaped my thinking on the cinema," Sarris writes in "Notes on the *Auteur* Theory in 1962" (*Film Culture*, Winter 1962–63). He then proceeds to establish three premises of the *auteur* theory: 1) "the technical competence of a director as a criterion of value"; 2) "the distinguishable personality of the director as a criterion of value"; and 3) the "ultimate premise of the *auteur* theory is concerned with interior meaning [which] is extrapolated from the tension between a director's personality and his material." Sarris goes on to say: "The three premises of the *auteur* theory may be visualized as three concentric circles: the outer circle as technique; the middle circle, personal style; and the inner circle, interior meaning. The corresponding roles of the director may be designated as those of a technician, a stylist, and an *auteur*." Some explanation of these three premises, or circles, is in order.

By "technical competence," Sarris means an "elementary flair for the cinema"; "simply the ability to put a film together with some clarity and coherence." After a director has made a fair amount of films he reveals a "pattern," or "certain recurring characteristics of style, which serve as his signature. The way a film looks and moves should have some relationship to the way a director thinks and feels." By "interior meaning," Sarris intends "not quite the vision of the world a director projects nor quite his attitude toward life. It is ambiguous, in any literary sense, because part of it is imbedded in the stuff of the cinema and cannot be rendered in noncinematic terms . . . Dare I come out and say what I think it to be is an *élan* of the soul? Lest I seem unduly mystical," he adds, ". . . all I mean by 'soul' is that intangible difference between one personality and another, all other things being equal. Sometimes, this difference is expressed by no more than a beat's hesitation in the rhythm of a film."

Pauline Kael, in "Circles and Squares: Joys and Sarris" (a well-known essay which originally appeared in the Spring 1963 *Film Quarterly*, and which is reprinted in *I Lost It at the Movies*), has taken on the *auteur* theory in her customary hard-hitting style. As Sarris wryly points out in *The American Cinema*, Kael's "attack on the theory received more publicity than the theory itself." According to Kael, all three of Sarris's premises are worthless. On occasion, she declares, a great film-maker ignores the "technical competence" that alone distinguishes the studio drudge: "For example, it is doubtful if Antonioni could handle a routine directorial assignment of the type at which John Sturges is so proficient." Didn't Dreiser in the novel triumph over "technical incompetence"? The great artist, she maintains, creates new standards.

Kael is so intent on pommeling Sarris that she will not even allow him to retain his least debatable premise. Surely Antonioni knows the basic principles of film-making; if the Italian master had to, he could put together a film so that it would have the same *mechanical* "clarity and coherence" as a picture directed by Sturges. Of course, Antonioni's heart—or "soul"—wouldn't be in the project; but for that matter, there is no "soul" in Sturges's films, either. Once the viewer understands what Antonioni is up to in *L'Avventura*, the film is seen to have its own form of "clarity and coherence." The great artist can indeed create new standards (but not without technical knowledge—how would that be possible?); nevertheless, the new standards are never completely isolated from the larger body of older standards. In "Tradition and the Individual Talent," T. S. Eliot argues that the artist "must inevitably be judged by the standards of the past. I say judged, not amputated by them . . . It is a judgment, a comparison, in which two things are measured by each other." In short, a "conformity" exists "between the old and the new." But Kael really knows all this, otherwise why would she say, in her review of *The Trojan Women* (*Deeper Into Movies*): "I question whether a director [like Michael Cacoyannis] with so little feeling for the most basic elements of movie-making can ever be a good movie director. A director with a 'film sense' knows where to put the camera so that you don't question the shot; for others every setup looks arbitrary." Most critics would concur that "technical competence" and "film sense" both point to the same meaning. Of course, Sarris doesn't always stick to his premises; when it is convenient, he can write: "Welles makes many more mistakes than Zinnemann ever could, and yet I wouldn't trade one shot from [*Chimes at Midnight*] for the entire oeuvre of Zinnemann" (*Confessions of a Cultist*).

Sarris's second premise—"the distinguishable personality of the director as a criterion of value"—is met with a question by Kael: "The smell of a skunk is more distinguishable than the perfume of a rose; does that make it better?" A recurrent criticism of the *auteur* theory is that its proponents place more value on the *auteur* than on the film itself. "When a famous director makes a good movie, we look at the movie, we don't think about the director's personality," Kael writes; "when he makes a stinker we notice his familiar touches because there's not much else to watch." (She admits: "Traditionally, in any art, the personalities of all those involved in a production have been a factor in judgment, but that the *distinguishability* of personality should in itself be a criterion of value completely confuses *normal* judgment.") Kael's criticism would appear to owe something to Bazin's essay "La Politique des Auteurs," which appeared in the *Cahiers* April 1957 issue, though she does not acknowledge a debt. In his article, Bazin (whom Sarris calls "the greatest film critic who ever lived") states that his fundamental disagreement with the *auteur* theorists "concerns the relationship between the work and its creator, [for] . . . as soon as you state that the film-maker and his films are one, there can be no minor films, as the worst of them will always be in the image of their creator . . . It is unfortunate to praise a film that in no way deserves it, but the dangers are less far-reaching than when a worthwhile film is rejected because its director has made nothing good up to that point." Bazin argues that "mediocre *auteurs* can, by accident, make admirable films," whereas "a genius can fall victim to an equally accidental sterility." The *auteur* theory, Bazin concludes, needs to be "complemented" by other approaches: "*Auteur*, yes, but what *of?*" In "Notes on the *Auteur* Theory in 1962," Sarris devotes more than half his space to a discussion of Bazin's essay, but without ever really coming to grips with the French critic's main argument.

A critique of Sarris's third premise must be preceded by some general remarks on film-making. Where the novel is concerned, it is easy to determine the author; there is no problem in saying: "*Anna Karenina* was written by Tolstoy." To speak of an "author" in terms of a movie, however, presents certain difficulties. Fellini helps write the scripts for his pictures, chooses the cast, gives instructions to his cameraman, and suggests the kind of music he wants to his composer. All the same, the purity of the term "*auteur*" as applied to a Fellini film is compromised by the fact that some of Tullio Pinelli's ideas find their way into the script, that a portion of Marcello Mastroianni's personality is expressed on the screen, that cameraman Otello Martelli is not always given precise instructions, and that composer Nino Rota is not wholly an organ on which the director plays his personal theme. Bergman writes most of his scripts without help; so in that sense, he is an even more complete film-maker than Fellini; yet he too depends on the work of associates. Does this mean that we can't speak of a "Fellini film" or a "Bergman film"? No—because the "signature" of these men, as the *auteur* critic would put it, is definitely on every picture they direct; but we should bear in mind that where movies are concerned the term "*auteur*" can only be used in an analogous sense.

Now, if we can say: "*La Dolce Vita* was made by Fellini"— since Fellini is in full control of a picture from beginning to end (or to the extent that the circumstances of film-making allow)— can we also say: "Such and such Hollywood film was made by such and such director?" No one, so far as I know, resists the idea of Fellini as an *auteur*. The opposition begins when Sarris's theory is applied to the studio system in America. On the Continent the director—even before the appearance of the *auteur* theory— was always accorded more homage than the Hollywood film-maker received from the American press and public (with the exception of a Griffith, say, or a Chaplin). The reason isn't hard to find.

In Hollywood, the director has traditionally exercised little or no control over script, casting, and editing. Hitchcock is an exception; but he has earned this privilege because his films have been consistently successful at the box-office. Few American directors, even today, enjoy the right of final cut (that is, the last editing of a picture before it is released). And since the recent film-director-as-superstar approach has not often enough guaranteed commercial success, the studios have increasingly returned to their authoritarian ways.

Whose "signature" is on an American film? That is the question. Some have answered that it is that of the studio head or the producer. Gazing back over the history of movies in America, proponents of this view point to Louis B. Mayer, Irving Thalberg, Jack Warner, and Harry Cohn as *auteurs*. In *The Liveliest Art*, Arthur Knight argues that each major studio had a style of its own; men like Dore Schary, Darryl Zanuck, and Frank Freeman "left their ideological imprint upon every picture that their studio released." The "signature" of the studio also appeared as a result of departmentalism: the organization of MGM, Paramount, and 20th Century-Fox into camera departments, music departments, sound departments, and processing laboratories. These various departments, headed by men who remained after producers and directors had passed off the scene, "determine[d] the physical appearance of their studio's pictures." For Knight, then, the "signature" on a typical American movie of the thirties and forties is a joint one: the producer's ideology combined with the stamp of the specialized departments of his studio.

Some claim that the writer is the true *auteur* of a Hollywood film, or at least that he ought to enjoy equal status with the director as the *auteur*. In *Cinema Eye, Cinema Ear*, John Russell Taylor points out that Carl Mayer, Jacques Prévert, and Ben Hecht achieved a personal quality in their scripts which is manifest on the screen. (Taylor contends, however, that such cases remain the exception rather than the rule.) In *The Hollywood Screenwriters*, editor Richard Corliss observes: "If this book has any message, it is not that the writer deserves to replace the director as *solus rex,* or even *primus inter pares,* but that the Hollywood film is a collaborative effort. Unless he writes his films as well, the Hollywood director is essentially an interpretive artist who steers the script, the actors, and the camera in the right *direction.* He is less an architect than a foreman, less a painter than an illustrator, less a composer than a conductor." Lawrence B. Marcus, who wrote the screenplay for *Petulia,* insists that the "jumpcut style" of that picture was his creation, not director Richard Lester's. "The length of time of the flashbacks and flash-forwards so that it all came out together at the end," according to Marcus, "—all that had been hinted at in the script" (quoted in *Variety,* February 5, 1969). "But, argue the *auteurists,*" writes William Froug, scenarist, "the screenwriter is often 'merely' an adapter, translating somebody else's work to the screen. In the past that has been largely true. [It is still "largely true." Over half the pictures made in America continue to be derived from plays and novels.] But who in film-making is not an adapter? Isn't the director's function to adapt to film the work provided him by the writer? . . . If, until recently, the screenwriter's efforts could not be considered 'original,' surely no one, by that narrow standard, was less 'original' than the director" (*The New York Times,* September 24, 1972). The solution to the scenarist-versus-director problem in American (and English) films will be resolved, as the authors surveyed in Corliss's book recognize, when the same man both writes and directs a picture.

It has also been argued that in some films the true *auteur* is the actor. Greta Garbo, Spencer Tracy, John Wayne, Clark Gable, Humphrey Bogart, James Cagney, Cary Grant, Katharine Hepburn, Marlon Brando—stars such as these, some have maintained, dominate a film with *their* personality. Others have made a case for the cameraman as *auteur.* Men like Stanley Cortez, Arthur C. Miller, Gregg Toland, James Wong Howe, Hal Rosson, Ted Tetzlaff, Burnett Guffey put *their* "signature" on a film, it is said, though the ignorant take the picture to be the director's creation. Undoubtedly, we will soon hear arguments in favor of the sound technician as *auteur,* the costumer as *auteur,* the art director as *auteur,* the special-visual-effects technician as *auteur,* and so forth. The problem seems much more complicated than either the Sarrisites or anti-Sarrisites have so far acknowledged, though the *politiques des auteurs* can be credited for initiating the discussion.

In "Notes on the *Auteur* Theory in 1962," Sarris says that "film for film, director for director, the American cinema has been consistently superior to that of the rest of the world . . . Consequently, I now regard the *auteur* theory primarily as a critical device for recording the history of the American cinema, the only cinema worth exploring in depth beneath the frosting of a few great directors at the top." So it is clear why Sarris and other *auteurists* stress the personality of a film-maker instead of his individual films. Since most directors in Hollywood lack the freedom of a Fellini or a Bergman, it is idle for the *auteurist* to search for value in American films considered as discrete entities. By viewing the pictures of a particular director en masse, however, the *auteur* critic can ignore the "incidental" contribution of collaborators and concentrate on the director's personality as it is revealed in his characteristic stylistic techniques.

"Because so much of the American cinema is commissioned," Sarris writes, "a director is forced to express his personality through the visual treatment of material rather than through the literary content of the material." Film is basically a visual medium. This means that character and theme, even in the sound film, should be expressed mainly in pictures. But this isn't what Sarris is saying. Because the immense majority of Hollywood films are scripted by one man and directed by another, and because their subject matter will not bear close inspection, the *auteur* critic focuses on the visual. What this amounts to is an aesthetically indefensible separation of form ("visual") and content ("literary"). "A Cukor, who works with all sorts of projects, has a more developed abstract style than a Bergman, who is free to develop his own scripts," Sarris declares. "Not that Bergman lacks personality, but his work has declined with the depletion of his ideas largely because his technique never equalled his sensibility." The preposterous assertion of Bergman's "decline" (between 1955 and 1962 Bergman directed *Smiles of a Summer Night, The Seventh Seal, Wild Strawberries, The Virgin Spring,*

Through a Glass Darkly, and *Winter Light*) is matched by the equally preposterous assertion of Cukor's superiority to Bergman. "Is Sarris saying what he seems to be saying, that if Bergman had developed more 'technique,' his work wouldn't be dependent on his ideas?" asks Kael. "I'm afraid that *is* what he means, and that when he refers to Cukor's 'more developed abstract style' he means by 'abstract' something unrelated to ideas, a technique not dependent on the content of the films." Hence the third premise of the *auteur* theory—"Interior meaning is extrapolated from the tension between a director's personality and his material"— means that unity as a criterion of value in a work of art is replaced by the criterion of "tension." (Or, as Kael puts it, the amount of personality the director can express "by shoving bits of style up the crevasses of the plots.") The concept of unity is not, however, completely abandoned. Instead, it is removed as *a* standard by which a film is evaluated and applied as *the* standard by which a true *auteur* is judged. For the three concentric circles coalesce in the work of a Pantheon Director, so that technique serves style and style expresses a personal vision.

Sarris has never attempted to refute Kael's premise-by-premise criticism of the *auteur* theory with a premise-by-premise defense. He had a chance to do so in his article "The *Auteur* Theory and the Perils of Pauline," which was published in *Film Quarterly* (Summer 1963), but he settled instead for some lengthy quotes from his earlier pieces. Nor does Sarris's "Notes on the *Auteur* Theory in 1972," in the Spring 1972 issue of *Film Comment*, reveal anything noteworthy. Kael is not even mentioned by name in *The American Cinema,* where she is merely referred to as "a lady critic with a lively sense of outrage." "Circles and Squares" does seem to have had an effect, however, on Sarris's later articulation of *auteurism* in "Toward a Theory of Film History," the introduction to *The American Cinema.*

Less oracular in tone than "Notes on the *Auteur* Theory in 1962," the later piece also is not encumbered by references to premises or circles. The first premise of the *auteur* theory is not in evidence at all, in spite of the fact that the "technical competence of a director as a criterion of value" remains the most secure premise of the three. The second premise, "the distin-

guishable personality of the director as a criterion of value,"
reappears as: "Ultimately, the *auteur* theory is not so much a
theory as an attitude, a table of values that converts film history
into directorial autobiography." And the third premise, the aesthetic worth derived from the "tension between a director's personality and his material," is buried in the middle of a paragraph
and reappears as: "The *auteur* theory values the personality of a
director precisely because of the barriers to its expression."

In "Toward a Theory of Film History," Sarris makes an effort
to reconcile some of the negative comments on his earlier essay
with the tenets of *auteurism*, but without much success. For
example, he argues that the critic need not make an "irrevocable
choice between a cinema of directors and a cinema of actors, or
between a cinema of directors and a cinema of genres, or between a cinema of directors and a cinema of social themes, and
so on." Still, any cinema other than a cinema of directors is
treated with scorn ("the weak director allows the personalities of
others to run rampant" . . . "*The Americanization of Emily* is
written but not really directed"). Sarris writes: "The auteur critic
is obsessed with the wholeness of art and the artist. He looks at a
film as a whole, a director as a whole. The parts, however entertaining individually, must cohere meaningfully."

These sentences suggest that Sarris is reacting to the charge
that *auteurism* splits form from content. Yet he in no way makes
clear how this aesthetic wholeness, or unity, squares with his
reiterated claim that value, for the *auteurist*, stems from the ability of a director to leapfrog over the obstacles of studio production in pursuit of individual expression. He says: "The whole
point of a meaningful style is that it unifies the *what* and the *how*
into a personal statement . . . [T]he best directors are usually
fortunate enough to exercise control over their films so that there
need be no glaring disparity between *what* and *how*. It is only on
the intermediate and lower levels of film-making that we find
talent wasted on inappropriate projects." This is begging the
question, or arguing in a circle, with a vengeance. Sarris assumes
to be true the assertion: "a 'meaningful style' equals 'the distinguishable personality of the director.' " He further assumes to be
true: "the 'best' directors have usually been free to exercise re-

sponsibility for their films." Finally, as "proof" that the "best" directors have usually had control over their films, Sarris points to the "meaningful style" which equals "the distinguishable personality" of these same directors!

"The critic can talk about meaning and style in the work of a director," Sarris writes. "But how does a critic determine whether a movie is good or bad? This is a more difficult question. . . . If Aristotle had been alive to write a *Poetics* on film, he would have begun with D. W. Griffith's *The Birth of a Nation* as the first definition of a feature film as a work of bits and pieces unified by a central idea. Griffith is thus one of the definitions of cinema . . . The bits and pieces have multiplied beyond measure. The *auteur* theory is one of several methods employed to unify these bits and pieces into central ideas." Notice the shift in meaning that occurs between the point where Sarris invokes Aristotle to suggest that a good film is one which is "unified by a central idea" and the reaffirmation of the *auteur* theory . . . a theory which states that a good film is one in which the director's personality triumphs over "the barriers to its expression." Sarris doesn't seem to realize that to see a film "as a work of bits and pieces unified by a central idea" is not the same as to see a film—or rather, bits and pieces of *films*—as "directorial autobiography." Aristotle praises the plot of *Oedipus*; he does not say a word about Sophocles's personality.

3

The major portion of *The American Cinema* is devoted to a ranking of Hollywood directors according to "aesthetic" criteria devised by Sarris: "This . . . study will start at the top with the bundles of movies credited to the most important directors, and work downward, director by director, movie by movie, year by year, toward a survey of what was best in American sound movies between 1929 and 1966." Until now, according to Sarris, film scholarship has been dominated by "forest critics"; that is, by critics who have focused on what Hollywood pictures have in common rather than on their individual differences. Whereas "forest critics" describe Hollywood as a factory run by capitalists and philistines, Sarris defends the studios: "Film for film, Hollywood can hold its own with the rest of the world. [In "Notes on the *Auteur* Theory in 1962," the reader will recall, Sarris declared that "film for film, director for director, the American cinema has been consistently *superior* to that of the rest of the world."] If Hollywood yields a bit at the very summit, it completely dominates the middle ranges, particularly in the realm of 'good-bad' movies and genres. . . . The theory of film history toward which this book is directed aims at nothing more than taking the moviegoer out of the forest and into the trees."

Sarris's first ranking of American directors appeared in the Spring 1963 *Film Culture*, where about 150 of them were graded under the following categories: Pantheon Directors; Second Line; Third Line; Esoterica; Beyond the Fringe; Fallen Idols; Likable But Elusive; Minor Disappointments; Oddities and One Shots; and Other Directors. In *The American Cinema* the number of directors totals nearly 200; there are eleven categories instead of ten; and the titles of all but one category have been changed. It would be impossible—and futile—to go over Sarris's rankings category by category, director by director, but a few observations are necessary.

Fourteen names appear under the heading of Pantheon Directors: Chaplin, Flaherty, Ford, Griffith, Hawks, Hitchcock, Keaton, Lang, Lubitsch, Murnau, Ophuls, Renoir, Sternberg, and Welles. In line with the *auteur* theory, these directors belong in the Pantheon because they "have transcended their technical problems with a personal vision of the world. To speak any of their names is to evoke a self-contained world with its own laws and landscapes." But then Sarris adds: "They were also fortunate enough to find the proper conditions and collaborators for the full expression of their talent." Is this statement consistent with the previous one, namely, that the Pantheon Directors "transcended their technical problems"? By "technical problems," doesn't Sarris mean the Hollywood system of production? And if these directors found the right scripts and co-workers, then what has happened to the *auteurist's* criterion of tension?

As lists of important film-makers go, Pantheon Directors is

probably par for the course. Even if one isn't an *auteurist*, one might on other grounds still agree that most of the fourteen directors have made some distinguished, even great, films. The list, however, seems padded. Flaherty doesn't belong in a book otherwise reserved for directors of the fiction film. Are Griffith and Keaton representative film-makers of the sound period? Sarris lists over 100 of Griffith's films; but the only all-talking pictures the great man directed are *Abraham Lincoln, The Struggle*, and possibly *One Million, B.C.*—scarcely masterpieces. Since *auteurists* hold that "as a director grows older, he is likely to become more profoundly personal than most audiences and critics can appreciate" ("Notes on the *Auteur* Theory in 1962"), Sarris announces: "Like all great artists, [Griffith's] art had become so deceptively simple by the time of *Abraham Lincoln* that most critics assumed that he was in decline." For the same *auteurist* reasons, the American films of Lang and Renoir are overrated. Padding is also in evidence further down from the Pantheon under Fringe Benefits, where we find Antonioni, Buñuel, Chabrol, Clair, Clément, Eisenstein, Pabst, Polanski, Rossellini, Truffaut, and Visconti listed. Even Sarris admits that these directors "occupied . . . a marginal role" on the Hollywood scene; yet he includes them anyway, in a book ostensibly written to prove that American film-makers are the equal of any in the world.

To the obvious question: If Hollywood is not the aesthetically destructive place it has been pictured to be by "forest critics," then where are the American Fellinis, Bergmans, Antonionis, Kurosawas, and Truffauts?—Sarris answers: "Undiscriminating champions of foreign films against Hollywood movies might profitably inspect the crisp authority of Samuel Fuller's *Merrill's Marauders* and Don Siegel's *Hell Is for Heroes*" (*Confessions of a Cultist*). For those who are looking for him, Fuller can be found with nineteen other directors on The Far Side of Paradise ("these are the directors who fall short of the Pantheon either because of a fragmentation of their personal vision or because of disruptive career problems"), where he is described as "an authentic American primitive" whose *I Shot Jesse James* has an "oppressive intensity" comparable to Dreyer's *The Passion of Joan of Arc*. "Fuller's ideas are undoubtedly too broad and oversimplified for any serious analysis," Sarris admits, "but it is the artistic force with which his ideas are expressed that makes his career so fascinating to critics who can rise above their political prejudices." In other words, *Merrill's Marauders* and *I Shot Jesse James* are idiotic in content, but their images are exciting. Siegel is in the category labeled Expressive Esoterica—the one just below Fuller's—where twenty other "unsung directors with difficult styles or unfashionable genres or both" are located. "Their deeper virtues are often obscured by irritating idiosyncrasies on the surface," Sarris declares, "but they are generally redeemed by their seriousness and grace." Because Sarris "would never endorse a Ptolemaic constellation of directors in a fixed orbit" ("Notes on the *Auteur* Theory in 1962"), there is still hope for Fuller and Siegel, both of whom may one day add their "crisp authority" to the Pantheon.

"The categories are obviously absurd," Dwight Macdonald notes of Sarris's rankings, "but even if they were more sensible (and fewer), matters would not be improved. It's at best a parlor game . . . Taken seriously, this kind of quality-grading simply makes it more difficult to evaluate works of art—as if it weren't hard enough already—by forcing them into Procrustean categories that always add or subtract something essential" (*Dwight Macdonald on Movies*). Sarris seems to have a compulsion to elevate one director at the expense of another (what Roger Greenspun, in the *New York Times* [*February* 16, 1969], calls "the Sarris law of gravitation"). Thus, Sirk is ranked high—he dwells on The Far Side of Paradise—but Huston—along with ten other directors whose "personal signatures to their films were written with invisible ink"—is consigned to the lower depths in Less Than Meets the Eye ("These are the directors with reputations in excess of inspirations"). The Huston who directed *The Maltese Falcon, The Asphalt Jungle,* and *The African Queen* is, according to Sarris, just a "competent craftsman"; *The Treasure of the Sierra Madre* is "overrated." But Sirk's *Written on the Wind* and *Tarnished Angels* "become more impressive with each passing year. Sirk requires no extreme rationalization, and his films require no elaborate defense. The evidence of his style is visible on the screen." Sarris likes to make a pseudo-scientific appeal to the "evidence"—which often means nothing more than a bald assertion on his part. (Yet he makes converts. In his review of *The American Cinema* in the *Times, auteurist* Greenspun remarks: "Back in 1963 some people did not realize that the director of *Taza, Son of Cochise* was greater by far than the director of *The Treasure of the Sierra Madre,* but Sarris did— and time and The Late Show have born [sic] him out." Here the "evidence"—"time and The Late Show"—means "*auteur* critics.") Similarly, Vidor is placed on The Far Side of Paradise and Milestone is sent to Less Than Meets the Eye. In the section devoted to Vidor, Sarris compares one scene from *The Big Parade* with one scene from *All Quiet on the Western Front,* and concludes from this deep and extensive analysis that Vidor is superior to Milestone. "Vidor's treatment is more forceful than Milestone's, and hence more emotionally satisfying," he writes. But the question arises: "More forceful and more emotionally satisfying *for whom?*" Sarris argues that it is not because he has been "arbitrarily designated" as such that Vidor is a better director than Milestone. Oh, no. "The *auteur* theory can only record the evidence on the screen," he declares. "It can never prejudge it." Methinks the critic doth protest too much. The *auteur* theory does not enjoy the epistemological status of Ohm's Law, say, or the Law of Refraction; furthermore, it is not the *auteur* theory which records the "evidence"—it is the *auteur theorist.* And too often Sarris leaves one with the uncomfortable suspicion that he *has* prejudged the evidence. Whether Vidor is superior to Milestone, or whether Milestone is superior to Vidor—or whether they are both equally good or both equally bad—are questions that need much more attention to particular details and general considerations than Sarris even begins to suggest in *The American Cinema,* a book which could only be a bible to those "critics" who want instant evaluations and smooth answers to thorny questions.

In "Notes on the *Auteur* Theory in 1962," Sarris confesses that he had "always felt a cultural inferiority complex about Hollywood." Now, in overcoming an inferiority complex, the sufferer frequently goes to an opposite extreme. Sarris has performed a commendable service by asking us to reevaluate American pictures: not all Hollywood movies are bad, not all foreign films are good. But Sarris often tends to disparage the foreign import in his efforts to boost the hometown product ("the Sarris law of gravitation"). Since foreign directors are freer to create than American film-makers, they naturally tend to produce more artistic pictures. Book editors in the United States don't remove chapters from novels without conferring with the novelist; yet in most cases, as noted, the final editing of a Hollywood film isn't in the hands of the director (where, of course, it belongs), but is at the discretion of the producer. Under the circumstances, it is remarkable that so many good films manage to get made—with or without clear-cut signs of a single *auteur*—but there is no reason to exaggerate the achievement.

4

The Films of Josef von Sternberg (1966) is a short book (slightly over fifty, double-columned pages) with large print and about twenty-five handsome stills. Sarris takes up in order each of the director's twenty-six films, from *The Salvation Hunters* to *Anatahan*, allowing himself about two pages for discussion of the better ones and about two paragraphs for the poorer ones. Obviously, *The Films of Josef von Sternberg* cannot be described as a study in depth.

Although "the art of Josef von Sternberg is too often subordinated to the mystique of Marlene Dietrich," Sarris writes at the outset, the director is very much an *auteur*. Sternberg's cinema of illusion and delusion transcended the personality of his star the better to reflect his own vision. He not only crossed the sound barrier and confronted the star system without sacrificing his style, he defended Hollywood when it was not fashionable to do so.

Sarris sees no reason to doubt that if the way to "purer personal expression" had been less closely tied to financial considerations, Sternberg's film output would have shown a higher art-to-craft ratio, though even as it is "his work can be measured more by his actual achievements than by his alleged aspirations."

Throughout his book, Sarris is concerned with the familiar *auteurist* criterion: *The Salvation Hunters* is Sternberg's "most explicitly personal work until the emotional recapitulation of *Anatahan* . . ."; "There is no known print of *The Case of Lena Smith*," which is "unfortunate because it appears to have been more personal than *The Exquisite Sinner* . . ."; "*The Devil Is a Woman* is the last of the Sternberg-Dietrich sagas, and never before has Sternberg seemed as visible as he does here in the saturnine silhouette of Lionel Atwill, the morose victim of frustration and folly"; "*Crime and Punishment* was a relatively impersonal assignment for the director", and so on.

In spite of his ability to see both the strength and weakness in the mystiques of montage and *mise en scène*, Sarris has generally shown a partiality for the latter concept. This bias can be explained by the *auteur* theory. "Most Hollywood directors of the thirties were disqualified from serious consideration because they did not supervise the final editing (montage) of their films, for editing was then considered, by the aestheticians, the supreme function of cinematic creation," he writes in "The Fall and Rise of the Film Director," his introduction to *Interviews With Film Directors* (1967). The montage mystique having collapsed, however, many directors of the thirties are now seen as undeniably personal artists. "Not only do the best directors cut 'in the mind' rather than in the cutting room, but montage is only one aspect of a directorial personality." So it is not surprising that Sternberg should appeal to Sarris (there are, of course, other reasons too); for Sternberg, Sarris continues in his monograph, "entered the cinema through the camera rather than the cutting room and thus became a lyricist of light and shadow rather than a master of montage . . . [H]e concentrated on the spatial integrity of his images rather than on their metaphorical juxtaposition."

Although Sarris gives some attention to the relationship between technique and meaning, he devotes most of his space to an analysis of plot, character, and theme. Which is strange. He argues that writing credits "will always be a bone of contention, but there is now little doubt that Sternberg participated, with or without credit, in the writing of his most meaningful films." Still, *auteur* criticism—which claims to be director conscious—should be especially concerned with the visual instead of with plot, character, and theme, elements which belong in large measure to the writer or *writer*-director. As Ernest Callenbach observes in his review of Sarris's book in *Film Quarterly* (Spring 1967): "surely, of all directors save perhaps Eisenstein of *Ivan the Terrible*, Sternberg demands treatment on the level of how his films *look*: what they are as visual works . . . [Sarris fails] to show why Sternberg, on the evidence of his *mise en scène*, should be considered an important artist . . . You would think that anybody interested in Sternberg would be able to tell us something of how he handled space and time, how he managed lighting and camera movement to obtain such a preeminent luster in his images, how he worked out visually his conceptions of character and action—in short, the nature of his style, and what we are to make of it."

Another reason why Sarris appears to have been drawn to Sternberg is the latter's "relative lack of interest in realist social themes." Sarris has frequently expressed an aversion for the sociological approach in either film-making or film criticism, in part because he tends to equate that approach with Marxism. In a review of Norman Mailer's *Beyond the Law*, he notes that his had been the only relief family in Brooklyn to vote for Alf Landon in 1936. "Mailer, I think, was for Henry Wallace, and hence remote from my relatively timid traumas. My own reaction to *The Naked and the Dead* at the time was fogged up by my complete ignorance of the political context in which literary reputations were established. The Trotskyist formalism of the *Partisan Reviewers*, for example, seemed needlessly polemical to a reader for whom Stalinist strictures had been not merely absurd but anathema in the most reactionary sense" (*Confessions of a Cultist*).

Sarris's writings are filled with disparaging comments on neo-realism, "Which was never anything more"—according to him— "than the Stalinallee of social realism." Following Raymond Durgnat, he dismisses such films by calling them "male weepies." At times, Sarris is able to damn Eisenstein (Marxism, montage) and neo-realism (Marxism, emphasis on content rather than style-as-a-mirror-of-the-director's personality) all in one breath. "For those who are wary of Batman, Captain Marvel, Superman, and Flash Gordon, but who still are not ready to return to revivals of *Potemkin* and *The Bicycle Thief*," he writes in *Confessions of a Cultist*, "I would like to recommend Georges Franju's *Judex* as a lovely bit of fun without foolishness." Writing on Ophuls (whose *Lola Montes* he once called "the greatest film of all time") in *Interviews With Film Directors*, Sarris says: "After the elementary montage theorizing on *Potemkin*, lesson two was the need for Human Brotherhood, World Peace, Social Reform, Class Struggle, and all sorts of related Big Themes. Realism—Poetic, Social, or Neo—was all that separated us from the convulsions of Caligari and the horrors of Hitler." De Sica is one of Sarris's favorite targets. In "A Movie Is a Movie Is a Movie Is a," which appeared in *The New York Film Bulletin* (No. 46, 1964), he remarks: "Most left-wing directors . . . prefer to deal in universals rather than specifics. Their concern is Man in general, not men in particular. *The Bicycle Thief* is their model, and who would dare call such an abstractly humanistic tract communist or even Marxist in orientation. After all, we are all brothers, and every man should have his own bicycle." According to Sarris, De Sica lacks "insight into the real world" (interestingly enough, this is a criticism which others have made repeatedly against Sarris himself). Unlike Agee, who praised *Man's Hope* and *Open City*, Sarris can't seem to rise above his political prejudices—though non-*auteurist* critics are asked to do so where Fuller's pictures are concerned ("Fuller belongs to cinema, and not to literature and sociology"). Bazin, a Catholic, could describe *The Bicycle Thief* as a "communist film" and yet announce, after a long sensitive analysis, that De Sica's picture is also "one of the first examples of pure cinema" (*What Is Cinema?*, II). Of course, Bazin never slavishly adhered to the *Cahiers* line. Sarris, however, can praise Rossellini's *Open City*, *Paisan*, and *Germany Year Zero* (he calls these films "neo-realistic classics"); and in his review of *La Chinoise*, he can manage the neat trick of not once mentioning Godard's Marxism . . . Like Whitman, Sarris contains multitudes.

On the first page of *The Films of Josef von Sternberg*, Sarris writes that Sternberg's work has "not been seriously evaluated since the mid-thirties, when movies were supposed to crackle crisply to the proletarian point." Two pages later he quotes from Sternberg's autobiography, *Fun in a Chinese Laundry*, wherein the director acknowledges his blindness to social and political reality. Sternberg recalls that he was in Germany when Hitler became Der Fuehrer, and he was in Austria shortly before the Nazis moved into that country, yet each time he had no knowledge or awareness of what was going on around him. Similarly, he was in Japan, Spain, and Italy during history-making periods without noticing anything significant. With charming candor, Sternberg admits to "a peculiar and specific block. . . . Certainly it did me no good not to know what went on in minds other than my own." Nevertheless, Sarris comments: "Sternberg's apology for his solipsism seems unnecessary today, but in the thirties he was castigated for not mounting the barricades." To Simon's statement: "My interest in politics is rudimentary," Sarris has replied: "a thinking man with only a rudimentary interest in politics is both a fool and a knave" (*New York Times*, February 14, 1971). Finally, Sarris does grudgingly admit in criticism of Sternberg: "An insufficient grasp of one's time and place is hardly a positive virtue even for the most lyrical poet."

Sarris's tendency, however, is to defend Sternberg's "block." In a discussion of his film version of *An American Tragedy*, Sternberg observes: "I eliminated the sociological elements, which, in my opinion, were far from being responsible for the dramatic accident with which Dreiser had concerned himself." Eisenstein had previously prepared a treatment of Dreiser's novel but Paramount had rejected it; the movie moguls, according to the Russian director, would have preferred a "simple, tight whodunit about a murder . . . and about the love of a boy and a girl." Dreiser, who had approved of Eisenstein's script, rejected the Sternberg-Samuel Hoffenstein treatment. "Under this creative cloud *An American Tragedy* has been reviewed less for the film it was than for the film it should have been," Sarris writes. When a subliterary work is brought to the screen, the critic can ignore the original (though perhaps a less cavalier attitude towards even subliterary sources would provide a fairer basis for evaluating the accomplishments of *auteurs*); where a classic novel like *An American Tragedy* is concerned, however, comparisons are inevitable. Naturally, final judgment must be based on the film *qua* film. But Sarris allows himself too little space for showing how Sternberg's film succeeds artistically on its own terms. "Where Eisenstein proposed a deterministic treatment of the subject to absolve Clyde of the crime committed in the name of a materialistic society, Sternberg preferred to consider Clyde guilty of an act conditioned by the furtive prurience of his environment," Sarris remarks. "To equate the difference between Marx and Freud would be an oversimplification, but the thirties were an epoch when desire ran a poor second to dialectics in serious discussions of the cinema." Sarris neglects to mention that *An American Tragedy* was published in 1925; that Eisenstein's "deterministic treatment" was faithful to Dreiser's original; that the novel contains both "desire" and "dialectics"; and that sex has always been more appealing to Hollywood than "the sociological elements . . . with which Dreiser had concerned himself."

The *Blue Angel* is normally considered Sternberg's best film. In *From Caligari to Hitler*, sociological critic Siegfried Kracauer devotes three pages to the subject: he summarizes the plot (one paragraph); he discusses Sternberg's *mise en scène* (one paragraph); he attributes the picture's success to Marlene Dietrich as "a new incarnation of sex" and to "its outright sadism" (one paragraph); and he then places *The Blue Angel* in a sociological perspective: "It is as if the film implied a warning, for these screen figures anticipate what will happen in real life a few years later. The boys are born Hitler youths, and the cockcrowing device is a modest contribution to a group of similar, if more ingenious, contrivances much used in Nazi concentration camps" (two paragraphs). In *The Films of Josef von Sternberg*, Sarris allows *The Blue Angel* two pages: there is some general introductory material (three paragraphs); a comparison of the careers of Emil Jannings and Marlene Dietrich with the roles they play in the film (one paragraph); analysis of one shot (one paragraph); the rest is character and thematic analysis, including repeated comparisons of *The Blue Angel* with Renoir's *La Chienne* and Bergman's *The Naked Night* (five paragraphs).

Clearly, there is not much to choose between Kracauer's so-

ciological method and Sarris's *auteurist* approach. It is interesting
to see how Sarris attempts to justify *The Blue Angel* as a serious
film. He argues that it "is not specifically Germany or the German character with which Sternberg is concerned here, but
rather the spectacle of a prudent, prudish man blocked off from
all means of displaying his manhood except the most animalis-
tic." *The Blue Angel*, Sarris seems to be saying, has a universal
theme: Sternberg himself, he notes, has explicitly exempted the
film from the socially significant path Kracauer has traced in
From Caligari to Hitler. And he adds: "If 'serious' criticism of the
cinema were not as puritanical as it is, the experiences of Lola
and the Professor would seem more pertinent to the hidden
world of domestic sexuality than is now the case. The idea that
all eroticism is hopelessly exotic has made Sternbergian cinema
seem much stranger than it is." Sarris is suggesting that *The
Blue Angel* is not a mere clinical study of abnormal types but a
representative picture of heterosexual relationships. Yet he also
argues that "the niggling necessities of economics intervene between the drab decor and any of its frivolously sado-masochistic
implications. It is not Lola who forces the Professor to peddle her
gamey photos, but rather the financial realities of the situation."
Sex and economics have a way of getting entangled in real life,
and a film that shows this phenomenon should require no apology. But then, why does Sarris *seem* apologetic—why does he
keep shifting his ground? Comparing the Renoir and Bergman
films mentioned above with the Sternberg, Sarris observes that
all three "personal" films deal with cuckoldry: "Where Renoir is
more realistic and Bergman more literary, Sternberg is more effective in resolving his tragedy within the form he has postulated
for it. Renoir arbitrarily ends his film as if it were a stylized
spectacle of the Paris streets, but his implication is clear: life goes
on, transcending pride, passion, and morality. For Bergman life
is a mystery which no amount of thought can solve. Renoir and
Bergman are thus concerned with ideas beyond the frames of
their films, whereas Sternberg remains within his frames." Obviously, Sarris can't make up his mind whether *The Blue Angel*
means something—or nothing. The last sentence quoted is rem-

iniscent of the confused argument in "Notes on the *Auteur* Theory in 1962," wherein Sarris elevates Cukor at the expense of Bergman, who supposedly lacks an "abstract style" unburdened by ideas about life.

Sarris's faults as a critic are mainly traceable to the *auteur* theory. In *The American Cinema*, he remarks: "*Auteur* criticism is a reaction against sociological criticism that enthroned the *what* against the *how*. However, it would be equally fallacious to enthrone the *how* against the *what*." Rarely does Sarris manage to strike a proper critical balance between the *what* and the *how*. Because he values design over detail and form over fact, he tends "to praise *The Cardinal* rather than seek to bury it" (*Confessions of a Cultist*). The *how* means form, technique, expression; the *what* points in two directions: the content of the film; and that reality beyond the movie screen which the picture in some measure is a commentary on—that is, if it hopes to be taken as more than pure entertainment. Because the average Hollywood film has nothing to "say"; and because it bears little or no relationship to reality; the *auteur* critic—theoretically—is left in the position of having not much else to write about except the *how*. Now, *The Blue Angel* is, according to Sarris, "the one Sternberg film the director's severest detractors will concede is beyond reproach and ridicule"; yet Sarris like the sociological critic ends up writing mainly about the *what* (character analysis instead of analysis of characterization, thematic analysis instead of analysis of the ways in which the theme is expressed visually). Here, one would imagine, is a perfect opportunity for the *auteurist* to justify Sternberg by showing the wholeness of his art. In place of the *how*-and-*what* approach, though, Sarris substitutes an indecisive, muddled defense of the *what*. One suspects that Sarris's "cultural inferiority complex about Hollywood" is functioning again. Deep down, he doesn't really believe that form is more important than content; he himself says ("Do I contradict myself?") that the one should not be enthroned against the other. Throughout *The Films of Josef von Sternberg*, Sarris focuses so much on plot, character, and theme because he wants to prove that the content of a Sternberg film can be taken just as seriously as the content of a Renoir or a Bergman film . . . He is not convincing.

If sociological criticism too often fails because it overemphasizes the *what, auteur* criticism too often fails because it overemphasizes the *how* (that is, when it is not itself perversely overemphasizing the *what*). *Auteur* criticism represents an eccentric but understandable reaction to sociological criticism. After the excesses of Warshow and Kracauer, the *auteurist* discussion of film as a visual art comes as a welcome relief. For reasons which have been made abundantly clear throughout this chapter, however, *auteurism* is not a critical method which can be recommended to take the place of a purely sociological approach.

5

Although Sarris claims, in his comments on Preston Sturges in *Interviews With Film Directors*, that he has "always believed in some version of the *auteur* theory," his criticism is at its best when he forgets the dogma of *auteurism* and concentrates on analyzing form and content in pictures which, by common consent, have achieved a recognized position in film history. I would like to end this chapter by discussing what I consider to be Sarris's two best essays, both of which were written *before* "Notes on the *Auteur* Theory in 1962."

The first essay, "*Citizen Kane*: The American Baroque," published in *Film Culture* (No. 3, 1956), is a stimulating job of critical work. Sarris attempts to confront three persistent criticisms of *Citizen Kane*: "1) its narrative structure is unduly complicated; 2) its technique calls attention to itself; 3) its intellectual content is superficial." All three points have surface validity, he concedes, but a closer examination of the film reveals an inner consistency of theme, structure, and technique.

Analyzing the mystery-story element of the picture, with brief but perceptive comments on each flashback, Sarris suggests that the complications are valid because the film is concerned with the meaning of a man's life. He defends the ending of the movie —the shot of the sled and the word "Rosebud" on it being consumed by fire—since "without this particular resolution, the film would remain a jumbled jigsaw puzzle." True, Welles's virtuosity is far from being unobtrusive; but the very showiness of the camera work, the editing, and the use of sound squares with the subject matter: for technique in *Citizen Kane* "is a reflection and projection of the inhuman quality of its protagonist." Though respectively attacked as pretentious and as anticlimactic, Sarris writes, the beginning and end of *Citizen Kane* subtly suggests its theme. "The intense material reality of the fence dissolves into the fantastic unreality of the castle and, in the end, the mystic pretension of the castle dissolves into the mundane substance of the fence. Matter has come full circle from its original quality to the grotesque baroque of its excess."

Although no deep thoughts are uttered in dialogue, Sarris implies that the involved technique—the shifting points of view, the various perspectives on Kane—indicate a profound theme. "The *apparent* intellectual superficiality of *Citizen Kane*," he writes (the italics are mine), "can be traced to the shallow quality of Kane himself"; in other words, Kane may be shallow, but the film is not. "*Citizen Kane* presents an intense vision of American life," Sarris concludes. Unchecked by principles or traditions, his very magnitude causes his spiritual ruin. He emerges as an extension of the nouveau-riche American searching for a living culture among dead relics of the past. Though he strives to transcend it, Kane is victimized by the power of his wealth to alter the moral quality of his behavior. "In the end, everything has been bought and paid for, but nothing has been felt." As a short piece of analytical criticism, in which all the elements of the film are touched on and its humanistic import also conveyed, "*Citizen Kane*: The American Baroque" is well-nigh perfect.

Three years before Sarris announced that Bergman's "work has declined with the depletion of his ideas largely because his technique never equaled his sensibility," he published an essay on *The Seventh Seal* in *Film Culture* (No. 19, 1959). Sarris begins by asserting: "Although Ingmar Bergman's *The Seventh Seal* is set in medieval Sweden, nothing could be more modern than its author's conception of death as the crucial reality of man's existence." The Bergman film, Sarris believes, is the first "existential" movie: "Quite obviously," he writes, "the time has come to talk of other things beside the glories of social reconstruction . . . If modern man must live without the faith which makes death meaningful, he can at least endure life with the aid of certain necessary illusions. This is what Bergman seems to be saying in *The Seventh Seal*, a remarkably intricate film with many layers of meaning."

Sarris's aim in his article is to explore the complexities of Bergman's picture. He observes that the structure of *The Seventh Seal* is shaped by the chess game between the knight and Death; that "towering overhead shots" alternating with "pulsating images of the sun" suggest the universal dimensions of the drama; and that once the "philosophical size of the film is established, Bergman's camera probes more intimately into his characters." Sarris leans rather heavily on plot synopsis; but since he attends to structure, technique, and theme too, he gives the reader a sense of not just what occurs but also of how it is shaped, how it looks, and what it means.

Of the scene in which Death traps the knight into revealing his chess moves, for instance, Sarris remarks: "Almost any other director would have sustained this great cinematic moment with either an immense close-up or a receding tracking shot to the ceiling of the church looking down upon mortal man in his fullest affirmation. Instead, Bergman truncates his effect with a quick cut to the squire entertaining the church painter with a Rabelaisian account of the Crusade. This abrupt transition from sublimity to ridicule is characteristic of Bergman's balanced treatment of the high-low dualism of human life." In spite of its thematic density, Sarris insists, *The Seventh Seal* is "entertaining" ("more and more critics are demanding," he observes in "The Fall and Rise of the Film Director," "that there should be more fun in art, and more art in fun"). "Bergman's achievement is that he projects the most pessimistic view of human existence with an extraordinary vitality. Conceding that life is hell and death is nothingness, he still imparts to the screen a sense of joy in the very futility of man's illusions."

Sarris—who concludes that Bergman's "camera technique is fully adequate to his theme"—helps us to see deeper into *The Seventh Seal,* and to see it whole . . . Why hasn't Sarris been able to do as much in his later criticism?*

---

* Sarris's *The Primal Screen: Essays on Film and Related Subjects* (1973) appeared after this chapter was completed. There is nothing in the most recent book, however, which makes me want to alter either the treatment of *auteurism* or the evaluation of Sarris advanced here.

CHAPTER FOUR

Parker Tyler and Psychoanalytic-Mythological Criticism

I'm sure that we who are serious desire that better film criticism stand for values, that it should be able to point and distinguish, speak a coherent language, and espouse, at its best, a vigorous, high-level doctrine.

—PARKER TYLER

1

Of all American students of the film, Parker Tyler has been by far the most prolific writer of books. The last time I counted (the number will probably have multiplied by the time this study appears), Tyler's collected works ran to twenty-one volumes. He has published a novel; three books of verse (he was awarded a Longview Award for poetry in 1958); a biography of Pavel Tchelitchew (who collaborated with Tyler on one book of verse); studies of Van Gogh, Renoir, Degas and Lautrec, Cezanne and Gauguin, and Florine Stettheimer; and nine books of what are generally—and, in most cases, charitably—referred to as "film criticism."

Aside from the sheer bulk of Tyler's writings, the would-be explicator of his thought faces several other formidable problems. One is inconsistency. Tyler has often demanded one type of approach to film while blithely practicing the opposite. Then there is his numbing reiteration of ideas, from volume to volume and within individual volumes. Tyler's books have no real organization—everything gets dumped into the hopper. Individually published articles are dusted off and become "chapters" in the next tome. Any thought which happens to cross the author's mind while writing, no matter how irrelevant to the matter at hand, is apparently deemed worthy of preservation for future doctoral candidates.

And then there is the famous Tyler style. Many times he searches over several pages for the *mot juste* without coming anywhere near discovering it. "Tyler's method of writing is so obtuse, and he is so personally in love with the sound of his own words," Philip T. Hartung observes in *The Commonweal* (September 1, 1944), "that it frequently becomes impossible to follow the line of his reasoning." A reviewer for the *Canadian Forum* remarks: "Tyler has evolved a peculiar, specialized language of his own which bears only a haunting resemblance to English, so that the entire book [*Magic and Myth of the Movies*] reads like a message from a hashish dream, still to be translated" (August 1947). The words "involuted," "convoluted," "wooly," "pretentious," and "incomprehensible" are repeatedly used by book reviewers to describe Tyler's style. Undoubtedly, the subject of this chapter has applied to his expository writing William Blake's remarks in defense of artistic obscurity: "that which can be made explicit is not worth my care."

It would be pleasant to report that the faults just mentioned (as well as those, alas!, not yet mentioned) have been corrected over the years; but, unfortunately, practice has not made Tyler perfect. Indeed, his two most recent books are even more loosely structured, more garrulously written, more ostentatiously empty than his first three ones.

Tyler has never suffered from excess of modesty. In "Is Film Criticism Only Propaganda?" (which was published in the Fall 1966 *Film Culture*, and from which I have taken the quotation that appears at the head of this chapter, a quotation which ironically bears no relation to Tyler's own efforts), he announces: "Perhaps I am the most unpopular film critic in the world and

maybe, despite my long record, I'm so unpopular because I'm
not a very good propagandist for modern doctrines *in* film and *of*
film." Translated, this means: "If I'm not widely read, the reason
isn't because my books are nearly impossible to read but because,
unlike Kracauer and the *auteurists* and spokesmen for the underground movie, I have no ideological ax to grind." (As we shall
see, Tyler himself is not above propagandizing.) Previously,
Tyler had boasted in a letter to *The Hudson Review* (Winter
1961–62) that his "merger of psychoanalysis, myth, free plastic
analogies, unconscious syndromes in the film industry, and
straight technical criticism, has already won recognition precisely
for establishing new criteria of integrity and coherence." (As we
shall also see, Tyler has used various approaches to film but he
has rarely, if ever, fused them in terms of aesthetic criticism. His
grandiose claim of having formulated unique evaluative criteria
is unsubstantiated, since these criteria are not known to anyone
but Tyler himself.)

2

In his preface to the paperback version of *Magic and Myth of
the Movies*, written in 1970, Tyler again protests that he is not
"selling ideas." He describes his method in *The Hollywood Hallucination* (1944) and *Magic and Myth of the Movies* (1947) as
" 'psychoanalytic-mythological,' often socially angled." Tyler's
thesis in his first two books is that American films are myth, not
art. The subject matter of *The Hollywood Hallucination* and
Magic and Myth of the Movies is the American film of the thirties and forties; however, since Tyler makes no distinction in his
preface between the product of the past and current production,
one must assume that for him nothing has changed.

Both art and myth remain fictions, and in this sense they are
related. There is, however, one important difference between
them. Art—or for that matter, pure entertainment too—is a
product of conscious creation; myth is unconscious fantasy. A
myth "is specifically a free, unharnessed fiction, a basic, proto-
typic pattern capable of many variations and distortions, many

betrayals and disguises, even though it remains *imaginative truth.*" The movie which the film-makers believe they have created may be compared to what the Freudian calls the "manifest content" of a dream; but the significance and value of the work, as Tyler sees it, lies in its "latent content." Like Kracauer—a critic with whom he has often quarreled—Tyler stresses the collective aspect of film-making. With the author of *From Caligari to Hitler,* Tyler maintains that "movies are dreamlike and fantastic." The second proposition largely depends upon the first; if the film experience allegedly expresses the collective unconscious, it remains incumbent upon the theorist to minimize individual responsibility. Since so many talents contribute to the making of a picture, Tyler contends, the rule of the lowest common denominator prevails, thus assuring that the same stereotyped kinds of manifest content will be projected. Like the *auteurists,* however, Tyler sees in this collective and commercial enterprise a salutary benefit; for the group effort reveals in symbolic form the yearnings of that larger mass which sits mesmerized before the movie screen, enjoying therapeutic release at bargain-basement prices. ("The movie theater," Tyler writes in *The Hollywood Hallucination,* "is the psychoanalytic clinic of the average worker's daylight dream.")

In *Theory of Film,* Kracauer regards art as a contaminating presence in a movie; Tyler is not punning when he insists that art on the screen is a myth. In his own way, each critic dispenses with form in the form-content unity of a movie—Kracauer by rhapsodizing over the "flow of life," Tyler by extolling the healing properties of the medium. In *The Three Faces of the Film* (1960), Tyler writes: "*Reality* in the movies reasserts 'content' in the classic aesthetic dualism, *hallucination* reasserts 'form.'" These definitions do not square with Tyler's use of the terms in his first two books, even though his explanation in the later volume is intended to be consistent with them. As Tyler repeatedly employs the word, "hallucination" equals "unconscious." "Form" for him, then, can only mean "the unconscious psychological-mythological hidden significance of a picture as experienced by the viewer."

In his preface to *Magic and Myth of the Movies,* Tyler clearly equates "form" and "art"; therefore, by denying that any Hollywood films are art—by insisting on their mythic nature—Tyler also denies that they have form. The *auteurist* severs form from content by asserting that the latter is unimportant; for him "form" (by which he intends "directorial style") alone matters. As Sarris states it: "Interior meaning is extrapolated from the tension between a director's personality and his material." Tyler doesn't care a rap for the American director's personality; his reasoning in one respect, however, is not unlike that of the *auteurist*. He points out that the situation in Hollywood provides "crevices [apparently he has read Kael's polemic against Sarris's third premise of the *auteur* theory] for whatever there be in actor, dialogue writer, cinematic trick shot, or directorial fantasy to creep through and flower." And predictably, he adds: "Under such conditions the factor most likely to succeed in Hollywood would unquestionably be the mythic."

Most of Tyler's attention in his first two books is devoted to the Hollywood stars and to what he conceives to be their mythological symbolism. For example, he argues that the "adulation, often so shockingly naive, given to movie stars independently of their screen roles and only as personalities, provides a basis for thinking of them as semi-divine, a vestigial form of the pagan divinities of classical Greece." Whereas Kracauer sees the film performing a quasi-religious function by "redeeming" physical reality, Tyler asserts that the glamourous personages on the screen fulfill "an ancient need, unsatisfied by popular religions of contemporary times." We know that the stars are human; "yet a magic barrier cuts across the texture of our mutual humanity; somehow their wealth, fame, and beauty, their apparently unlimited field of worldly pleasure—these conditions tinge them with the supernatural." According to Tyler, the movie theater is not only a psychoanalytic clinic but also a temple or a church. By the logic of their premises, the *auteurists* must desire to see the Hollywood system perpetuated, since the barriers to directorial expression produce a fruitful tension in films. Similarly, it follows from Tyler's premises that the star system should not be allowed to perish —even though it has already perished, or at least is far from being what it once was—since that system gratifies so many sociocultural needs. No wonder Tyler insists that his "'psycho-analytic-mythological,' often socially angled" method is not intended to "test the high or low aesthetic content of a given movie," that he does not "analyze the best movies as the *artistic best* but as the *mythological best*" (italics in original).

In other words, whatever Tyler is up to in *The Hollywood Hallucination* and *Magic and Myth of the Movies*, it isn't film criticism. For the most part, the author discusses bad old movies in a patronizing way, except when he is ferreting out their concealed psychoanalytical and mythological meanings. When faced with a great picture like *Citizen Kane*, he dismisses it—as though it were just another *When Ladies Meet*. (Does anybody remember that one?)

If the *auteurists* exaggerate the number of worthy accomplishments produced within the Hollywood studio system, Tyler goes to an opposite extreme. (Extremes often meet. Gore Vidal perhaps unwittingly points to an affinity between the *auteurists* and Tyler in *Myra Breckinridge*. One of the chapters in the title character's book is called "Parker Tyler and the Films of the Forties; or, the Transcendental Pantheon." Tyler, by the way, is mentioned ten times in Vidal's *chef-d'oeuvre*.)

Although Tyler's own method is noncritical, the mythological approach remains a valid tool of criticism. No sane theorist would deny that film, like literature, *sometimes* deals with myth in one or another form (whereas Tyler sees mythic profundities in *every* grade "B" movie). Obviously, there are mythic or archetypal characters, plots, images, symbols, and themes. Tyler has admitted to being influenced by Sir James Frazer. Myth criticism also owes a debt to Nietzsche's *The Birth of Tragedy* (1872), which anticipated much of what has been of interest to later students of the method. Other figures who have inspired the approach are the Cambridge anthropologists (Jane Ellen Harrison, F. M. Cornford, and A. B. Cook), Gilbert Murray, Freud (especially in *Totem and Taboo*, published in 1913), Carl Jung (particularly in *The Archetypes and the Collective Unconscious*, published in 1959), Bronislaw Malinowski, Ernst Cassirer, and Claude Lévi-Strauss.

Since the basic premise of the myth critic is that narrative art is an unconscious projection of the collective experience of men, he draws freely on anthropology, religion, psychology, and folklore in an effort to "get at" a specific movie. Like the sociological critic, the myth critic holds that film and society interact, each one influencing the other. Like the psychological critic, the myth critic assumes a close relationship between dream and film story. At his best, the myth critic simultaneously illuminates a film from aesthetic, psychological, and social perspectives. The proper interest of the myth critic is not in myth by itself but in the motion picture as a vehicle of myth in *artistic* form. To express the point differently: it is the job of the myth critic to explain how the archetypal subject matter relates to the movie's design and meaning. The central task for the myth critic—as for any other kind of critic—is to analyze, interpret, and evaluate the film itself as a whole. Tyler's lack of concern with the unity of a movie is a characteristic failing of the mythological critic, who often locates the archetype but overlooks the art.

3

Tyler's *Chaplin: Last of the Clowns* (1948; revised 1972) is a psychoanalytic study. According to Tyler, the death of Chaplin's father when the future comic was five traumatically arrested his development. Already burdened with an Oedipus complex, Chaplin now felt constrained to take over the role vacated by his father; however, he was too small to provide the economic and emotional support required by his mother. The famous image of the Tramp—from clumsy shoes up through baggy pants and narrow shoulders to derby hat—symbolizes the adult as viewed from the low angle of the child. In brief, the Tramp is "really" a small boy in adult clothing, buffeted about by a hostile environment and held back by his cumbersome, outsized shoes. Because Chaplin grew up in poverty, Tyler also sees the Tramp as "an aristocrat turned inside out, a knight turned clown. Yet, although visually, from the child's viewpoint, he is a caricature of a man, he is also, in his moments of humiliating flight, a caricature of the aristocrat . . . So Charlie's flight as the Tramp was, both in the literal and symbolic-retrospective senses, a flight from the 'punishment' of poverty." In private life Chaplin became rich and famous but inwardly he remained frustrated, haunted by his past. Gradually, the comedian began to take a critical attitude toward his fantasies, so that in *The Great Dictator* the "common man"—formerly apotheosized—is found to harbor in his psyche not only the lovable Tramp but also the power-hungry Hynkel.

The method used in *Chaplin* is in the worst tradition of psychoanalytic criticism. Tyler begins at the beginning—and stays there. Every development in Chaplin's life is reductively seen in terms of the past. Aside from the necessarily speculative nature of the thesis itself, Tyler is often guilty of an extremely crude application of Freudian insights. For example, the balloon that Hynkel dances with in *The Great Dictator* is "the maternal breast, unmoored." The machine which traps the Tramp in *Modern Times* is a "womb."

As can be seen, Tyler's psychoanalytic approach largely takes place in a historical and social void. Chaplin's pantomime is associated with the infant's "dream at the mother's breast, broken into by the father's word, the father's voice . . . Charlie's dream of happiness, essentially wordless, could have been connected perfectly logically with an essentially wordless action of life." When Charlie drinks the tea offered him by a mother figure in *Modern Times*, his "audible gastric reactions . . . stand for sexual speech, and thus, in general, for the psychic relations and their consequences." Chaplin resisted the sound film, Tyler argues, because his silent acting represented unconscious Oedipal satisfaction; only when the comic felt pressed to rationalize his inner conflicts in words did he accept talking pictures.

The foregoing interpretations also indicate that Tyler's method takes scant cognizance of aesthetic problems or professional questions. At no point in the book does Tyler come to grips with any one film as a complete work of art. *Chaplin* not only fails as film criticism but is also suspect in its use of psychoanalytic material. How much Tyler has read in depth psychology is an open question; he never advances a single authority in support of his readings. When the starving Big Jim chases Charlie with a knife in *The Gold Rush*, the action—according to Tyler—is a "paradigm for the child's fear of the father-devourer." And when, in the same film, Charley eats his shoe, he is symbolically devouring in turn the father. The literature of psychoanalysis records sundry instances of unconscious infantile fantasies of being eaten by the mother. This is sometimes explained as a reversal of thinking on the part of the suckling: "It is not I who wish to devour Mother, but Mother who wishes to devour me." If there are case histories containing infantile fantasies of being devoured by the father, I am unfamiliar with them. (There is, of course, the famous myth about Kronos and Zeus.) This does not mean of course that Tyler is necessarily wrong. It does suggest, however, that on occasion it behooves the psychoanalytic critic to offer clinical evidence along with his intuitions and free associations.

Like the mythological approach to film, the psychological, or psychoanalytic, method can be of value to a critic. It is important to add, however, that probably no other approach to the arts— not even the Marxist—has proved so unsatisfactory as the Freudian. Some of the faults are inherent in Freud's system itself—for example, in the pansexualism of psychoanalytic theory. Other faults stem from the vulgarization of Freudian concepts and methodology, resulting in a mechanical and oversimplified search for incest symbols (or whatever) with no effort to place those symbols into a film's total aesthetic and thematic framework.

To psychoanalyze the characters in a movie is risky, since none of the techniques available to a clinician in establishing a relationship with his patient in real life are available to the critic in the screening room or later at his typewriter. For a layman to psychoanalyze a film artist without ever having met him is likewise no easy task. The biographical approach—psychoanalytic or otherwise—can never tell us whether a film is great or trash, although it can suggest why the same motifs recur in a filmmaker's work. In other words, the biographical approach can be of interpretive help to a critic but it cannot aid him in evaluation. It is necessary for the explicator to be as interested in film as art as in the psychological or psychoanalytic method. If Freudian criticism is to make a genuine contribution to our understanding of film, then, it must cast light on the work of art as a whole, otherwise it destroys the integrity of the picture. Therefore, the biographical method—psychoanalytic or otherwise—can enrich film criticism only when it is joined with a formalistic, aesthetic approach.

4

Cinema can be apprehended, Tyler argues in *The Three Faces of the Film*, under three aspects: 1) art, 2) dream, and 3) cult. In his 1967 introduction to the revised edition of the study (entitled "The 'Hollywood Hallucination' Rampant," in which he argues that the thesis of his first two books is still pertinent, and will continue to be so), Tyler writes that "*cult* is to be distinguished from *art*, and *dream* from both." He adds: "At the same time, since most of the films I shall discuss here start with the premise of being fiction, and thus 'art,' the dream and the cult can never be wholly isolated from the art: organically, they remain interrelated. Hence the classifications in this book represent emphases and not categories; viewpoints and not final definitions."

Kurosawa's *Rashomon* is an example of the film as art. Whereas Kracauer reserves his highest praise for the film as non-art, Tyler holds that art "represents destiny as opposed to chance, form as opposed to formlessness." Whereas Kracauer views with horror any correspondence between film and the other arts, Tyler maintains that "the film has to invent not only in terms of its own exclusive nature but also in terms of the formal law which it shares with painting."

Tyler sees a relationship between structure, point of view, and theme in *Rashomon* and a Futurist multiple-image canvas, even though film is a time art and painting a space art. The Futurist suggests the dynamics of movement by a blurred image. "The analogy of *Rashomon* with such procedures of stating physical movement is that, for the single action photographed, a complex action (or 'episode') is substituted, and for the single viewpoint toward this action, multiple (and successive) viewpoints," Tyler explains. "The camera in this movie is actually trained four times on what theoretically is the same episode; if the results are different each time, it is because each time the camera represents the viewpoint of a different person; a viewpoint mainly different, of course, not because of the physical angle (the camera is never meant to substitute for subjective vision) but because of the psychological angle." Both the Futurists and Kurosawa deal with a multiform, as opposed to a uniform, plastic reality. Tyler compares *Rashomon* to Picasso's *Girl Before Mirror*. Just as the Picasso depicts the subject, through the use of a mirror, in profile and in fullface—that is to say, just as the painting reveals "different 'phases' of the same person"—the Kurosawa depicts different versions of the same event, and "people as they think of themselves and as they are to others."

The mistake of too much film-making, Tyler believes, is the effort—lauded by Kracauer—to project "reality" in a documentary, journalistic, scientific way. Fact in such movies is enthroned but fiction becomes a "dream to be shunned rather than explored." Experimental pictures challenge the theory that film aspires to the condition of nonart, that Kracauer's "camera-reality" equals "material reality." As Tyler points out, "reality" is also subjective, "fiction as well as fact." Film-makers should not reject the imagination. Art "has its genesis within man, and without this basic innerness, man is not a living soul but a living thing." The camera is a passive recording device; however, it is also an active transformer of material "reality" into "*imaginative* reality." The dream symbols of experimental films should be interpreted "not as psychoanalytic, but as *poetic*, material." This is, of course, just the opposite of what Tyler does in his first three books, wherein the contents of the commercial film are treated as "manifest" and "latent." Here, however, he informs us that "documentary film does almost nothing to mend the dream/reality split so insidiously and irresponsibly nurtured by Hollywood, while at least in theory, experimental film is dedicated exactly to mending this split." Isn't this statement a negation of Tyler's thesis in his first two books that the Hollywood film performs a curative function, that the commercial movie theater represents the equivalent of a psychiatric clinic?

The film as cult can be most clearly seen in the concept of Hollywood as a "Universal Church absorbing both Jewry and

Christianity by means of a rigid social-professional creed." The success story is a familiar Hollywood theme. By projecting certain physical characteristics and personality types on the screen and by showing them as leading to success in life, Hollywood creates "the lay religions of snobbery and social climbing." Although anti-Semitism is explicitly condemned in movies, Tyler argues that the bobbed nose is held out as the way to achieve status through "conformance with a given personality norm." By refusing to divulge any information about the religious affiliations of its stars, the Hollywood studios further promulgate the tenets of the Universal Church.

The last essay in *The Three Faces of the Film* is called "Movies and the Human Image." "Film is the art—and this is a pivotal definition—where the finished 'form' is the most easily soluble into raw 'content' or ingredients of meaning," Tyler observes. "Both psychologically and technically, the photographic lens is a mirror, even if a sometimes flattering one. For this reason, the relation of photography to the classic human image is simple and direct. Classic Western art evolved through the aesthetic desire to come as close to nature (or 'content') as possible while in the same act 'idealizing' it: giving it a flattering look (or 'form')." Elsewhere in the same essay, Tyler adds: "Historically, classicism is nothing but the moral preeminence of Man—man as a theoretically, or 'rationally,' perfectible if not perfect being. Preferably and conventionally, man is inspired by God, but at least he is given his basic meaning by the ability to reason, to relate himself to gods, other men, and nature as well as to art." Because nonobjective, nonrepresentational painting appears, "in comparison with the whole of human experience, both narrow and tending to barrenness," Tyler looks to film "as the probable savior of the classic human image in our age."

Of Tyler's first four books on the movies, *The Three Faces of the Film* is by far the best. The tripartite conception of a movie as simultaneously art, dream, and cult is a suggestive one, in that it properly stresses the complexity of the subject rather than oversimplifying and distorting it. Whether every film is in fact open to Tyler's three approaches is a separate matter. Although not entirely free from the usual Tyler windiness and the typical looseness of construction (a number of chapters in the revised edition were published in magazines after the original edition of the book appeared), *The Three Faces of the Film* is relatively intelligible and generally dedicated to serious concerns. Tyler's focus on art, his argument that surrealistic films are as cinematic as so-called realistic ones, and his espousal of humanistic values provide *The Three Faces of the Film* with a critical relevance too rarely attained elsewhere in his work.

5

Classics of the Foreign Film (1962) is Tyler's fifth book on the movies. Actually, it is less a "book" in the ordinary critical sense than an attractive pictorial history featuring over four hundred stills. Tyler has selected seventy-five "classics" from France, Spain, Italy, Germany, Scandinavia, Poland, Czechoslovakia, Russia, India, and Japan. For the most part, the films are an irreproachable selection (one of the "classics," though, is *Mondo Cane*). The earliest film discussed is *The Cabinet of Dr. Caligari* (1920), the most recent one *The Silence* (1963). Whereas in his first two books Tyler almost never identifies the director of an American film (since he regards Hollywood as an impersonal dream-myth factory), he begins *Classics of the Foreign Film* with a short essay entitled "A Gallery of Directors: Some Men Who Have Created Foreign Film Classics." However, except for the captions underneath pictures of Eisenstein, Gance, Lang, Buñuel, and seven other directors, the essay is mainly a statement on the meaning of the terms "classic" and "myth."

By "classic," Tyler first of all intends a film which embodies values that have survived the test of time. A "classic" is also a formally preserved slice of the historical past. And finally, a "classic" represents a "myth." According to Tyler, myth "is an inalienable function of every art; myth is not what makes art difficult to understand but what makes it easy to understand. The popular misconception that a 'myth' is something that was never true—or, once true, true no longer—is unworthy of the well-equipped filmgoer. A myth, in *that* sense, is only a colloquial figure-of-speech. In the responsible sense, it is a permanent pattern in stories of all kinds, making it possible for the same person to understand and relate Shakespeare's plays, Aesop's Fables, the Bible, Eisenstein's film epics, and Cocteau's modernized-myth films." Tyler concludes that films which use mythological patterns are "classics—the things of enduring values, balanced and undiminishing truths."

Such definitions—namely, of "classic" and "myth"—mean everything and nothing. So many "values" have survived, for example, that it is not very helpful to learn that the mere capacity for endurance confers upon a picture the status of a "classic." Some "classics" involve "myth"; but "myth" is not a synonym for "classic." Tyler also seems to equate "myth" and "universality." The latter term indicates the presence in art of qualities which appeal to all people in all places and in all times. "Universality" points to those "undiminishing truths" Tyler speaks of; or, as Faulkner put it in his famous Nobel Prize speech, to those "old universal truths lacking which any story is ephemeral and doomed—love and honor and pity and pride and compassion and sacrifice." However, "myth" as a "permanent pattern" in stories refers to such archetypal motifs as The Quest, The Initiation, Death and Rebirth, The Adam and Eve situation (mentioned by Tyler), and some others. Obviously, mythic patterns have universal significance; but neither "classic" nor "universal" are convertible as terms with "myth."

Fortunately, Tyler forgets his fuzzy reflections on myth in "A Gallery of Directors" and except where appropriate (such as in his discussion of Cocteau's *Beauty and the Beast*) his commentary in the rest of the book is innocent of mythopoeic musings. Since the critic allows himself only about two pages of text per film, however, he has little analysis to offer that is either sustained or profound. His basic aim remains a *"vivid evocation* of a film." Unhappily, Tyler does not possess the style or sensibility to accomplish such a task. Compare his commentary on *The Passion of Joan of Arc* (which, considering most of Tyler's observations in other books, is well-written and perceptive) with Vernon Young's essay on the same picture in *On Film* ("Fugue of Faces: A Danish Film and Some Photographs"). In about the same

amount of space that Tyler allows himself, Young takes the
reader up close to Dreyer's masterpiece—makes him see it, feel
it, and understand it—and afterwards, makes him want to go
back to the film itself for another viewing. The difference between Tyler's approach and Young's is the difference between
merely competent writing and film criticism at its best.

6

The Hollywood movie, according to Tyler, remains commercial nonart. Even though it is also commercial, the foreign film is
capable of rising to aesthetic heights. Yet, because a picture by
Fellini or Bergman or Kurosawa is intended to make money in
addition to delighting the artistic sense, Tyler's greatest hope
resides in the underground cinema . . . notwithstanding the fact
that he himself admits that little gold has been mined so far in
that particular region.

In *Underground Film: A Critical History* (1970), Tyler argues
that, for the most part, the experimental film has been traveling
downhill since the early days of the avant-garde. Tyler's touch-
stone remains Cocteau's *Blood of a Poet*. Among American films,
he can only recommend a trilogy by Maya Deren, *The Lead
Shoes* by Sidney Peterson, and a handful of other nuggets. Up to
1930 the avant-garde film was carefully structured—"built, as it
were, to last." The typical underground movie today, however,
remains chaotic in form: "The main strength of the underground
film per se . . . is currently to use the camera as the self-sufficient
reporter of vital activity. It is as if to say: The technique and the
form do not matter, only the message matters. And yet here the
message is what makes the medium look messy—*that* is the ultimate message!"

The underground film, Tyler maintains, exploits those areas
which have heretofore remained taboo for the camera: "One of
the strongest motifs in underground films is the drive toward
sloughing off civilized dignity and indulging amoral naked im-
pulses in the sight of all." What Tyler calls "infantile psychology"
prevails among underground film-makers; yet he adds: "The

child and the lunatic . . . are sources of much interest and charm, being (at the very least) highly instructive as subjects of study. I have no wish at all to demean underground films by isolating their infantile and lunatic traits." All the same, the main point of Tyler's argument is that the underground movie tends to be not only slovenly in form that also moronic in content: "In our psychedelic age it is possible that people (including film-makers) depend too much upon the optical 'explosions' occasioned by drugs, too little upon the parallel explosions of the creative imagination."

Yet the avant-garde of yesterday—notably the Surrealists—and the undergrounders of today possess one aim in common: "the desire to use film as an instrument going beyond the real, in that it goes beyond surfaces and penetrates reality *especially* where protective conventions frustrate the eye." Naturally, the author of *The Three Faces of the Film* applauds this aim. However, if the underground film is to command serious attention, Tyler insists, artistic standards have to be invoked to judge experimental pictures. For a given film-maker to merely express himself is not enough. The personal movie-maker must "have something unforgettable to contribute to human sensibility through film." Undergrounders must dedicate themselves to rediscovering that "organic sense of form possessed by the best avant-garde films of the past, even when those same films are not quite successful." The cardinal sins of the underground cinema are *anti-aestheticism* and *anti-intellectualism*.

Part of the responsibility for the lamentable state of affairs in Warhol-land resides with film critics. "By and large, underground film criticism is an occupation to be termed blurbing; statistically, it is most inaccurate unless both film and commentary are viewed as one homogenized life style," Tyler writes. "Then the argument . . . becomes entirely empiric, and really is neither argument nor criticism, but an appeal or invitation to join up." The result is still another cult. In "Is Film Criticism Only Propaganda?," Tyler states a proposed new slogan for undergrounders: "The Independent Cinema Independent Of Its Independence Of Criticism." Elsewhere in that same piece, he gloomily observes that the underground cinema is the "social and economic antibody of the commercial film and directly tends to substitute for the vices of its opponent its own peculiar vices." Very few independent film-makers, Tyler concludes, are producing anything of value better than Hollywood with its commercial fare.

Underground Film is one of Tyler's better books. It is well-organized, fairly well-written, and, on the whole, intelligently argued. The trouble is that Tyler's pains are exercised on basically trivial material. Since by his own admission few works of art have surfaced from the underground, the reader can't help asking: Is the subject worthy of a book? Even the Hollywood commercial movie can claim a more impressive list of accomplishments than the experimental film, avant-garde or underground. As for comparisons between the foreign film and the underground—well, the latter is nowhere. In sum: *Underground Film* appears to be "Much ado about nothing."

7

Sex Psyche Etcetera in the Film (1969) is a potpourri of essays divided into four main topics: "Sex Ritual," "The Modern Psyche," "The Artist in Crisis," and "Film Aesthetics Pro and Con." Even if the reader familiar with Tyler's previous books had not read most of these pieces originally in *Film Quarterly, Sight and Sound, Film Culture, Kenyon Review, Accent, Kulchur,* and elsewhere, he would still experience the sensation of having visited the territory before.

Under the first heading—"Sex Ritual"—Tyler discusses Warhol, a subject whose meager talents were scrutinized in *Underground Film.* In the earlier study, Tyler expressed critical reservations about Warhol; here *Fuck*—released as *Blue Movie*—is compared to "great art" and is said to be "exciting to the intelligence." Later in the book, however, Tyler reports: "Warhol's current topical importance has very little to recommend the aesthetic status of his work" ("Film as a Force in Visual Education"). Tyler's praise for *Fuck*, strategically placed at the beginning of the book, signals a development in the aging writer. Weary perhaps of being "the most unpopular film critic in the world," Tyler manifests an embarrassing willingness in his last three volumes to hop on the latest cultural and countercultural bandwagons. His apparent desire for acceptance comes at a time when, as suggested, he does not appear to have anything really new to say. In "The Awful Fate of the Sex Goddess," he reworks material first offered up in *The Hollywood Hallucination* and *Magic and Myth of the Movies*. He takes credit (if that is the proper word) for having been the first writer to describe Mae West in terms of a female impersonator—a subject which he rehearses for still a third time in his next book.

"The Horse: Totem Animal of Male Power—An Essay in the Straight-Camp Style" reveals Tyler using the psychoanalytic approach with the same ludicrous results achieved earlier in *Chaplin*. Now we are informed that horse racing is symbolic of the sex act. ("The obsessional temper of racing fans and the emotional build-up to a minutes-long suspense—the race itself—accompanied by the wildest excitement and breathlessly climaxed, are factors of racing that testify to its sexual parallel.") Also, the Western—or at least those "significantly totemic" examples of the genre—is a product, in Tyler's vision, of the Oedipus complex. If "The Horse: Totem Animal of Male Power" is written in a "straight-camp style," then *Chaplin* must have been similarly composed, although there was no evidence back in 1948 that such was Tyler's attitude toward his vaporous outpourings.

Chaplin is revisited in *Sex Psyche Etcetera* in the essay "Autobiographic Artist." Originally—and this shows how far down the barrel Tyler had to reach—the Chaplin essay was published in a 1947 issue of the *Kenyon Review*; it was later worked (naturally enough) into the Chaplin book. The comic is also discussed in *The Hollywood Hallucination, Magic and Myth of the Movies*, and *The Three Faces of the Film*; not surprisingly, he shows up again in the last two books.

The psychoanalytic method—or what passes for that method in Tyler's hands—is also brought to bear on *L'Avventura, La Notte*, and *L'Eclisse* ("Maze of the Modern Sensibility: An Antonioni Trilogy"). Tyler attempts to explain the problems of Antonioni's characters, their fear of the "moral unknown," by reference to abnormal psychology. Freud's view of "paranoia," Tyler glibly assures us, "supplies the answer." Like most of *Sex Psyche Etcetera*, the essay on Antonioni makes for unrewarding reading.

As bad as *Sex Psyche Etcetera* is, however, *Screening the Sexes: Homosexuality in the Movies* (1972) and *The Shadow of an Airplane Climbs the Empire State Building: A World Theory of Film* (1972) are worse. Tyler's last two books are so bad as to be beyond description or belief.

Screening the Sexes runs to over three hundred and sixty pages (Tyler's longest book), but it seems easily twice that length. The subject is announced in the subtitle; the method—to the extent that one can legitimately speak of a "method"—is bald summarizing and tortured psychoanalyzing. Tyler discusses two kinds of films: those which treat homosexuality overtly, and those which, in Tyler's judgment, treat homosexuality covertly. Some movies that fall into the first category are *The Sergeant, Advise and Consent, The Damned,* and *Staircase.* Tyler classifies these films under various headings, such as "Homeros in Uniform" and "Homeros as Chameleon," and redundantly explains their contents. It is a mere compilation, unencumbered by anything even slightly resembling an idea. Platitudes are rapped out with an air of having discovered Truth in its pristine state. For example: "No matter which sexes are involved, I want to emphasize that the sex act is an act of basic and extreme physical intermingling . . . Perfect union is merely the *logical extreme* of the mutual drive that brings two people together in bed for sexual reasons." If nothing else, *Screening the Sexes* proves that Tyler doesn't need the likes of a Gore Vidal to parody him—he can expertly perform that service for himself.

Tyler really warms to his subject, though, when he goes to work on films in the second category—those films, according to him, with unconscious homosexual themes. Oscar Wilde was a homosexual, and the homosexual writer always writes about himself. Ergo *The Importance of Being Earnest* is "really" a homosexual charade. Every cucumber is a phallic symbol. Jack and Algernon eat cucumber sandwiches in the film made from Wilde's play. Ergo Jack and Algernon (but especially Jack) are "really" performing fellatio. "The animal gusto of this scene (a perfect icon of repressed homosexual hysteria) does not come through so well in the British film," Tyler observes; "it was positively juicy as acted by Sir John Gielgud and a colleague in a British stage production I saw in New York. What best brings out the sex-charade quality in the movie . . ." And so on.

Then there is Tyler's twelve-page Freudian investigation into the heretofore concealed homosexual dynamics of *The Great Escape.* "When I say that *The Great Escape* is a homosexual mystery story, I am prepared to hear the worst charges against me that could possibly assault a critic's integrity," Tyler begins. "People may go so far as to say that I'm not only homosexual myself, but a systematic fantasizer determined to use the movies as propaganda to slander normal sex and completely innocent motives. I shall be brave." When Tyler gets finished with John Sturges's entertainment film, it is barely recognizable. The movie has an all-male cast, a fact which in itself would be enough to arouse Tyler's suspicions; in addition, eight of the characters look like "couples"—at least to Tyler. "I imagine," he remarks, "that by now some must really think I have a distorted mind. Yet in the interests of truth and humanity, I refuse to give up my position." And so, Tyler plunges bravely on . . .

Before long we learn that the escape depicted in Sturges's film is "anally oriented rather than vaginally or womb oriented"—those secret, underground tunnels, you know. Why aren't the escape passages named after women? Why are they called Tom, Dick, and Harry? Tyler has the answer. It's all part of a—or *the*—homosexual plot—or subplot. As Tyler perceptively puts it: "the tunnels [are] excretory passages and the escape itself [is] an anal climax." Again, the psychoanalytic critic expresses some uneasiness and stoutly defends the purity of his motives. No doubt some Hollywood people will see his "logical" speculations as dirty jokes or an impudently malevolent critical attack. "I am not evil, I think, because I believe so much *good* of the movies. As for being thought scandalous or impudent, I don't mind that at all. To the 'critical attack,' I plead guilty, because always I speak for the truest aesthetic values I know. But by all means, and in any event, the matter here is *no joke*. It is humanly fine and has a considerable majesty of its own, this symbolic substratum of *The Great Escape*." And so, Tyler plunges gravely on . . .

In the introduction and conclusion of *Screening the Sexes*, Tyler delivers a message to mankind; that is, he indulges in propaganda. The terms "male" and "female," he announces, are but crude signposts on the road to authentic human sexuality. Henceforth there shall be no more Establishment sex—away with artificial barriers to the free play of the libido! "At the peak of erotic ecstasy, no matter what carnal technicalities are involved, the sex organs literally possess each other, and so saturatively that all awareness of *difference* between the partners is momentarily submerged. At the moment of the purest and most satisfying orgasm, sexual differentiation ceases to exist as a conscious fact." Therefore, Tyler concludes that homosexuality is the ideal towards which heterosexual love is "really" tending. These rich thoughts are uttered in an oracular manner, as though Norman O. Brown (another profound thinker of our time) had never existed, or as though the words "unisex" and "polymorphous perverse" were not crashing clichés. However, Tyler knows in which direction the vogue-minded are rushing, and he doesn't want to be found hanging back; at the same time, he wants to pretend that he is leading the mob instead of following it . . . Is film criticism only propaganda?

And, one might ask, is film theory only hot air? Certainly that's the impression one gets from reading—or rather, *trying* to read—Tyler's *The Shadow of an Airplane Climbs the Empire State Building* (which, in the interest of economy, and because the book has no real substance, shall hereafter be referred to merely as *The Shadow*). Tyler claims to have spent three years researching and rewriting his latest tome; however, it gives the impression of having been spontaneously dictated, in nonstop fashion, in the course of one lost weekend. The thought is impenetrable (reviewers again concurred that they didn't have the foggiest notion as to what Tyler was saying). Throughout *Screening the Sexes* and *The Shadow*, Tyler addresses the reader as follows: "Do you think I'm kidding?," "Do I seem to be camping?," "Do I sound absurd?" Well might Tyler be possessed by doubts! Although the author assures us that no part of *The Shadow* has had previous publication, the book is padded out with long discussions of *Blow-Up* and *Persona*, both of which are treated at length in *Sex Psyche Etcetera*, and *Fellini Satyricon*, which is also examined in *Screening the Sexes*. In between the seemingly endless chapters devoted to specific films, Tyler keeps promising the reader his "world theory of film." ("Where, now, does my theory emerge? Not from the clouds of a quandary but from the sole clear brightness of a quintessence." The quintessence—methinks—of dust!) But before Tyler gets around to delivering the goods, he is off on another jet of steam, hoping no doubt that somewhere, somehow, the semblance of a theory will providentially turn up.

It never does. At best, the reader can faintly discern—through the gassy fumes of Tyler's prose—a few reiterated ideas. As in *The Three Faces of the Film*, Tyler opposes the view of cinema as a mere record of a given, objective, physical world. To present "the naked truth" is not art. Art enters when the film-maker transforms "the naked truth" into *his* truth. Real space and time give way to filmic space and time. So far, so good. But Tyler goes beyond this sensible, unoriginal position in his desire to counteract the Kracauerian school of thought. "A world theory of film must be as much about the world as about film," he observes at the beginning of his introduction; "else it is only a stab at a theory, a shadow of one." However, if Kracauer ends up by ousting art for the sake of the world, Tyler eventually does away with the world for the sake of art. To the question: What does the camera photograph?, Tyler replies: It photographs the mind of the film-maker. True film art is mind objectified; what was subjective becomes objective.

This, of course, is nonsense. In the creative process there remains a constant interaction between the objective and subjective: the camera photographs parts of the real world, but the choice of which parts are dictated by the artist's design. Although the film-maker confers upon the selected content a new aesthetic existence, the "world" which he puts on celluloid never wholly loses its referential quality, or its link to that which is "out there." Tyler is right to insist that unity is not achieved by "the mere imitation of the world of appearances"; film must be judged by artistic standards. It is precisely the responsibility of a film theorist, however, to formulate such evaluative criteria. Yet Tyler fails to do so. "Unity in any respect—logical or aesthetic, elementary or complex," he writes, "must be attained by unification, or the act of being united." Now, isn't that helpful?

In *The Three Faces of the Film*, Tyler remarks: "Undoubtedly I have not been, by a long shot, the world's most *constructive* film critic." Fair enough. Parker Tyler has composed his own epitaph.

(This essay on Parker Tyler was written prior to his death on July 24, 1974.)

CHAPTER FIVE

John Simon, Judicial Critic

The first and last responsibility of the film critic is—
prepare yourselves for a thundering truism—to raise
the standard of motion pictures.

—John Simon

1

John Simon has published four books of film criticism: *Acid Test* (1963), *Private Screenings* (1967), *Movies Into Film* (1971), and *Ingmar Bergman Directs* (1972). In addition to the section on film, *Acid Test* includes criticism of drama, poetry, fiction, the fine arts, and other critics. With the exception of *Ingmar Bergman Directs*, Simon's books are collections of his weekly reviews for *The New Leader* and occasional pieces for other magazines.

A student of comparative literature with a knowledge of five languages, Simon has taught at Bard College, MIT, and Harvard, where he also took his Ph.D. For a time he was theater critic for WNDT, the educational television station in New York; at present he reviews plays for *New York* magazine and *Hudson Review*, and films for *Esquire*. In 1970, Simon won the George Jean Nathan Award for Dramatic Criticism. Probably no other American film critic writing today has such a broad familiarity with the arts as Simon. The pity is that, too often, his practical criticism has failed to live up to the high standards he has set for himself and others in the theoretical portions of this writing.

In *Private Screenings*, Simon prefaces the chapters devoted to criticism of specific films with "A Critical Credo," originally a lecture delivered before the National Film Board of Canada.

"The most important thing to remember about film criticism," he begins, "is that it is not fundamentally different from any other kind of criticism." The critic's job is to make "explicit the achievements and shortcomings of art"; criticism is "a kind of poetry, a poetry of hate for what is ugly or false, and of love for what is beautiful and true." Because art and life are ultimately "coextensive," bad art is a sin and should be treated accordingly; that is to say, the critic should carry a big stick and use it without compunction whenever chastisement is called for. "If the critic is mistaken or too harsh, time eventually proves him wrong," says Simon; besides, the "genuine artist cannot be destroyed by words." So much for squeamishness.

The bad critic is most often merely a reviewer. He is the drudge who is hired to "see with the eyes of the Average Man or Typical Reader (whoever that is)"; he has no training or background in the arts. The good critic is a specialist: he is a teacher, artist, and thinker. As a teacher, the critic "informs, interprets, and raises the ultimate questions, the unanswerable ones that everyone must try to answer nonetheless." As an artist, the critic gives us a "work of the contemplative imagination." As a thinker, the critic becomes a philosopher: "Nothing is more suspect in criticism nowadays than a moral position, and yet there can be no criticism without one. The moment something appears to us better or worse than something else, we are being moralists—for aesthetics is the morality of art, just as morality is the aesthetics of living." Simon doesn't believe that the specific moral position of the critic is too important. He thinks it best, however, if the morality is not hardened into a system of some kind, established or otherwise: "It should be, as nearly as I can describe it, a relevance to human life, an elegance of spirit, a generosity and adventuresomeness of outlook, and above all, a concept or intimation of what the ideal solution to an artistic problem would be, and the dogged insistence on measuring every performance against the envisioned model."

Few films made since the inception of the medium are, according to Simon, genuine works of art. "The main thing the critic can do while waiting for the day when it will be possible to limit oneself to writing serious criticism about serious films for serious publications is," he says, "with every means at his command, to help bring about that day." Clearly, the task is a difficult one. Like opera and ballet, film remains a complex art; but film, unlike any other complex art, has, as Simon views it, two elements of equal importance: "word and image." The "ideal film critic" would have to be knowledgeable about "cinematography, literature, acting techniques, painting and sculpture (form and composition), music, dance (film musicals), and in view of the generally poor subtitles, as many foreign languages as possible."

But what makes film criticism particularly difficult is that the reader can't verify the critic's statements because the picture, in most instances, is not available for study; in addition, the critic cannot quote from the film: "If you use technical terminology to explain shots and camera movements, you may very well lose your reader, and will certainly end up boring him; if you use impressionistic, imaged prose, unless you are very skillful indeed, you may wander far afield." Furthermore, the critic is never given enough space in a review to satisfactorily consider the film in all its complexity and depth. But if the critic has a "poetic style to evoke the loveliness, the subtleties, the excitement of film," a "coruscating wit," and "conviction," he will enter the fray well-armed. "Of course, one is not infallible," Simon adds; "but one must believe that one is." So much for humility.

Although Simon makes clear that the "Credo" is not intended as "a whole critical philosophy," some of his ideas are so important that they call for elaboration, if not in *Private Screenings* then elsewhere. One would like him to be more precise, for example, about the relationship between art and life, and between art and morality.

It is doubtful whether any responsible film critic or theorist would agree with Simon that the word is equal in significance to the image. Sound has greatly extended the reach of film as art; speech allows the film-maker to reveal character in greater depth and to explore theme in more detail than was possible in the silent-film period. But to say that sound is now an integral part of film is not to argue that word and image are of equal importance. Film is still (I say "still" because even in Griffith's day words appeared on the screen) a basically pictorially medium. If this were not so, then why does Simon himself say that "dialogue conveys only a fragment of what happens in a film"?

Opponents have charged that Simon is more of a literary critic than a film critic; and, as we shall see, there is a good deal of evidence in support of this view. For one who places as much emphasis on training and background as Simon does, there seems to be a curious lack of long-range perspective in the "Credo," and elsewhere. The theories of Eisenstein, Pudovkin, Arnheim, Balázs, Kracauer, and Mitry (to name just some of the more obvious ones) are never cited in Simon's work; Bazin is dismissed, in about fifty words, as a "buff." I'm not saying that a critic should quote film theorists—reverently or not—in order to prove he has done his homework; what I *am* saying is that references to film theorists would seem to be at least as pertinent to the discussion of film as the literary references that are such a conspicuous feature of Simon's writing. One wonders how many pictures made before, say, 1939—the release date of Renoir's *The Rules of the Game*, one of Simon's all-time favorites—Simon has actually studied. Although Simon tells us in the "Credo" that he can't make up his mind which one of Chaplins' films—*The Gold Rush, City Lights,* or *Modern Times*—he likes best, not one of these movies is discussed along with his other favorites in the next section of the book. Throughout Simon's criticism, Griffith and Eisenstein are treated—when they are referred to at all—as non-entities; Murnau and Pudovkin are completely ignored.

Finally, Simon complains that a review frustrates the serious critic because it doesn't allow him to do full justice to a film. But what is to prevent the critic—if he *is* serious—from developing his analyses at greater length in book form?

2

No other critic writing about film in America at present uses the word "art" more often than Simon; yet he has never given an extended definition of the term. If one wants to understand what

Simon means by "art," then, one must skip around in his prefaces and numerous reviews for whatever transient, general remarks he makes on the subject.

Although not all entertainment is art, Simon points out in the introduction to *Movies Into Film*, "all true art is entertaining." Not everyone, however, may be capable of being entertained by art. To enjoy some films, one must be intelligent, educated, sensitive, and experienced. "In this sense," Simon writes, "I would define art as entertainment of the most far-ranging and penetrating sort; or, conversely, as matters of the most encompassing and profound human concern couched in the most moving or amusing, tragic or comic, form."

He goes on to say that art is different from lower forms of entertainment "by its greater human relevance or, more simply, truth." Nonart, he insists, can be entertaining: "Only there need be a sense of distinctions, proportions, values. We must not confuse pleasures with higher pleasures, fleeting with lasting goods, laughter with laughter that taught us something, carefree moments with moments which, by making us face them, might actually free us from our cares." To confuse mere entertainment with art is, Simon argues, aesthetically wrong and, in some cases, morally wrong.

In *Private Screenings*, Simon concludes a review of *The Spy Who Came in from the Cold* by saying: "Art is that which gets better with reexperiencing; nonart is what can be fully relished only once." Of *Dear John* he asks: "What is it that . . . prevents the film from attaining full artistic stature?"—and answers: "the splendid parts fail to build a whole greater than their sum." In *Movies Into Film*, Simon argues that *Patton* fails to measure up as art because the protagonist is not explored in depth, there is no strong antagonist, the dialogue is as flat as the characters, and there is no "poetry." *Midnight Cowboy* is very "efficient": "But art, real art, isn't like that at all. It is full of asperities, rugosities, the inexplicable. . . . *Midnight Cowboy* is just a little too knowing, pert, and pat."

Simon's distinction between "art" and "entertainment" sounds good, until we begin to ask what he intends by such vague expressions as "the most encompassing and profound human concern," or "human relevance," or (gulp)—"truth." Since Simon is fond of lumping films into such categories as "art," "pseudoart," and "nonart" ("pseudoart" is "trash"—a form of "nonart"— masquerading as "art"; and "nonart"—which is superior to "pseudoart"—is . . . well, *nonart*), this lack of conceptual precision is a serious failing.

After reading much of Tyler, however, it is good to find a critic who, like Simon, raises questions of value. But it isn't enough for the judicial critic to erect hierarchies; the reader wants to know by what standards the films are being evaluated and classified. Most critics would agree that *The Spy Who Came in from the Cold* is good for one viewing only; but what of a film like *The Birds*, which Simon calls "tawdry" but of which Robin Wood, the fine English critic, remarks: "My own experience with *The Birds* has been varied and disconcerting. At first it seemed to me a great disappointment; now, after repeated viewings, it seems to me among Hitchcock's finest achievements" (*Hitchcock's Films*). One might agree with Simon that both *Patton* and *Midnight Cowboy* are overrated, superficial films; but what is screen "poetry" (a honorific term for Simon, as well as for sundry other film critics), and what is the difference between "art" and "real art" (one is reminded here of Willy Loman's distinction between being "liked" and "well-liked")? And what, precisely, is the nature of that whole which makes a film more than the sum of its parts, and which elevates the film into Simon's pantheon?

As can be seen from the "Credo," Simon's view of art is closely linked to moral or humanistic values. "The New Wave is wavering. Having, with a few notable exceptions, waived sense for the sake of scintillation, and pushed this to the limits of available technical resources," he observes in *Private Screenings*, "it seems now to have nowhere to go but up into narrative and (I write the word with trepidation) *human* significance." He then goes on to praise *Sundays and Cybele* because its hero "is a human being, flanked by other human beings, about whom we can actually care." In a review of *A Woman Is a Woman*, he says: "today, a large body of film-makers, film reviewers, and film consumers have lapsed into a tacit agreement: the brainless, trashy, anti-human—provided only that it be tricky or pretentious—shall be

accepted and hailed as art." And in a review that appeared in
The New York Times (August 29, 1971), he begins: "If there is
such a thing as a film that makes its viewer a better human
being—and I dearly hope there is—*Hoa Binh* is it." (The film
dealt with the wartime experiences of two Vietnamese children.)

One of the categories into which Simon has divided his reviews
in *Movies Into Film* is entitled "Sex"; and a look at what he has
to say on that subject, here and elsewhere in his writing, will
further reveal the moral emphasis of his criticism. In the brief
introductory note to "Sex," Simon points out that film has come a
long way since 1963 when Bergman's *The Silence* was censored
because of "some rather chaste masturbation footage and a fairly
briefly and dimly seen bit of copulation." Simon hails this advance in freedom of treatment for a basic human activity, but
acknowledges that "besides film-makers who have important
truths about sex to convey, the open door admits every kind of
opportunistic hack whose sole aims are titillation and turning a
quick buck along with an incidental stomach or two." Still, Simon
is persuaded that the good of sexual permissiveness "far out-
weighs the bad." He argues: "One of the unquestionable good
things about this freedom is that, because it is equally available
to film artists, it may to some extent undercut the success of skin
flicks. For the film artist can, among other things, make his sexuality more powerful than that of the crass skin-flick-maker."

Simon began to observe a change in sexual attitudes in *Private
Screenings*, where he asks: "What has happened to 'normal love'
. . . in contemporary movies? Or even to 'normal sex'?" An exception is Kaneto Shindo's *Onibaba*, which Simon lauds as an "ardent and unflinching celebration of sex. It shows with equal
faithfulness the ecstasies of its fulfillment and the agonies of its
frustration. The people involved are far from admirable, and the
conditions of their intercourse are downright grubby. Yet what
radiates from this sex is, in its humble way, comparable to the
last chapter of *Ulysses*: a glorious affirmation of release, joy, and
appeasement." Later in the same book, in "Notes Toward a Definition of Pop Culture," he says that the "older escapist fare" with
its conventional happy ending at least made "a plea for quality
over quantity in man-woman relationships. Once that standard is

unconditionally reversed, not only love becomes meaningless, but even sexuality escalates itself out of being a refined pleasure into becoming a production-line opiate."

Simon's moral approach, however, leaves something to be desired. Reviewing *The Strawberry Statement* in *Movies Into Film*, he asks: "What is pornography? Or what is pornocinematography? The question is frequently asked and even more frequently, and boringly, answered. Yet it is a subject one cannot entirely avoid at a time when so many new films, directly or indirectly, touch upon it—or, more often, burrow into it. There are even some films around that have hardly any overt sex in them but manage, nevertheless, to generate a subliminally pornographic atmosphere." Simon never gets around to answering—boringly or otherwise—the question posed in his first two sentences. Inasmuch as Simon is convinced that the critic should go about his task with an air of infallibility, he never grapples with the vexing problem of how one is to know for certain, in every instance, whether sex is being treated artistically or inartistically, morally or immorally. The reader looks for a debate on the issues but Simon gives him categories.

There is, for example, a category which Simon calls the Loathsome Film. *Boom!*, *Secret Ceremony*, *Candy*, *End of the Road*, *Myra Breckinridge*, *Beyond the Valley of the Dolls*, *Something for Everyone*, and *Performance* belong to the genre. None of these films "try to win you over by wit, seriousness, humor, plot, characterization, logic, dialogue, or any other such outmoded paraphernalia." The structure of a Loathsome Film resembles "a series of electroshocks . . . administered . . . by a misprogrammed computer." Simon finds "something promiscuous and amoral about the very construction and editing" of *Performance*; and he suggests: "The MPAA might consider whether such already existing ratings as G, GP, etc., for the guidance of parents, should not be supplemented by others, like H, S-M, etc., for the guidance of perverts."

It is not certain whether every Loathsome Film is also a pornographic film. *Beyond the Valley of the Dolls*, however, is clearly tagged. "Now this film is true pornography," Simon points out. (Is there "false pornography"?) "There is sex and intercourse all over it, but staged and photographed to look merely like an unusual way of playing mahjong . . . There is no stab at believable characterization or narrative; everything simply leads to yet another prettified and disembodied scene of sexual activity. It is meant to turn you on, but the very people it can arouse are those whose idea of sex is totally divorced from reality."

Simon then makes what he calls an "important distinction" (the "distinction" leads, in effect, to a Simonian subcategory): "whether a film incites to masturbation or intercourse. There seems to exist a pornography for potency, and a worse pornography for impotence." The expression "a worse pornography" suggests that all pornography is bad. Yet elsewhere in "Sex," Simon remarks: "This is Buñuel's tragedy: he could make the greatest works of film pornography ever—nothing to be sneezed at—but no one will subsidize him. Instead, he is forced to make more or less respectable films, which he nudges as best he can toward pornography, and which, as a result, tend to fall between two stools (no pun intended)."

Of *Censorship in Denmark*, Simon says: "It is, I am afraid, hard-core pornography [still another subcategory]—which does not make me want to ban it . . . but does make me wish it were at least good hard-core pornography . . . What we see was not staged directly for this film, but only recorded or rerecorded by it, thus diminishing its chance to stir up our healthy lusts and appetites." Although *I Am Curious* is not without artistic weaknesses, the film is a serious one—according to Simon—and thus receives his imprimatur: "Though varied, the sexuality is never erotic. (Whether that makes the film better or worse is a question I leave open.)" *Elvira Madigan* is praised because of "its subdued but unquenchable sensuality, which can forgo spilling over into explicit sexuality. There is no more nudity on display than the briefest glimpse of the beginnings (the French, beautifully, call it *naissance*) of one breast, yet it conveys everything."

Perhaps Simon could argue a clear and consistent rationale behind these various pronouncements; it seems doubtful, however, whether anyone else could. He appears to be of two minds about pornography (whatever *that* is): sometimes it's bad, sometimes it's good. Is he for showing sex on the screen? Or is he against it? Are there times when the direct presentation of sexual activity is more artistic than the indirect? Is the reverse also true? And how can we tell which times are which? Simon leaves *too* many questions open: he substitutes dogmatic evaluations for patient analysis, arbitrarily chosen categories and subcategories for hard thinking. In the "Credo" Simon argues that the critic as teacher should engage and stretch the reader's faculties. If so, one is forced to conclude that Simon himself fails to pass the test.

3

In *Private Screenings*, Simon lists his twelve "all-time greats, in no particular order": Bergman's *The Naked Night* and *Smiles of a Summer Night*, Fellini's *The White Sheik* and *I Vitelloni*, Antonioni's *L'Avventura*, Kurosawa's *The Seven Samurai*, Welles's *Citizen Kane*, Renoir's *The Rules of the Game*, Clément's *Forbidden Games*, Carné's *The Children of Paradise*, Wajda's *Kanal*, and, as noted earlier, one of three Chaplin films—he cannot decide which. He then devotes a single chapter to these "favorites" (except for a Chaplin film), treating the majority of them in a page or two. For the most part, his method in "Favorites"—and elsewhere—consists in summarizing the action; he rarely makes the reader "see" the film he is discussing. Nor does he evince much historical or sociological awareness. The Carné, Clément, Wajda, and Renoir films are naturally linked to the Second World War; but the Bergman, Fellini, Antonioni, Kurosawa, and Welles pictures are discussed in a void.

However, some of Simon's observations are illuminating. In *Private Screenings*, for instance, he says: "a great novel has yet to make a great film. . . . Rarely, very rarely, an estimable achievement comes along . . . But always either the book or the film is less than absolutely first rate." And in *Movies Into Film*, he adds that if a film version of a novel "stays close to the original, it finds the fictional devices unassimilable or only awkwardly translatable into film; if it takes liberties, it ends up, being usually made by lesser men than Flaubert or Mark Twain, proportionately inferior to the original. First-rate cinematic talents tend not to bother with adaptations." However, Simon the theorist does not always seem to know what Simon the practical critic is doing. In a review of *All the Way Home*, we are told that plays "never work on the screen, for these two media are fundamentally antithetical." Before *Private Screenings* is over, though, *Alfie* (a film version of a play) has been called the "best comedy and the best serious film seen in New York so far this year."

It is instructive to trace Simon's comments on an individual director throughout his books. Take, for example, his approach to Fellini. For Simon, Fellini's early work was his best work. *The White Sheik* is praised as "a model of a *comédie larmoyante* in which laughter and tears are blended in perfect proportions." It is not made clear why *I Vitelloni* is Fellini's "most beautiful film." *Il Bidone* is called "choice Fellini." Although Simon evidently likes *La Strada* and *The Nights of Cabiria*, they are nowhere analyzed.

La Dolce Vita is seen as the pivotal film in Fellini's alleged decline as an artist. The picture is treated in *Acid Test*, wherein Simon nicely focuses on the "visual refrains" which unify the structure; but his conclusion that the "most important point" in the film is that "there is no cure for human insufficiency and unhappiness" obviously misses "*the* most important point." ("*La Dolce Vita* is only a substitute title," Fellini has said. "I wanted to call it *Babylon, 2000 Years After Jesus Christ*." The opening and closing shots in the film suggest Fellini's intentions.) *La Dolce Vita* is still a work of art, Simon says, even though Fellini "surrounds what he hoped would be images of hope with so much gloom that they, too, become suspect [does "hope" equal "art"?]; Steiner's intellectual crowd seems phoney and pretentious [again, Simon misses the point!]; Paola, a little girl [!!] who beckons Marcello away from his degenerate companions, looks like an Umbrian angel but suggests a Roman nymphet [if Simon had put this last statement into one of the other languages he commands, perhaps it would make sense]."

8½ is discussed in *Private Screenings*. Simon, in his role of Rhadamanthine critic, begins by saying: "Things started going wrong with the Steiner episode in *La Dolce Vita*." He admits that the "creeps" surrounding Steiner were meant to be fake intellectuals; but he tries to save the day by arguing that Steiner was portrayed as "the genuine article." Instead of trying to understand what Steiner intends when he confesses to Marcello that he has made a womb out of art; what Steiner's fears of the irrational and the incalculable represent; and what the relationship between Steiner's isolation from nature, his suicide, and the whole framework of symbols means in the film—Simon utters an unsubstantiated assertion about Steiner's unconvincing motivation, and then moves on to a sweeping condemnation of 8½. All of Fellini's later films, according to Simon, are bad: 8½ "is a disheartening fiasco"; *Juliet of the Spirits* "is a dreadful film: a little less arrogant, but no less vacuous and even tawdrier than 8½"; *Fellini Satyricon* is "a gimcrack, shopworn nightmare". In Simon's judgment, the "decomposition of what was once one of the greatest talents in film history" can be traced to Fellini's ambition to treat subjects and themes beyond his intellectual range.

Even if one agreed with Simon's evaluation of Fellini's later work, one would still be disturbed by his overall approach to the director. In the "Credo," the reader will recall, Simon tells us that the true critic hates "what is ugly or false" and loves "what is beautiful and true." Simon devotes all of three pages to *I Vitelloni*—Fellini's "most beautiful film"—but gives five pages to 8½, five pages to *Juliet of the Spirits*, and over eight pages to *Fellini Satyricon*. The evidence of Simon's books (*Ingmar Bergman Directs* aside) indicates that he hates "what is ugly or false" more than he loves "what is beautiful and true."

And Simon is an expert hater. Indeed, he hates Godard with a hate that is probably unparalleled in film criticism anywhere. *My Life to Live* (a "piece of legalized abortion") is discussed in the following terms: "crass and pointless experimentation for its own sake, tiresomely indiscriminate revival of silent-film techniques, perverse disregard of the audience, pretentious dabblings with pseudoprofundities, deliberate trampling of psychology in the mud of wantonness." *Alphaville* "is a pretentious bore afflicted with pseudointellectual diarrhea." *The Little Soldier* is full of "the customary Godardian philosophomorizings"; the picture merely gives Godard "a chance to masturbate on the screen." *Sympathy for the Devil* is an "abomination"; *Le Gai Savoir* strikes a "balance between inanity and insanity"; and *La Chinoise* is "a piece of mitigated trash." The chapter "Godard and the Godardians" in *Private Screenings* runs to twenty-six pages, four pages more than "Favorites," in which Simon discusses his *eleven* "all-time greats." To Sarris's assertion that Godard's "allegedly revolutionary position is comparable to the positions of Stravinsky, Picasso, Joyce, and Eliot," Simon replies: "About the only place where Godard's position might be comparable to that of the other four is on the toilet seat. But Godard, alas, also expels his works fron that position."

Simon rationalizes his obsession with Godard by saying that the director, though "insignificant as an artist," is "highly significant as a disease." There is little to choose between Warhol and Godard: both do violence "to coherence, causality, point of view, responsibility, form—any of the things that might hold a work of art together." Godard has "no respect for anything: meaning, communication, significant form, men, women, or life"; his work represents "infantile self-indulgence": it reveals "a hatred of language, [a] desire to desecrate the word." As Simon sees it, Godardism is everywhere: it is the "single worst influence . . . on all film." At times, Simon sounds like Tom Buchanan in *The Great Gatsby*, whom Fitzgerald describes as seeing himself—after one outburst of "impassioned gibberish"—"standing alone on the last barrier of civilization." Simon has some perceptive criticism to offer on Godard's films; and he challenges critical evaluations that are often unthinkingly uttered. Yet he spoils what is valuable in his work with hysterical, excremental rant.

The one director Simon values above all others is Bergman. In *Acid Test*, he remarks: "Bergman, indeed, seems to me the Shakespeare of our moving picture theater." *The Naked Night* and *Smiles of a Summer Night* are discussed under "Favorites" in *Private Screenings* (both films are also dealt with briefly in *Acid Test*). Bergman has a section all to himself in *Movies Into Film*, wherein Simon devotes himself mainly to plot summaries of *Persona, Hour of the Wolf, Shame*, and *The Passion of Anna*. "After seeing . . . *Persona* twice, I still cannot be sure that I understand it," Simon admits. Hence, perhaps, the reason for his escape into mere description. Simon concludes that *Persona* is, "with luck, a magnificent film" (a curious statement, to say the least). *Hour of the Wolf* is called a "disheartening" failure; but no judgment—or even attitude—emerges from the review of *Shame*. ("If I have related plot and technical highlights in such detail," he says at the finish, "it is for a reason. *Shame* is so tightly packed that you can fully appreciate it only on second seeing. This review hopes to make it possible for you to start, as it were, with a second viewing [!]"). *The Passion of Anna* is said to have a "central weakness . . . But it is a weakness that reinforces two of the main themes . . ."

"Ingmar Bergman is, in my most carefully considered opinion," Simon writes in *Ingmar Bergman Directs*, "the greatest film-maker the world has seen so far." ("Ingmar Bergman is, in my opinion," Simon writes in *Movies Into Film*, "the truest, most self-sustaining, least exhaustible genius of the cinema.") In *Movies Into Film*, Simon finds Bergman's excellence to lie in his "full-ness, which is both a variety—the continuing elaboration of themes and elucidation of problems; and a unity—the blending of all Bergman films into a sustained questioning of the universe, a heroic struggle to come up with a clearer understanding of the questions at least, where answers seem to be increasingly unobtainable." In *Ingmar Bergman Directs*, Simon—because he continues in the delusion that picture and language are co-equal in importance on the screen—asserts that Bergman is "the true lord of the medium," the master "whose word is as good as his image." Once again, Simon praises the thematic continuity of Bergman's pictures.

Ingmar Bergman Directs is a study of what Simon considers to be Bergman's "four most important films to date," namely, *The Naked Night, Smiles of a Summer Night, Winter Light,* and *Persona.* Few would quarrel with Simon's selection, so far as it goes. The one surprise is the inclusion of *Winter Light*, which Simon had found wanting in *Private Screenings*, where we read statements such as: "*Winter Light* is inferior Bergman . . . *Winter Light* is one of Bergman's rare disappointing films . . . *Winter Light* is scarcely even a 'good' film, much less a 'great' one." In

Ingmar Bergman Directs, Winter Light is said to be "in many ways Bergman's most extraordinary film." Although no explanation is provided for the change in critical status, Simon notes parenthetically that Bergman was "very much against inclusion of [*Through a Glass Darkly*] in this book, and urged the choice of *Winter Light* in its stead." When Rolf Fjelde referred to this problem in his *New York Times* review (November 26, 1972), Simon responded with a letter to the editor (January 14, 1973): "Eight years and many viewings after the initial one in 1963 have radically changed my estimate of *Winter Light*," he declares. "It is not my first change of mind—I hope I'll never be so inflexible as to be unable to extend my understanding, or so ungenerous as to be unable to admit I was wrong. If I did not in the present book explain what Mr. Fjelde calls my 'spectacular mark-up,' it is simply because I consider the different dates affixed to the books explanation enough." According to Simon, Bergman "did not in any way dictate the film's inclusion." He closes: "I may err in many ways but, contrary to Fjelde's slur, my 'independence' has in no way been 'compromised.'"

Simon's "independence" notwithstanding, *Ingmar Bergman Directs* is a poor book. By focusing on just four pictures, Simon should be able to analyze their complexities in depth; otherwise, why ignore *Wild Strawberries, Through a Glass Darkly, The Virgin Spring,* and other worthy films? The book runs to over three hundred pages; but included is a long interview with Bergman, the print is exceedingly large, and there are over four hundred photographs. The length of the chapter on *Winter Light* comes to roughly ten thousand words—about twice the length of Robin Wood's section on the same film in his book. However, in less than two hundred pages, Wood covers all of Bergman's films up to *Shame*, and his various analyses in no way suffer by comparison with Simon's. In his discussion of *Winter Light*, Simon devotes one paragraph to structure (what he calls the "three movements" of the film); six paragraphs to theme; and two paragraphs to Bergman's visual approach (and one of those two paragraphs is quoted from Wood!). The bulk of the essay is nothing more than straightforward description of character and action. Simon has so little visual sense that, in comparing Bergman's use of the monologue in *Winter Light* to the same device in *The 400 Blows*, he can say that Truffaut employs "jump cuts to suggest the passage of time"—when the dissolves used in the French picture remain unforgettable to any viewer with normal cinematic literacy.

In *Acid Test*, Simon writes: "Those who have not seen Bergman's films can enjoy the screenplays as excellent dramas or novellas in their own right." Now, even though Bergman's scripts are better written than most, Simon's statement is a gross exaggeration; yet it points to a fundamental limitation in his critical approach. Believing as he does that word and image are equally important on the screen, Simon tends to write about motion pictures as though they *were* "dramas" or "novellas." *Ingmar Bergman Directs*—which might better have been called *Ingmar Bergman Writes*—is the result of such thinking.

4

Simon hates Godard's arrogance but he displays the same quality in his own work. In *Movies Into Film* he tells us that *War and Peace* is too bulky for his taste, so he has never been able to finish it. Still, that doesn't prevent him from comparing Sergei Bondarchuk's film version of the novel with the original. He has not read *In Cold Blood*; "from even a cursory scanning of the book," however, he knows that the film fails to be a faithful adaptation. "I have not read the Oakley Hill novel from which [*Downhill Racer*] was made, but a glance at the book tells me that [James] Salter [the scenarist] has wrought enormous changes." Simon hasn't read Bernard Malamud's novel, *The Fixer*, either; however, he can say that the adaptation is a failure. "I am going to be brief about . . . *Catch-22*," remarks Simon, "because I am one of those illiterates who did not read the novel . . . But I have skimmed it, and I can tell that Mike Nichols's conception and Buck Henry's screenplay, though ostensibly faithful to the book, have really tried to turn its absurdities into a kind of superabsurdism." Like Simon, Agee would often admit to not having read a novel; but Agee, unlike Simon, did not then go on to criticize the film version as though he *had* read the original. Although Simon gives high marks to such film classics as *Mondo Cane, Lawrence of Arabia*, and *I Am Curious*, he finds little else on the screen that pleases him. Not only do Griffith, Eisenstein, Godard, the later Fellini and Antonioni, and much of Truffaut get the back of his hand but also Dreyer, Stroheim, Visconti, Hitchcock, Sternberg, Pasolini, Chabrol, Bresson, and Rohmer (among others). Except for *The Rules of the Game* and a few other "respectable films," Renoir is a "vastly overrated *petit-maître*: a plodding simple-minded, stagy director, a man with an infantile vision and a wobbly style." In a piece that appeared in *The New York Times* (December 6, 1970) entitled "A Critic Asks What Is Taste," Simon writes: "plays of various types survive: comic and tragic, realistic and surreal, naturalistic and poetic. If a reviewer seems to favor one or two kinds at the expense of the others, chances are that he does not have a catholic enough taste." In *Movies Into Film*, Simon tells us that the epic is "an infantile form of art," and that the "film to the extent that it wants to achieve maturity, must outgrow the western." He is "not overfond of crime pictures" (though he likes *Bullitt*); "usually [has] little love for the big sports competition story" (still, he likes *Downhill Racer*); thinks good musicals are rare; and finds the tyical student film "boring, pretentious, arty, self-conscious, self-righteous, and false."

Simon—more often prosecuting attorney than judge—has a penchant for attacking the man instead of analyzing the work. In *Private Screenings*, Ophuls is said to have had "the taste and mentality of a chambermaid." (Simon's "criticism" is filled with tiresome derogatory remarks about chambermaids, football players ["puckish golems"], poor hicks from Duluth and Tulsa, and "mean-looking geezers" from Hollywood Boulevard and Flatbush Avenue.) In *The New York Times* (October 29, 1972), Rohmer is referred to as "a timid, intensely Catholic, basically Puritanical husband and father"; and his filmic themes appeal to others like him—that is, to "Puritans, weaklings, sexual failures," and "self-styled moralists." (There is also a distasteful anti-Catholicism in Simon's work. Bazin is patronizingly described as "a cultivated, extremely well-meaning, Roman Catholic critic—and, essentially, a buff." As Sarris has noted, observe "the boldly bigoted placement of 'Roman Catholic' in the ascending order of abuse" [*The New York Times*, February 14, 1971]. Agee could say, in a review of *The Fugitive*, that his "feelings about the Catholic Church" were "mixed"; but Agee, unlike Simon, was candid about his feelings and directed his remarks to an institution, not to an individual.) Also in the *Times* (February 25, 1973), Simon refers to Buñuel's *The Discreet Charm of the Bourgeoisie* as the product of "an old, exhausted film-maker," a "sadistic" and "impotent" old man.

Simon's abuse of directors is exceeded only by his abuse of actors and actresses. Obviously, the face and figure of a performer are relevant to criticism only if there is a question of miscasting; yet Simon continually ignores this guideline in order to ridicule those who, unfortunately, are not as prepossessing as himself. For example, Judy Garland's face, in her last pictures, had "become that of a wizened child" and her figure resembled "the giant economy-size tube of tooth paste in girls's bathrooms: squeezed intemperately at all points, it acquires a shape that defies definition by the most solid geometrician." Walter Matthau is an "actor who looks like a half-melted rubber bulldog." Essy Persson "has an ugly face, squat body, unsightly bosom, bad legs, stubby fingers"—and, oh yes, "no acting ability." Anne Wiazemsky has "the face of a horse, the teeth of a rabbit, and the expression of an amoeba." Barbra Streisand "is clearly the darling of the hordes of homely women who have no trouble identifying themselves with her in full face, and feeling superior to her in profile." Michael York has "the head of a blond rat." What has any of this to do with the aims espoused in the "Credo"? How will this "raise the standard of motion pictures"?

Simon also enjoys disparaging other critics. In *Ingmar Bergman Directs*, Tyler is referred to as "that prime purveyor of critical logorrhea." In *Private Screenings*, Kael is described as "that curious combination of lively shrewdness, sentimental-hysterical self-indulgence, and dependably plebeian tastes." Sitting with his back to the mirror, Simon can even say that Kael fails to convey her enthusiasm for pictures she likes, and that she shows a "frequent inability to write *about* a film at all, preferring to write *around* it instead."

In *Private Screenings*, Sarris is accused of "godardliness (which, in style, is next to uncleanliness)." Elsewhere, in *Movies Into Film*, Sarris is called a "buff," that is, one who uses "movies as an escape from reality." Buffs like to utter "vague, prestige-conferring words" like "poetic," "lyrical," and "myth." (But Simon fails to add that he likes to mouth these words, too: "But what may distinguish *Citizen Kane*," he asserts in *Private Screenings*, "is its extracting the mythic from under the humdrum surface of the American experience . . .") "Perversity," Simon informs us, "is certainly the most saving grace of Sarris's criticism, as well as the only deliberate one, the humor being mostly unintentional." Although Simon presents some valid arguments against the excesses and weaknesses of the *auteur* approach, we are not spared the following: "Only a crazy *auteur* theorist (if that is not sheer redundancy) . . ."; "But the *auteur* critics, who with characteristic lack of taste . . ."; ". . . Renoir, rapturously extolled by *auteur* critics everywhere, and, indeed, by normal critics as well"; and so forth. For a man who claims to believe in the importance of love, Simon shows little of it in his writing.

Apparently, Simon revels in his title: "the critic you love to hate." Wilfred Sheed, a former movie reviewer for *Esquire*, has defended his friend's "famous nastiness" by calling it "the most theatrical thing since Bela Lugosi: Simon must be understood primarily as a man of the Stage" (*The New York Times*, March 7, 1971). Sheed doesn't seem to realize that Simon's hammy posturing as a Transylvanian vampire is incompatible with his stance as a judicial critic seriously concerned with elevating the aesthetic quality and moral tone of the movies. As for Simon's "standards," they are those grand fuzzy commonplaces which mean little until the critic applies himself to particular cases. And when the critic cannot find one good word to say about *Bonnie and Clyde*, or cannot discover one significant weakness in *Alfie*, the reader is inclined to be skeptical of his vaunted exquisite taste. Simon's limitations result from his inability or unwillingness to discuss a film whole (in the "Credo" he says that form and content cannot be separated, "except for purposes of classroom demonstration," but he separates them all the time by focusing mainly on what a film "says"); his perverse refusal to see that film is a primarily visual medium, and his resultant failure to do justice to the pictorial element in his analyses of specific movies (amply demonstrated in *Ingmar Bergman Directs*); his lack of scholarship in film history (which he vainly attempts to conceal by a snobbish dismissal of the silent and early sound film nearly in toto); his inability or unwillingness, most often, to view a picture in its socio-historical setting (which is peculiar, considering his moral approach, since the validity of moral judgments cannot be easily weighed in a temporal-spatial vacuum); his preference for discussing what he hates rather than what he loves (a sure indication of a second-rate mind and a defective sensibility); and his vitriolic personal abuse (which often takes up more space than the matter at hand, probably because of a lack of more productive insights and of a confused desire to be "a man of the Stage").

The conclusion remains inescapable: John Simon is not a critic who thus far has shown the capability for raising the standard of motion pictures.

CHAPTER SIX

Pauline Kael and Pluralistic, Nonaesthetic Criticism

> The role of the critic is to help people see what is in the work, what is in it that shouldn't be, what is not in it that could be. He is a good critic if he helps people understand more about the work than they could see for themselves; he is a great critic, if by his understanding and feeling for the work, by his passion, he can excite people so that they want to experience more of the art that is there, waiting to be seized. He is not necessarily a bad critic if he makes errors in judgment. (Infallible taste is inconceivable; what could it be measured against?) He is a bad critic if he does not awaken the curiosity, enlarge the interests and understanding of his audience. The art of the critic is to transmit his knowledge of and enthusiasm for art to others.
>
> —PAULINE KAEL

1

Pauline Kael is regarded by many as the best movie critic now writing in America. One of the most influential of contemporary reviewers, she is also one of the toughest. Compared to twenty-six other critics, according to a report published in *Variety* (October 25, 1972), Kael is considered by distributors as the third hardest-to-please (Kauffmann and Simon, in that order, are just ahead of her). She has a vast knowledge of movies, a caustic wit, a flair for polemic, and a brilliant style. Indeed, Kael is one of the

finest stylists writing on any subject—anywhere—in the English
language today. Her prose is lucid, idiomatic, sophisticated, and
zestful. (Sometimes *too* zestful. She has a tendency to overwork
words like "dumb," "crummy," "crappy," and "lousy.")

Kael's first book, *I Lost It at the Movies*, appeared in 1965; it
quickly became the best-selling volume of film criticism ever
published in this country. Covering the period from 1953 to 1964,
the collection contains essays and reviews that appeared originally in *Film Quarterly, Sight and Sound, Film Culture, Moviegoer, Art Film Publications, Partisan Review, Kulchur,* the
Atlantic Monthly, the *Massachusetts Review,* and the *Second
Coming.* "Don't ask me about the title of my book," Haskel
Frankel quotes Kael as saying. "I didn't pick it. I submitted all of
the serious titles I could think of but my publisher didn't like any
of them. I was tired and in the middle of doing the index when I
sent in *I Lost It at the Movies.* It was chosen but I don't know
what it means. So far as I am concerned, 'it' refers to my normal
life. Your whole pattern is changed when you become a FOOF.
That's a trade term. Friends of Old Films. We FOOFs are movie
addicts. We are all night people, and we can pick each other out
of crowds. We are a special breed of nut" (*Saturday Review,*
May 1, 1965).

Kiss Kiss Bang Bang was brought out in 1968. The material in
this volume, most of it written after the publication of *I Lost It
at the Movies,* previously appeared in *The New Yorker, Life,
Holiday, Vogue, McCall's, Mademoiselle,* the *Atlantic Monthly,*
and *The New Republic.* Kael's second book also includes "Notes
on 280 Movies," brief descriptive and evaluative comments
culled from "about four thousand" such jottings written since
1953. "A Note on the Title" reads: "The words 'Kiss Kiss Bang
Bang,' which I saw on an Italian movie poster, are perhaps the
briefest statement imaginable of the basic appeal of movies. This
appeal is what attracts us, and ultimately what makes us despair
when we begin to understand how seldom movies are more than
this."

Between the publication of *I Lost It at the Movies* and *Kiss
Kiss Bang Bang,* Kael was briefly a reviewer for *McCall's* (an
unfavorable evaluation of *The Sound of Music* is said to have

been responsible for her fleeting tenure there); later she became the regular critic for *The New Republic*. In January 1968, Kael moved over to *The New Yorker*, where she was offered for the first time a regular weekly column, and where she has been ever since. (At present, Kael reviews films from October through March, Penelope Gilliat takes over from April through September.) The pieces in *Going Steady*, which was published in 1970, represent her work for *The New Yorker* (January 1968 to March 1969), except for a long essay entitled "Trash, Art, and the Movies," which first appeared in the February 1969 *Harper's*. The title of Kael's third book suggests her deepening love affair with the screen.

In 1971, *The Citizen Kane Book* was published; it includes a long essay by Kael (nearly 100 pages) as an introduction to the shooting script by Herman J. Mankiewicz and Orson Welles. Originally "Raising Kane," the title of her piece, appeared in *The New Yorker*. Two years later, *Deeper Into Movies*, a collection of her reviews from the same magazine for September 1969 to March 1972, came out.

2

In a review of Bazin's *What Is Cinema?*, Volume I, Kael calls Vachel Lindsay, James Agee, and Robert Warshow "the best American movie critics" (*The New York Times*, September 10, 1967). As I have tried to suggest, Agee and Warshow both approached films in a personal way. So does Kael. Kauffmann has complained, in his review of *I Lost It at the Movies* (*Harper's*, June 1965), that the first eight paragraphs of Kael's opening essay—"Zeitgeist and Poltergeist; Or, Are Movies Going to Pieces?"—have "nothing at all to do with her subject." He's right.

But Kael's strategy in presenting herself as Katharine Hepburn playing Alice Adams—an unsophisticated, down-to-earth woman from San Francisco, out of her depth among the decadent Hollywoodians of Los Angeles—is intended to disarm the reader, to get him to identify with her, and thus to make him more receptive to the arguments which follow. Later in the book, in the course of reviewing *Hud*, Kael tells us that she grew up on a ranch and that her father was both a charitable man and a whoremonger. She draws from her own experience here in order to refute Bosley Crowther's charge that Hud is evil simply because he commits adultery. In her review of *Shoeshine*, Kael explains that she first saw the picture after a lovers' quarrel; she emerged from the theater, in tears, not certain whether she was crying over the picture or reacting to her personal loss. Subsequently, she learned that her partner in the quarrel had also gone to see the De Sica film that same night, and he had likewise left the theater with tears in his eyes. "Yet our tears for each other, and for *Shoeshine*, did not bring us together," she reflects. "Life, as *Shoeshine* demonstrates, is too complex for facile endings."

Although Kael reacts to films in a personal way, she does not—at least at her best—substitute emotion for thought. She uses both. As her comments on *Hud* and *Shoeshine* make clear, Kael cites her own experience in order to judge the veracity of a picture, to weigh and evaluate different interpretive responses. However, there are times when the subjective approach gets her into serious difficulties.

Kael's view of the critic's function over the years, though, has undergone significant changes. In "Movies, the Desperate Art" (published in *The Berkley Book of Modern Writing No. 3*, edited by William Phillips and Philip Rahv, and reprinted in Daniel Talbot's *Film: An Anthology*), she notes that the American film critic is in a curious position because his rage and negativism is likely to be in direct proportion to his interest in the medium. He can amply assert and document his disgust, but then what? Haunting film societies to reassess the classics only results in increased disgust, since Hollywood did not take the directions indicated in those classics. "A few writers, and not Americans only, have taken a rather fancy way out: they turn films into Rorschach tests and find the most elaborate meanings in them (bad acting becomes somnambulism, stereotyped situations become myths, and so forth). The deficiency of this technique is that the writers reveal a great deal about themselves but very little about films." In this same piece, in which she attacks Tyler's mythological criticism and impressionistic noncriticism, Kael also takes a parenthetical shot at the sociological method: "To a sociologist, movies can be a constant source of material on up-to-date habits and manners. But one interested in film as an art form finds these surface shifts about as significant as a sculptor finds the cosmetic lore of Forest Lawn . . . Skilled teamwork, having already destroyed movies, will now take over movie criticism." Elsewhere in this same essay, she writes: "may one propose simple basic terms for the evaluation of film: does the frame of meaning support the body of photographic, directorial, and acting styles; and conversely, do these styles define the frame of meaning?" In other words, Kael is reaffirming the familiar standard that form and content ought to cohere in a work of art. So it would seem that her primary concern, in 1956, is the work itself: the film regarded as an autotelic, self-contained, self-sufficient entity—an entity which is to be evaluated solely by criteria intrinsic to its own mode of existence.

In *I Lost It at the Movies*, Kael again scores the "Rorschach-blot approach" to pictures like *Last Year at Marienbad*, because the method turns "criticism into autobiography." She points out in "Circles and Squares: Joys and Sarris" that "criticism is an art, not a science"; this remark would appear to put not only Sarris and the other *auteurists* in their place, but also the sociologists. Still, Kael insists on the relevancy of the critic's own experience. "Those, like Sarris, who ask for objective standards seem to want a theory of criticism which makes the critic unnecessary," she writes. "And he *is* expendable if categories replace experience." Whenever people ask her to explain her method of evaluation, Kael informs us, she tells them "that new films are judged in terms of how they extend our experience and give us pleasure, and that our ways of judging how they do this are drawn not only from older films but from other works of art, and theories of art, that new films are generally related to what is going on in the other arts, that as wide a background as possible in literature, painting, music, philosophy, political thought, and so forth, helps, that it is the wealth and variety of what he has to bring to new works that makes the critic's reaction to them valuable." Discussing Kracauer's *Theory of Film* in the same volume, she declares: "I should like to see motion picture art brought back into the world of the other arts (which it has never left, except in film theory) and see movies judged by the same kind of standards that are used in other arts, not by the attempt to erect a 'reality' standard. Reality, like God and History, tends to direct people to wherever they want to go."

Thus far, Kael has been saying that art is not life; that a work of art is divisible into form and content; that evaluation of a specific film is based on the degree of coherence it manifests between form and content; and that, though sociology remains irrelevant to evaluation, the critic's own experience of life and his knowledge of other arts and disciplines *is* relevant. It is not clear whether she believes in objective criteria in 1956. By 1963, though, her essay on Sarris (see also her review of the Bazin book) leaves no doubt on the matter.

Why should the critic reject the sociological approach to film, however, and accept the data of his personal experience, including his own social experience? Kael wants art to receive its due; she does not want it to be confused with sociology. Yet she admits that in evaluating a picture, not only other arts but also "philosophy, political thought, and so forth, helps"—which would also seem to leave the door open for sociology. That Kael's developing critical theory is not purely a formalistic one—or one which regards a film as an autonomous whole—remains clear from her remarks on *Last Year at Marienbad* in "Zeitgeist and Poltergeist": "Robbe-Grillet . . . may say that the film is a pure construction, an object without reference to anything outside itself, and that the existence of the two characters begins when the film begins and ends ninety-three minutes later, but, of course, we are not born when we go in to see a movie. . . . This can only sound like pedantry to those interested in 'pure' art who tend to consider analysis as an enemy."

The tension in Kael's thought between the concept of a film as an object in itself and the view of it as an object which interacts with life becomes more evident in *Kiss Kiss Bang Bang*. In "A Sense of Disproportion," she says: "There are not—and there never were—any formal principles that can be used to judge movies but there are concepts that are serviceable for a while and so pass for, or are mistaken for, 'objective' rules until it

becomes obvious that the new work that we respond to violates
them." About twenty pages further, she writes: "conceivably it's
part of the function of a movie critic to know and indicate the
difference between a bad movie that doesn't much matter because it's so much like other bad movies and a bad movie that
matters . . . because it affects people strongly in new, different
ways. And if it be said that this is sociology, not aesthetics, the
answer is that an aesthetician who gave his time to criticism of
current movies would have to be an awful fool. Movie criticism
to be of any use whatever must go beyond formal analysis—
which in movies is generally a disguised form of subjective reaction to meanings and implications, anyway." Are *all* "current
movies" inartistic? In "Circles and Squares," Kael says that the
auteurists have an anti-art aesthetics and that this is the "most
serious charge that can possibly be brought against an aesthetics." Can't the same charge be leveled at her own theory?

Whether the critic uses the inkblot, impressionistic approach or
a rigorous analytical method, the result—for Kael—seems to be
equally the same: subjective evaluation. Yet she ridicules those
wives who "identified" with the heroine of *Red Desert*, because
"reacting to the movie meant for these women not an interpretation which could be validated by checking it against the meanings and connections in the work, but anything that happened to
occur to them as they saw it or thought about it afterward, they
didn't necessarily care that it didn't make sense." When it suits
Kael's purposes, she is an analytical critic who will argue that the
meaning of a picture can be determined through a logical investigation of its organization, and she will use this position as a
weapon to batter those whose judgment runs counter to her own.
But on other occasions, when for one reason or another she wants
to go outside a film, she argues that formal principles are a myth,
serviceable concepts transient, and objectivity impossible.

In "Circles and Squares," Kael defends critical pluralism: "I
believe that we respond most and best to work in any art form
(and to other experience as well) if we are pluralistic, flexible,
relative in our judgments, if we are eclectic. But this does not
mean a scrambling and confusion of systems." Eclecticism, not to
be confused with a lack of scruple, is the selection of superior

standards and principles from different systems of ideas. The pluralist has to be more careful and orderly than the critic who applies a single theory, she argues.

Granted, pluralism is preferable to monism in criticism. The critic ought to be clear, however, about the terms he uses and the weight he attaches to the different critical systems. Words like "standards," "principles," and "concepts" appear repeatedly in Kael's writing, but without any visible means of support. Now she is a formalist and hostile to the sociological method; now she is a sociological critic and opposed to the formalist approach. Kael has never coherently articulated her critical theory; consequently—as we shall see—her practical criticism is frequently muddled and self-contradictory.

3

Formally, a movie can be broken down into a number of basic elements: the visual approach, structure, point of view, characterization, and the expressive use of sound. These elements amount to what Sarris calls the *how*. Character and theme comprise the *what*, the content, the paraphrasable result of the filmmaker's stylization of experience. Need I add that this bifurcation enjoys a logical existence only, that it allows the critic to discuss with some precision what actually remains, in a fully realized work of art, a single entity? Even the formal elements themselves are separable only at the convenience of the critic. For example, point of view (the perspective from which the film-maker presents the action, or how he shoots a scene—now from the angle of one character, now from that of another—which necessarily shapes the viewer's response to the story being enacted) could also be considered under the visual approach or regarded as a structural component.

Now, if we study Kael's criticism we find that she hardly ever has anything to say about the visual nature of the medium, or the pictorial quality of a specific film; in other words, she generally ignores what should properly be the starting point for any discussion of a movie. Similarly, she rarely, if ever, has anything to say about point of view. And her comments on sound are sparse, normally being restricted to dialogue. As far as the *how* is concerned, Kael's chief interest resides in structure and characterization. Her later books reveal an increasing awareness of acting, a subject which most film critics ignore. (Kauffmann is a notable exception.) Mainly, Kael focuses her attention on the *what*: what characters stand for; what the film is "saying"; what it means to her ("I write," she says in the "Author's Note" of *Deeper Into Movies*, "because I love trying to figure out what I feel and what I think about what I feel, and why"); and what it means to others—an interest that frequently carries her into sociological criticism, just as the interest in her own feelings often carries her into impressionistic criticism (or noncriticism).

In "Zeitgeist and Poltergeist," Kael faults audiences for not caring about structural coherence (she cites the ending of *The Bridge on the River Kwai* as an example of poor editing and calls *What Ever Happened to Baby Jane?* a "mess"). Perhaps, she muses, contemporary viewers simply want sensations: "Audiences that enjoy the shocks and falsifications, the brutal series of titillations of a *Mondo Cane*, one thrill after another, don't care any longer about the conventions of the past, and are too restless and apathetic to pay attention to motivations and complications, cause and effect." Kael sees processes of structural disintegration are at work in movies of all types, and is uneasy about the disappearance of old forms. "The art-house audience accepts lack of clarity as complexity, accepts clumsiness and confusion as 'ambiguity' and as style." If audiences have come to prefer structural incoherence, she concludes, it must be because modern man feels that life doesn't make sense, so he enjoys movies that reflect his own experience.

Kael is far from being consistent on film structure. In *I Lost It at the Movies*, she attacks *La Dolce Vita, La Notte*, and *Last Year at Marienbad* (she refers to these films as "the-come-dressed-as-the-sick-soul-of-Europe parties"), calling them structural "disasters": "The episodes in these films don't build, they are all on the same level." According to Kael, the Fellini, Antonioni, and Resnais pictures compare unfavorably with *The Rules of the Game*: "Renoir's film was a dazzling, complex entertainment, brilliantly structured, building its themes toward a climax."

When Kael likes a movie, however, then structural neatness doesn't always seem to count for much. She tells us that "the greatness of *Shoeshine* is in that feeling we get of human emotions that have not been worked-over and worked-into something (a pattern? a structure?) and cannot really be comprised in such a structure. We receive something more naked, something that pours out of the screen." "I was exasperated by the defects of *The Music Room* when I saw it," she says; "now, a month later, I realize that I will never forget it. Worrying over its faults as a film is like worrying over whether *King Lear* is well constructed: it doesn't really matter." And to those critics who have complained of structural irrelevancies in the New Wave films, Kael replies that a film-maker like Truffaut or Godard is trying "to find some expression for his own anarchic experience, instead of making more of those tiresome well-made movies that no longer mean much to us. . . . For the meaning of these films is that these fortuitous encounters illuminate something about our lives in a way that the old neat plots don't."

As the reader can see, Kael has become one with that audience which, earlier in *I Lost It at the Movies*, she had castigated for not caring sufficiently for "the logic of the plot." It comes as no surprise, then, when the second review in *Kiss Kiss Bang Bang* begins with the previously noted announcement that there never were any formal principles and that "good construction" is a bore. According to Kael: "There was a clue right at the beginning of movies that perhaps dramatic structure wasn't so important: the serials, which were even more primitive—and more flexible—in construction than the simplest stage dramas. They were constructed *serially*, just one incident after another without regard to logic or dramatic coherence." Kael pauses in her praise for the vitality of comic-strip structure, however, to ask how this kind of form can hold an audience's attention for two or more hours "unless the material is somehow deepened and organized dramatically?" She doesn't attempt an answer to her question: perhaps because an answer might point in the direction of those

formal principles which—supposedly—never existed. In his review of *I Lost It at the Movies*, Kauffmann remarks on the
"untidiness" of Kael's "whole mental discipline." . . . Is he unfair?

Kael—who views *The Big Sleep* as a milestone in the evolution
of the ill-made film—apparently can't see that *The Rules of the
Game* belongs to one structural tradition and that *La Dolce Vita*,
for example, belongs to another. Isn't it naive to assume, as she
does, that because *The Rules of the Game*, *La Dolce Vita*, *La
Notte*, and *Last Year at Marienbad* all involve parties, all four
should be structured identically? *The Rules of the Game* has a
plotted, dramatic structure, whereas *La Dolce Vita* has an epi-
sodic, thematic structure. Although Fellini's form is looser than
Renoir's, each sequence remains strictly controlled by the major
theme. Within the different episodes, a number of subthemes
appear which contribute to the complexity of the picture; as the
action develops, the subthemes coalesce into rhythmic patterns
which support the main structure of meaning. It is untrue to say
that *La Dolce Vita* doesn't progress, since the central character,
Marcello Rubini (played by Marcello Mastroianni), spiritually
deteriorates, sequence by sequence. In its own way, *La Dolce
Vita* is just as "brilliantly structured" as *The Rules of the Game*,
and in its own way it builds "its themes toward a climax."

Kael's reflections on character, characterization, and theme are
similarly inconsistent, erratic, and unfair. In *I Lost It at the
Movies*, she complains that the characters in *La Dolce Vita*, *La
Notte*, and *Last Year at Marienbad* are alienated; "but," she
adds, "unless we know what they are alienated from, their alienation is meaningless—an empty pose." Now Fellini, for instance,
makes it perfectly clear what his characters "are alientated from";
yet Kael refuses to see.

"*Jules and Jim* is full of character and wit and radiance as *Last
Year at Marienbad* is empty, and the performance of Jeanne
Moreau is so vivid that the bored, alienated wife of *La Notte* is a
faded monochrome," Kael observes. "In *Jules and Jim* alienation
is just one aspect of her character and we see how Catherine got
there: she *becomes* alienated when she can't get her own way,
when she is blocked. It is not a universal condition as in *La
Notte*." The latter picture fails because Antonioni presents aliena-

tion as a universal condition; still, Kael calls *L'Avventura*—which has, of course, the same theme—"a great film." We are never told why she thinks *L'Avventura* is "a great film"; and the few differences she cites between *L'Avventura* and *La Notte* ("in *La Notte*, the architectural sense, integral to the theme and characters of *L'Avventura*, begins to dominate the characters, and as the abstract elements take over, the spatial becomes glacial, drama and character and even narrative sense are frozen") scarcely account for her strong pro-*L'Avventura* and con-*La Notte* reactions ("I dislike *La Notte*. Perhaps detest is the better word"). Yet the mystery which allegedly surrounds Robert Altman's characters in *McCabe & Mrs. Miller*, reviewed in *Deeper Into Movies*, appeals to Kael: "Lives are picked up and let go, and the sense of how little we know about them becomes part of the texture; we generally know little about the characters in movies, but since we're assured that that little is all we need to know and thus all there is to know, we're not bothered by it."

Kael is one of the few critics, however, who attends to film acting and who is worth quoting on the subject. Reviewing *Falstaff* in *Kiss Kiss Bang Bang*, she says of Welles: "Audiences are alert to him, as they often were to John Barrymore, and later to Charles Laughton, as they sometimes are to Bette Davis, as they almost always are to Brando—actors too big for their roles, who play the clown, and not always in comedy but in roles that for an artist of intelligence can only be comedy." She notes that large *latent* talent is required to communicate to an audience that even though what you are doing isn't worth doing, you are doing it very well. Previously, Welles had always been betrayed by his voice, she writes. Merely an instrument that he played, it seemed to point to shallowness and lack of feeling even in his best performances, becoming most fraudulent when he tried to infuse it with tenderness. "In *Falstaff* Welles seems to have grown into his voice; he's not too young for it anymore, and he's certainly big enough. And his emotions don't seem fake anymore; he's grown into them, too."

In her review of *No Way to Treat a Lady* (*Going Steady*), she writes: "When an actor dies, he does impersonations; when an actor has poor material to work with, that's often all he can do—and it's a form of death, though he can go on working and perhaps become a bigger star. Rod Steiger is playing not multiple roles in this picture but a psychopath who employs various disguises. Yet the masquerades are played as comic turns, and we are invited by the script and the director to enjoy them as if they were night-club impersonations." Calling to mind Steiger's acting in *The Mark, In the Heat of the Night, The Big Knife, Across the Bridge, The Pawnbroker,* and *Doctor Zhivago,* Kael concludes: "Except for the flashback scenes in *The Pawnbroker,* I've never seen Steiger so bad, so uninventively, ordinary bad as he is in his undisguised role in this movie, and he's only a little better in his disguises, acting high on the hog."

4

"Who cares whether the objects on the screen are accessible or inaccessible to the stage, or, for that matter, to painting, or to the novel or poetry?" Kael writes in her polemic against Kracauer's *Theory of Film.* And she goes on to argue that "what motion picture art shares with other arts is perhaps even more important than what it may, or may *not,* have exclusively" (*I Lost It at the Movies*).

True, film and drama have many features in common. Both use actors and speech, both can tell a story, both involve a formalization of experience, both convey themes. But once such generalizations are made, the differences between the two mediums—for example, in the *way* that the stage tells a story, and in the *way* that action is projected on the screen—are also plain. Not to recognize the differences as well as the similarities between stage and screen is to court theoretical and practical confusion. And this is what occurs in Kael's criticism.

In her review of *What is Cinema?,* she says of Bazin that his "essays help the reader see movies as part of a continuity and interaction with circus and music hall and theater and literature; Bazin undermines the media-infatuates who know so little of theater that they consider movies as a separate art without a past." Admittedly, film interacts with other arts: it has been influenced by, and it has in turn influenced, various media. But surely, film is a separate art! Although some continuity exists between theater and film—for instance, in the sense that the nineteenth-century stage foreshadowed (as A. Nicholas Vardac has shown in *Stage to Screen*, 1949) some of the techniques later used by the movies—the history of film began when a projector first threw moving images taken by a camera on a screen. Because Kael has never given the primarily visual nature of the medium the attention it demands, she has too often blurred the distinction between film and theater, and between film and literature.

Contradictions and fuzzy thinking distinguish Kael's reflections on adaptation. "I don't think that anybody who tries to put a great work of literature on the screen stands much of a chance of reproducing its *greatness* in another medium and probably much of its richness will be lost," she admits in a review of *The Innocents* (*I Lost It at the Movies*); "but there is an irresistable and certainly not-to-be-condemned desire to visualize works we love." Perhaps. If films were customarily adapted into plays and novels, however, would Kael also have a desire to see pictures theatricalized and literarized? The possibility that half the plays and novels written could be adaptations of movies seems absurd.

Yet Kael defends her longing to see Euripides and Hardy on the screen—and frequently she defends the adaptations—even though she admits that the greatness of the original stands little chance of surviving the transfer before the cameras. "One can understand, if not be very sympathetic toward, the purist monotony that Shakespeare is for the stage, Henry James for the printed page," Kael remarks. "(Suggested parlor game: try to think of five good movies *not* adapted or derived from any other medium.)" In 1963, the year Kael suggested her "parlor game," one could cite the following pictures as examples of original work for the screen: *The Last Laugh, Potemkin, The End of St. Petersburg, Intolerance* (which Kael, in *Going Steady*, calls the greatest film ever made), *Storm Over Asia, The General, Zéro de Conduite, M, Citizen Kane, The Children of Paradise,* all of Chaplin's and Fellini's films, *The Naked Night, Smiles of a Summer Night, The Seventh Seal, Wild Strawberries, Through a*

Glass Darkly, Winter Light, The 400 Blows, Viridiana, and *Los Olvidados.* Nevertheless, Kael can say in *Going Steady* that "almost all memorable movies are based on novels or biographies or some kind of book." She's right when she adds that movies based on second-rate books are better than ones made from first-rate books, because what distinguishes a great book is "the writer's way of seeing, and the film director cannot do justice to that."

All the same, the distinction does not prevent her from wanting to see Henry James on the screen, even though she realizes that *The Ambassadors* or *The Golden Bowl* are not for filming. Just as *Ulysses* is not for filming. "But how does one photograph intellectual pride? . . . But how does one photograph *thoughts* about food or desire?" Kael asks these questions in her review of James Joyce-into-Joseph Strick. And the reply to both questions, obviously, is: one can't. Which means that Joyce's subject is "inaccessible" to the camera. Which means that the differences between the page and the screen are more important than the similarities. And one wonders if, in spite of *The Birth of a Nation, The Treasure of the Sierra Madre,* and *Jules and Jim* (films mentioned by Kael as made from less than great literature), the most creative course for film artists still doesn't lie in the making of original works for the screen. If playwrights and novelists can generally think up their own material, why can't film-makers?

In "Filmed Theater" (*Going Steady*), Kael tells us that, because she grew up on a ranch, her experience of plays was derived from adaptations. "But, beyond that," she says, "I think play adaptations are one of the many *kinds* of movies and should simply be accepted as such. . . . I *like* filmed theater; I think there is a charge and a glamour about filmed plays and revues and vaudeville and music hall that one rarely gets from adaptations of novels or from those few screen 'originals.'" (*Few?* About half the films made are "originals"!) Now that Kael lives in New York City, one wonders why she simply doesn't go to the theater instead of filmed theater, if theater is what she's interested in. Why should film-makers be expected to bring plays to the provinces, any more than dramatists should be required to adapt films which are currently unavailable from distributors? To each his own.

"Filmed plays are often denigrated, somewhat dishonestly, by people who learn a little cant about what is said to be proper to the film medium and forget about the pleasure they've been getting from filmed plays all their lives," Kael writes. "Some of them don't realize . . . that, for example, the Marx Brothers comedies came direct from the stage, and that W. C. Fields was doing his stage routines on the screen, just as Chaplin and others before him had done." But there is a difference between using some comic "stage routines" on the screen and adapting *Hamlet* or *Phaedra*, plays which exist mainly because of their language. Chaplin's art was visual; Fields struck a balance between the verbal and the pictorial; to some extent, so did the Marx Brothers —though, as Arthur Knight points out in *The Liveliest Art*, the early "*The Coconuts* and *Animal Crackers* were nothing more than crudely photographed versions" of plays and one was always aware, even in the Marx Brothers's best films, of a recalcitrant staginess.

An almost ludicrous dualism on the subject of adaptation runs throughout Kael's essays. In "Movies, the Desperate Art," she writes: "The film *Miss Julie* treats the play as if stage and screen were opposed media and the play had to be subjected to a chemical change. (What is chemically changed in the process is the material and meaning of the play.)" According to Kael here, there is no basic conflict between stage and screen; and Alf Sojöberg, in "opening up" Strindberg's play for the cameras, changed the content because he altered the form. In "Ciphers" (*Going Steady*), however, we learn that plays—"because the dialogue and the action are conceived for the stage"—"don't give a movie director what he needs. . . . From the theater we can get a sense of human passions, we can learn what is *in* men, but we don't get the sense of man's environment that we get from movies." While movies give us a drama's setting, theater merely offers the drama itself, she notes. However, the contrast "isn't clear-cut, it's not an aesthetic law; it's just a generally observable difference."

Yet in *Kiss Kiss Bang Bang*, Kael writes of *Long Day's Journey Into Night*: "After such an experience, I don't see how one can niggle over whether it's 'cinema' or *merely* 'filmed theater.' Whatever it is, it's great. (And I am prepared to defend it as a movie.)" (But she doesn't!) Kael praises *The Member of the Wedding*: "The finest qualities of this film are in its sense of language and in the extraordinary performances"; and also *A Streetcar Named Desire*: "Elia Kazan's direction is often stagy, the sets and arrangements of actors are frequently too transparently 'worked out'; but who cares when you're looking at just about the best feminine performance you're ever going to see, as well as an interpretation by Brando that is just about perfection. This film has some of the best dialogue ever written by an American." The dialogue in *The Member of the Wedding* and *A Streetcar Named Desire is* good; but it's dialogue written for the stage, not for the screen. And Kael herself admits—in another book, in another mood—that concentration on performance is "not the most exciting way to approach movie-making" ("Cheaters," *Deeper Into Movies*).

Kael can even declare: "Shakespeare translates to film so extraordinarily well [!] because his plays are open in structure. . . . The greatest dramatist is also, as it happens, the greatest scenarist" (review of *King Lear, Deeper Into Movies*). Kael is correct on the score of Shakespeare's open form; but is there no opposition apparent between all that unforgettable language in his plays and the pictorial requirements of the screen? "One may long for the ideal—for a great play transformed by a great movie artist into a great movie. But great movie artists are not often tempted to tackle great plays, and when they do, it sometimes turns out that they don't have the right skills," she observes in her review of *The Trojan Women*. "Short of the ideal, what it comes down to is whether in seeing a movie version one can still respond to what makes the play great" (*Deeper Into Movies*). Now, even though some of the quality in a great play will come through any reasonably competent adaptation, how can a work of art created for one medium really be said to yield its uniqueness when transferred to another medium? If form and matter are inseparable (except for purposes of analysis), and if, as Kael admits, there is an "observable difference" between stage and screen (where we get a greater "sense of man's environment"), then doesn't it follow—even short of the "ideal"—that in seeing a

movie we can *not* "still respond to what makes the play great"?
Kael can argue just the opposite, however, because she has
come to believe that "content" equals "the work itself."

5

Perhaps the best way of comprehending Kael's "aesthetic" is to
examine "Trash, Art, and the Movies," one of her most famous
essays.

"The romance of movies is not just in those stories and those
people on the screen but in the adolescent dream of meeting
others who feel as you do about what you've seen," Kael writes.
"You do meet them, of course, and you know each other at once
because you talk less about good movies than about what you
love in bad movies." Kael's first sentence suggests that movies
represent a form of escape from adulthood, a subject which will
be dealt with more fully in due course. Her second sentence
means—to put the matter bluntly—that she would rather discuss
trash than art.

"People who are just getting 'seriously interested' in film always ask a critic, 'Why don't you talk about technique and the
visuals more?'" Kael observes. "The answer is that American
movie technique is generally more like technology and it usually
isn't very interesting." Granted . . . But Kael doesn't find discussion of technique "very interesting" even where great films are
concerned. "Technique is hardly worth talking about unless it's
used for something worth doing . . . And for the greatest movie
artists where there is a unity of technique and subject, one
doesn't need to talk about technique because it has been sub-
sumed in the art."

But isn't it part of the critic's job to show how technique *becomes* art? "One doesn't want to talk about how Tolstoy got his
effects but about the work itself." Here our best known film critic
equates "the work itself" with "content," with the *what*. "One
doesn't want to talk about how Jean Renoir does it; one wants to
talk about what he has done." "What" Renoir has done is the
"art"; "how" Renoir has done it is "technique"; so "form" equals

"technique," and "art" equals "content." "One can separate it all out, of course, distinguish form and content for purposes of analysis. But that is a secondary, analytic function, and hardly needs to be done explicitly in criticism."

Kael has a curious notion of "criticism" if she really believes that analysis is unimportant to the critical act. Unless we are made to see *how* Renoir has done it, we can't appreciate his art; unless we are given formal analysis, we are left with the ink-blot approach. "Taking it apart is far less important than trying to see it whole." Yes; but can we value the whole unless we have first taken it apart? Isn't unity—of structure, of characterization, of theme, of symbolism, of style—a criterion of value? And how can the critic persuade us that a film *is* unified—*is* a whole—without making explicit the necessary relationship of its various elements? By refusing to explain how a film-maker achieves his effects, a critic is left with nothing but bald assertion to recommend his judgment. And what can be baldly asserted, can be baldly denied.

An important clue to an understanding of the disorder in Kael's thinking—the many perverse statements, the sundry contradictions—appears in the fifth section of "Trash, Art, and the Movies." In it she argues that we enjoy movies for reasons that have little to do with art. Indeed, our most intense pleasure in movies may be the nonaesthetic one of eluding the responsibilities of the approved responses required by the middle-class values of home and school. Paradoxically, this may help us to develop an aesthetic sense because the obligation to pay attention and "appreciate" often works against art by making us too tense for pleasure. Our own responses are freer to develop when we are liberated from duty and constraint.

The critic goes on to argue that understandably enough it is easier for Americans to see "*art*" in films made abroad, because of how we think of art. "Art is still what teachers and ladies and foundations believe in, it's civilized and refined, cultivated and serious, cultural, beautiful, European, Oriental: it's what America isn't, and it's especially what American movies are not."

Kael still sees moviegoing in terms of her juvenile past: still sees herself as a kind of Huck Finn running away from attempts by the Widow Douglas and Aunt Polly to "civilize" her: still wants to "light out for the territory" of the silver screen—where she can discover a freer, brighter, happier, more intense form of experience than that offered by "official (school) culture." One reason why Kael, in an essay entitled "Trash, Art, and the Movies," has so much to say about trash but so little to communicate about art, is that art means for her the values of school and society, whereas trash represents escape from all that "falsity." Of course, she argues that there is more trash than art; and of course, she's right. But there are many examples of film art available— why should a critic refuse to discuss any of them in a piece ostensibly devoted in part to art and movies? Isn't Kael guilty of what she has elsewhere condemned others for doing—namely, turning "criticism into autobiography"? The dominant impression she conveys in her essay is that there is trash and pseudo-art— nothing else. What remains is an adolescent vision: an anti-intellectual, anti-art, nonaesthetic "aesthetic."

"Movie art is not the opposite of what we have always enjoyed in movies, it is not to be found in a return to that official high culture, it is what we have always found good in movies only more so," she explains. "It's the subversive gesture carried further, the moments of excitement sustained longer and extended into new meanings." During the sixties it became fashionable to describe various modes of activity as "subversive." Back in the fifties, in "Movies, the Desperate Art," however, Kael wrote: "A great film is one in which the range of meaning is so imaginatively new, compelling, or exciting that we experience a new vision of human experience (*Grand Illusion*). One might also call a film great because it triumphantly achieves a style (René Clair's *Le Million*) or because it represents a new method and approach (*Potemkin*)." Are *Grand Illusion*, *Le Million*, and *Potemkin* "subversive"? Is *Intolerance*? *L'Avventura*? Do these films bear any relation to that childish nose-thumbing gesture directed at society which Kael now calls "subversive" and which she now equates with "art"? Even if we agree that some great films are "subversive," in the sense that they assume towards "official culture" a critical attitude—I mean, a *mature* critical attitude—must we insist that all great films follow suit? Aside from striking an already dated posture of "radical chic," what does Kael gain by calling art "subversive"?

"I don't trust anyone who doesn't admit having at some time in his life enjoyed trashy American movies," Kael informs us; "I don't trust *any* of the tastes of people who were born with such good taste that they didn't need to find their way through trash." Kael expresses a similar notion in "Movies on Television" (*Kiss Kiss Bang Bang*): "The educated person who became interested in cinema as an art form through Bergman or Fellini or Resnais is an alien to me (and my mind goes blank with hostility and indifference when he begins to talk)." In order to be a FOOF, as Kael sees it, one is obliged to come up through the rank of trash. Who would deny that relaxation and enjoyment can be found in *The Thomas Crown Affair*, a film which Kael describes as "pretty good trash"? But when Kael goes on to say: "Trash doesn't belong to the academic tradition, and that's part of the *fun* of trash—that you know (or *should* know) that you don't have to take it seriously," she suggests that "trash" means "fun" and that "art" means "boredom."

"Who at some point hasn't set out dutifully for that fine foreign film and then ducked into the nearest piece of American trash?" Kael asks. "We're not only educated people of taste, we're also common people with common feelings. And our common feelings are not all *bad*. You hoped for some aliveness in that trash that you were pretty sure you wouldn't get from the respected 'art film.'"

There is a conflict in Kael between her democratic faith in the wisdom of the "great unwashed" and her aristocratic scorn for the "booboisie." In "It's Only a Movie" (*Film Study in Higher Education*, edited by David C. Stewart), written in 1966, she informs teachers (those dry-as-dust representatives of "official [school] culture"): "If *Ten Days That Shook the World* bores a student, there is no proof, no power on earth, to say he has got to like it. If a lady says, 'That man don't pleasure me,' that's it. There are some areas in which we can decide for ourselves." But in "Movies, the Desperate Art", she tells her fellow critics: "You will be reproved with 'What right have you to say *Samson and Delilah* is no good when millions of people liked it?' and you will be subjected to the final devastation of 'It's all a matter of taste and one person's taste is as good as another's.' One does not make friends by replying that although it *is* all a matter of taste (and education and intelligence and sensibility) one person's taste is *not* as good as another's." Similarly, in "War as Vaudeville" (*Going Steady*), she says: "College students study Ionesco and Beckett and Artaud and then respond to—*Charly*. A surprising number of people seem to be educated beyond their own tastes; despite education and literacy, they still want this guck."

Kael ends her essay as follows: "If we've grown up at the movies we know that good work is continuous not with the academic, respectable tradition but with the glimpses of something good in trash, but we want the subversive gesture carried to the domain of discovery. Trash has given us an appetite for art." This idea—if it can be dignified as such—is not new in Kael's "aesthetic." "If debased art is kitsch, perhaps kitsch may be redeemed by honest vulgarity, may become art," she writes in "Zeitgeist and Poltergeist." "Our best work transforms kitsch, makes art out of it; that is the peculiar greatness and strength of American Movies."

Since Kael has never really defined either "art" or "kitsch," the foregoing statements are semantically meaningless. The same criticism can be made of Kael's concluding sentences in "Trash, Art, and the Movies". What does she intend by "the academic, respectable tradition"? If *The Birth of a Nation* and *Intolerance* don't belong in that tradition, then what films do? Kael conveniently overlooks Griffith, as well as other accepted masters (and by "accepted," I mean accepted by Kael, too, elsewhere), because—as a result of her Huck Finn complex—she feels a need to justify trash and denigrate "art." Earlier, in "Movies, the Desperate Art," Kael argued that "the directions indicated in [the] classics are not the directions Hollywood took." Now she tells us that the directions Hollywood *did* take—for the most part, in the directions of trash—were the right ones. Since she refuses to "re-experience and reassess the classics"; since she chooses not to focus most of her attention on those films (mostly foreign but some American too) which follow in the traditions of the classics or establish new traditions; since she regards study of the ex-

pressive side of good films as merely "a secondary, analytic function, a scholarly function"—since, in brief, she would rather
watch the latest and "nearest piece of American trash"—is it any
wonder that she has grown hungry for art?

6

Three of Kael's other essays—*"Bonnie and Clyde,"* "Movies on
Television," and "Raising Kane"—also warrant detailed discussion.

In *"Bonnie and Clyde,"* which appears in *Kiss Kiss Bang Bang,*
Kael has a subject ideally suited to her interests. At the time of its
opening, the Arthur Penn movie caused a critical controversy:
some hailed it as a masterpiece of American film-making; others
condemned it for its depiction of violence, its sympathetic treatment of the title characters, its historical inaccuracies, and its
mixture of tragedy and comedy. Kael liked the picture. She has
always relished quarreling with other critics (too much so, as
most reviewers saw it, in *I Lost It at the Movies*), though since
joining *The New Yorker* her personal attacks have disappeared
(reportedly, because of a clause in her contract which forbids
it). So *Bonnie and Clyde* gave Kael an opportunity to defend an
outstanding American movie: one that could hold its own with
the best foreign films, one that embodies qualities Kael has always valued—vitality, humor, social meaning—and one that
would permit her to work off some hostility against the picture's
detractors (but without mentioning any names).

Significantly, Kael begins: "How do you make a good movie in
this country without being jumped on?"—a sentence which sets
the tone of a St. Joan riding out to do battle against the Enemy.
Her next sentence—*"Bonnie and Clyde* is the most excitingly
American American movie since *The Manchurian Candidate"*—is
scarcely high praise for Penn's film, even though Kael thinks it is.
Immediately she introduces her personal, Huck Finn motif: "Our
experience as we watch it has some connection with the way we
reacted to movies in childhood: with how we came to love them
and to feel they were ours—not an art that we learned over the

years to appreciate but simply and immediately ours. When an American movie is contemporary in feeling, like this one, it makes a different kind of contact with an American audience from the kind that is made by European films, however contemporary."

Kael defends the comedy in *Bonnie and Clyde* because it "keeps the audience in a kind of eager, nervous imbalance— holds our attention by throwing our disbelief back in our faces. . . . Instead of the movie spoof, which tells the audience that it doesn't need to feel or care, that it's all just in fun, that 'we were only kidding,' *Bonnie and Clyde* disrupts us with 'And you thought we were only kidding.'" As for historical accuracy, Penn's film "is far more accurate historically than most," and besides, "historical accuracy hardly matters anyway." Kael adds that those who use the historical argument against *Bonnie and Clyde* are merely seeking an excuse to attack a good film which upsets them in ways they don't want to acknowledge (though she admits that this charge is "based on some pretty sneaky psychological suppositions" and could be called "an argument *ad hominem*").

The violence in the picture is justified, Kael believes, because "violence is its meaning. When, during a comically botched-up getaway, a man is shot in the face, the image is obviously based on one of the most famous sequences in Eisenstein's *Potemkin*, and the startled face is used the same way it was in *Potemkin*— to convey in an instant how someone who just happens to be in the wrong place at the wrong time, the irrelevant 'innocent' bystander, can get it full in the face. And at that instant the meaning of Clyde Barrow's character changes; he's still a clown, but *we've* become the butt of the joke." Yes, Bonnie and Clyde are treated sympathetically, Kael admits; but that doesn't mean that we're all going to go out and become killers: "Part of the power of art lies in showing us what we are *not* capable of. We see that killers are not a different breed but are *us* without the insight or understanding or self-control that works of art strengthen." Kael points out that Louis B. Mayer "did not turn us into a nation of Andy Hardys, and if, in a film, we see a frightened man wantonly take the life of another, it does not encourage us to do the same, any more than seeing an ivory hunter shoot an elephant makes us want to shoot one. It may, on the contrary, so sensitize us that we get a pang in the gut if we accidentally step on a moth."

Kael has little to say about the structure of *Bonnie and Clyde*, except to observe that it "is a story of love on the run." Likewise, the visual quality of the picture is largely ignored, though she remarks that Penn's "squatter's-jungle scene is too 'eloquent,' like a poster making an appeal, and the Parker-family-reunion sequence is poetic in the gauzy mode." However, the "end of the picture, the rag-doll dance of death as the gun blasts keep the bodies of Bonnie and Clyde in motion, is brilliant." About the music, she has nothing to remark. Twice she complains that Clyde's "sexual success"—or his "triumph over impotence"—is unsophisticated, "a kind of sop to the audience," thus badly misunderstanding the event and failing to grasp an important aspect of the theme—that in nonsexual terms he remains impotent. (This failure might have been prevented by closer attention to the structure of action.) Kael relates *Bonnie and Clyde* to previous movies based on the lives of the killers, with particular emphasis on Lang's *You Only Live Once*.

The final portion of *"Bonnie and Clyde"* is devoted to an attempt to separate the contributions of the scriptwriters, Robert Benton and David Newman, from that of the director. Unlike Bergman and Fellini, Kael argues, Penn does not create "out of his own experience." Penn is "remarkable" when, as in *Bonnie and Clyde*, he has a good script; but he is not, she suggests, a great director. She writes: "Though one cannot say of *Bonnie and Clyde* to what degree it shows the work of Newman and Benton and to what degree they merely enabled Penn to 'express himself,' there are ways of making guesses." And her "guesses" lead her to conclude that, often, the writing is better than the directing. Kael's championing of the writers at the expense of the director—whatever one might think of it (and in part it can be interpreted as an overreaction to the *auteur* theory)—anticipates her more controversial thesis in "Raising Kane."

Aside from Kael, no other American critic has considered the influence of television on the motion picture and its audience. In "Zeitgeist and Poltergeist," she suggests that "television viewing, with all its breaks and cuts, and the inattention, except for action, and spinning the dial to find some action, is partly responsible for destruction of the narrative sense—that delight in following a story through its complications to its conclusion." Kael is afraid, as she points out in "The Making of *The Group*," that the television-trained director will come to dominate film-making, with the result that the movie screen will be converted into a television screen: all foreground, no background; all surface, no depth. Film directors who come from television, she argues, tend not to know how to handle masses of people for the large screen. "Television has been destroying the old show-business belief in giving everything you have to an audience," Kael writes in "Elfskin" (*Deeper Into Movies*). "With the skimpy material they're handed, performers can't give much. . . . A man like Carl Reiner or Woody Allen spreads himself so thin that he may never discover his full self; there just isn't enough of him together at any time in any one place. Now that such men are making movies, they treat the movie audience like the television audience; their movies are as thin as skits."

Kael's most extended discussion of television and film appears in "Movies on Television." Now that old movies are available morning, noon, and night on television, she observes, the movie past is completely out of perspective for those who did not live through that past, because the pictures "are all jumbled together, out of historical sequence." The good films are preserved along with the bad, "and so it all begins to seem one big pile of junk. . . . If the same thing had happened in literature or music or painting—if we were constantly surrounded by the piled up inventory of the past—it's conceivable that modern man's notions of culture and civilization would be very different." The better films are still good on the small screen, in spite of the shrinkage and visual distortion and structural violations, because "the bare bones of performance, dialogue, story, good directing, and (especially important for close-range viewing) good editing can still make an old movie more entertaining than almost anything new on television." The more visual a movie, the more it suffers on television; the more verbal a film, the better it seems on the home screen. "What looks bad in old movies is the culture of which they were part and which they expressed—a tone of American life that we have forgotten," Kael writes. Although most of the films are trash, they "probably taught us more about the world, and even about values, than our 'education' did."

And why—Kael asks defensively—shouldn't we enjoy trash? "Why should we deny these pleasures because there are other, more complex kinds of pleasure possible? It's true that these pleasures don't deepen, and that they don't change *us*, but maybe that is part of what makes them seem our own—we realize that we have some emotions and responses that *don't* change as we get older." However, three paragraphs later she remarks: "there is always something a little shameful about living in the past; we feel guilty, stupid—as if the pleasure we get needed some justification that we can't provide." Too bad Kael has never worked through the implications of this insight to a more adequate conception of film art and film criticism.

There is no space to do justice to all the material in "Raising Kane"—which combines film criticism, film history, film theory, biographical information on Welles, Herman J. Mankiewicz, William Randolph Hearst and others, and even some autobiographical data. Perhaps Kael's main thesis, however, is that much less credit should go to the director of *Citizen Kane* and considerably more to the writer. Earlier, in *Kiss Kiss Bang Bang*, Kael had a different view; there she called *Citizen Kane* "the most controversial one-man show in film history . . . staged by twenty-five-year-old writer-director-star Orson Welles." Mankiewicz is only mentioned parenthetically.

The first draft of *Citizen Kane*, Kael writes in "Raising Kane," was dictated by Mankiewicz, early in 1940, without the help of Welles. According to Kael, Welles "probably made suggestions" to the writer; "but Mrs. Alexander, who took the dictation from Mankiewicz, from the first paragraph to the last, and then, when the first draft was completed did the secretarial work . . . on the rewriting and the cuts, and who then handled the script at the studio until after the film was shot, says that Welles didn't write (or dictate) one line of the shooting script of *Citizen Kane*." Kael also argues that the contribution of Gregg Toland, the cinematographer for the picture, went "far beyond suggestions and technical solutions. I think he not only provided much of the visual style of *Citizen Kane* but was responsible for affecting the conception, and even for introducing a few elements that are not in the script." Toland had worked on an American remake of a German movie, *Mad Love*, which was directed by Karl Freund, who in turn had been the cameraman on such German films as *The Last Laugh, Tartuffe, Metropolis*, and *Variety*. So—according to Kael—the Germanic look of *Citizen Kane* (its "Gothic atmosphere") can be traced through Toland back to Freund and the styles of Murnau, Lang, and E. A. Dupont, and even back to Wiene, because the man who directed *The Cabinet of Dr. Caligari* also directed the German version of *Mad Love!*

The torturous reasoning Kael indulges in to show the supposedly pervasive influence of Toland on *Citizen Kane*, suggests that her article should have been entitled "Razing Welles," since she seems less concerned with giving due measure of credit to the writer and the cameraman than with deflating the director and the director's admirers. Kael seems to have done this partly because she has always been overly fond of the literary element in film; partly because she wants to continue her feud with Sarris and the *auteurists*; and partly because—well, partly out of sheer perversity, just to provoke a general reaction. Not even literary men, however, have rushed to defend Kael's thesis. Reviewing *The Citizen Kane Book* in the *New York Times* (October 31, 1971), author Mordecai Richler, for example, observes: "Kael's excellent case for Mank is in the end more than somewhat vitiated by the publication of the script itself. The script . . . albeit clever, even technically brilliant, is also superficial and without one quotable line. To Welles, then, however vain and objectionable his manner, rococo his style, must go the ultimate credit for the miracle of *Citizen Kane*."

The most detailed refutation of "Raising Kane," however, is Peter Bogdanovich's "The Kane Mutiny" (*Esquire*, October 1972). Bogdanovich, who is not only a well-known film director but also a critic and the author of a forthcoming book on Welles, writes: "The Chairman of the Critical Studies Program at U.C.L.A., Dr. Howard Suber, who conducted a seminar on *Citizen Kane* in 1969, did very thorough research on the film and its various extant drafts. Because, at one point, they were to collaborate in writing the prefatory material to the published screenplay, Kael had full access to this material. She takes full credit for whatever use she made of it, and gives none at all to Suber. What upsets Suber, however, are Kael's conclusions: 'After months of investigation,' he told me, 'I regard the authorship of *Citizen Kane* as a very open question. Unfortunately, both sides would have to be consulted, and Kael never spoke to Welles, which, as I see it, violates all the rules of historical research.'" Bogdanovich quotes screenwriter Charles Lederer as saying that the original draft of Mankiewicz's script was "pretty dull," and that Welles made considerable changes in it. He also refers to the Spring 1972 issue of *Sight and Sound* in which actor George Coulouris (Thatcher in *Citizen Kane*) calls Kael's essay "twaddle" and Bernard Herman (who wrote the music) refers to it as "rubbish." Mankiewicz's secretary "could have had no knowledge of Welles's script," argues Bogdanovich; "she was never present during the working meetings between" Mankiewicz and Welles "when the conception and basic shape of the story were developed, nor could she have known what happened to the Mankiewicz drafts *after* they were passed on to Welles, changed and rewritten by him, and incorporated in his own screenplay."

Welles claims that the original idea of a film "telling the same thing several times" was his; that Mankiewicz liked the idea; that, after concurring on character and plot, they each wrote their own script; and that he used what he liked in Mankiewicz's version and kept what he liked in his own. Katherine Trosper, Welles's secretary, relates that the director kept making changes in the script throughout production; Richard Barr, executive assistant on *Citizen Kane* supports Trosper's testimony. Both these witnesses, Bogdanovich points out, live in New York City: "Neither received so much as an inquiry about his participation in the making of *Citizen Kane*. But then, neither did Welles. In fact, there is nothing to show that Kael interviewed anyone of real importance associated with the actual making of the film."

As for the alleged Toland Influence, Bogdanovich notes that photographs of Welles's stage productions, as well as the evidence of all his other films, reveal the "same chiaroscuro" manifest throughout *Citizen Kane*. Nor is there any similarity in *mise en scène* between *Mad Love* and *Citizen Kane*; furthermore, the cinematography in both pictures is also different. "This is not surprising," Bogdanovich writes, "since Toland, far from being the sole cameraman on *Mad Love*, is listed *second* in the credits, after photographer Chester Lyons, who was responsible for most of the filming. Kael avoids that bit of information."

No doubt, the last word has not been written on the authorship of *Citizen Kane*. Although Bogdanovich is scarcely a neutral observer, he has managed to bring together an impressive array of evidence. Kael, it would seem, did not do her homework. Accordingly, her thesis remains unconvincing.

7

Pauline Kael has won many followers because she writes in a dazzling style, because she has a strong personality which is conveyed in everything she says, because she makes whatever interests her at the moment—even a trashy film—sound important, and because she discusses with intelligence subjects which most readers want to hear discussed . . . Unfortunately, what most readers want to hear discussed is not the *art* of the film: they are more interested in matter, not form; in sociology, not aesthetics. Either Kael's interests genuinely coincide with most of her readers', or else she is deliberately writing on their level of concern. In any case, her criticism has a tendency to suffer from a lack of attention to what makes film an art form. To be sure, as an analysis of "Trash, Art, and the Movies" suggests, Kael has ambivalent notions about art; and, as "Movies on Television" indicates, she has guilt feelings over her enjoyment of trash. No wonder her criticism is often perplexing!

Godardian in her love for spontaneity and improvisation, Kael seems never to have glanced backward at her previous writings in an effort to reconcile conflicting statements—on adaptation: pro and con, for example, or on the formalistic versus the sociological method—with the result that no consistent theory of either film or film criticism emerges from a study of her work. On the whole, Kael's criticism has *not* been getting deeper into her subject. In spite of some contradictions and confusions, her finest writing appears in "Movies, the Desperate Art" and *I Lost It at the Movies*, because in these early works she discusses—often incivisively—subjects of permanent value to criticism.

Kael has remarkable gifts. If she would discipline her thinking, take more care in her research, show more love for art than trash, and devote as much attention to form as to content—then she might truly become what many commentators have prematurely dubbed her: the best film critic now practicing in America.

CHAPTER SEVEN

Stanley Kauffmann and Pluralistic, Aesthetic Criticism

> The best critic is one who illuminates whole provinces of an art that you could not see before, who helps to refine the general public's taste (which is never good enough—they haven't time, they're busy studying something else or doing their jobs) and who serves as a sounding board for serious artists. . . . But fundamentally you take a critic's hand and let him lead you further, perhaps higher, only if you are initially convinced of a substantial area of mutual sympathy and interest.
>
> —STANLEY KAUFFMANN

1

Stanley Kauffmann has published two collections of film criticism: *A World on Film* (1966) and *Figures of Light* (1970). Most of the reviews in both books were originally published in *The New Republic*, the material in the first volume dating back to 1958. Kauffman studied drama in college and afterwards worked for ten years with a repertory group in which he wrote, directed, and acted in plays. Between 1963 and 1966, Kauffmann was drama critic for educational television in New York City; in addition, he served for eight months in 1966 as theater critic on *The New York Times*. It has been reported that at one time

Kauffmann also wrote anonymous movie reviews for *Playboy*. In 1964, he received a Ford Foundation Traveling Fellowship, which allowed him to study film-making for three months in eight countries. Author of seven novels, Kauffmann has also edited the section on film in *The Cosmos Reader* (1971), and co-edited another anthology, *American Film Criticism* (1972); he has written the introduction to the reissue of Vachel Lindsay's *The Art of the Moving Picture* (1970); and over the years he has been an active book reviewer and frequent guest on television shows devoted to film. At present, Kauffmann is film and drama reviewer for *The New Republic*, Visiting Professor of Drama at Yale, and Distinguished Professor of Film at City University of New York.

"I discovered film criticism some time in 1933," Kauffmann writes in his introduction to *American Film Criticism*. "Up to then, although I had already been an avid filmgoer for some ten years, it had not occurred to me that film could be discussed in terms relative to those used by good critics of the theater or literature or music. Then one day in my college library I picked up a copy of *The Nation* and read a review by William Troy—I can't recall the title of the film—in which he compared a sequence in a new picture with a similar sequence in a previous one to show relations of style. I'm not sure that my jaw actually dropped, but that's the feeling I remember."

For Kauffmann, the film itself is central to the critic's task. In his review of the reissue of Warshow's *The Immediate Experience* in *The New Republic* (January 22, 1962), he remarks: "There is plentiful room for more than one kind of critic, and social-intellectual attitudes are obviously a valid area of criticism. But Warshow's reviews remind us inescapably of the medical student who prepared for an exam by studying the stomach, was asked about the heart, and replied: 'The heart lies near the stomach. The stomach is constructed of . . . and so forth, and so forth.'" Kauffmann's basic criticism of Warshow is that the latter treats movies as sociological indexes. Or, as he puts it in his review of Kael's *I Lost It at the Movies* (*Harper's*, June 1965), the "sociological school is chiefly concerned with the film as treasury of social myth and cultural trait." In the latter review,

Kauffmann also scores the *auteur* approach and what he calls
" 'Free' criticism": "since it is apposite to the 'free' cinema, which
holds that any criterion is applicable or, if one chooses, none at
all; and which makes much of the latest vogue-word 'sensibility,'
as opposed to standards."

By " 'free' criticism," Kauffmann is apparently referring to
Susan Sontag's approach. "These schools—and others—seem to
me to twine about a center without which they would all col-
lapse," he goes on to say. "That center is a view of the film as a
descendant of the theater and literature, certainly *sui generis* but
not without ancestors or cousins, to be judged by its own unique
standards which are yet analagous to those of other arts: a view
that is pluralistic, aesthetic but not anti-science, contemporary
but not unhistorical, and humanistic. I need hardly add, after this
flattering description, that I subscribe to this last school, which
seems to me so sound and comprehensive that it can hardly be
called a school." The foregoing description of the film critic's
proper approach seems to me the finest brief statement on the
subject that any American critic has written. I wish, though, that
Kauffmann would—sometime—treat the subject at greater
length.

Whereas most film critics complain that their burden is a
heavy one because the medium is "impure"—being made up, as
it is, of moving pictures, dialogue, music, and dance—Kauffmann
speaks, in *The Cosmos Reader*, of a lack of aesthetic standards in
film. In other words, whereas most critics argue that the complexity of the medium, as Sarris expresses it in *The Film*, "requires no
less than a renaissance man to encompass all its aspects," Kauffmann begins with the broader philosophical questions posed by
movie criticism. "The aesthetics of all the arts is in flux," he
contends, "but the situation is at its least clarified in film. . . .
There simply has not been time, compared with other arts, to
evolve comparable critical theory. Part of the reason also is the
fact that film arrived in an era of drastic social, religious, and
political turbulence, to all of which aesthetics is closely knit." The
question: "What standards shall I use to judge films?" has no
"answer," Kauffmann insists. In view of what he has said elsewhere, he obviously intends *no single answer*, otherwise his own

approach would be no different from " 'free' criticism." Kauffmann's stance, it should be emphasized, is not (as he describes it
in his review of Warshow's book) "hyper-aesthetic." His humanistic concerns are evident in his remark that the "impulse" which
lies "behind" the search for viable critical standards "is, at its
base, a moral one." Yet after making this statement, Kauffmann
abruptly begins a new paragraph and says no more about the
relationship between morality and aesthetics.

But if Kauffmann starts with philosophical speculation, he
soon gets down to the practical problems of criticism. For example, he points out that film is a collaborative medium; consequently, an ability to evaluate "the different artistic and technical
contributions is essential" in a critic. Furthermore, film is not only
an art but a business; and business has "an effect, ultimately, on
aesthetics . . . [H]owever, not the slightest concession should be
made because of these facts, else we would quickly end up with
lopsided patronizing standards or sheer economic-sociological
history; but neither should analogies with other, 'individual' arts
be facile." Nevertheless, although the "options for film aesthetics
remain open," and although film critics should perhaps be thank-
ful that they have no tradition of Aristotelian and Hegelian
scholarship to weigh down upon them, "the search for values is
very strong and very persistent."

Accordingly, Kauffmann proceeds to lay down a few "general
propositions." He begins by asserting that "film is an art with a
popular base. It is made for groups of people, for audiences, not
for individuals." This far from lucid distinction is followed by
some surprisingly essentialist nonsense: "It is possible to enjoy a
film when seeing it alone . . . but that is not the nature of the art,
as it is the nature of the novel to be enjoyed alone." In the
nineteenth century it was a common practice for the head of a
family to read aloud from a novel to his wife and children. In the
latter half of the twentieth century it has been a far from un-
common practice to watch films alone—sometimes in front of a
television set, sometimes even in a theater (attendance being
what it is today). The introduction of the electronic cassette,
which Kauffmann himself writes about later in his piece, will

certainly encourage this trend. Granted, today novels are normally read alone; but there is nothing in the "nature" of either
novels or films which necessarily determines that they shall be
read or seen either alone or in company with others.

Next Kauffmann points out that the image-making power of
the medium "is absolutely central to film." However, he then
confusingly adds: "and [this power] creates a consanguinity between Bergman and a routine director that does not exist com-
parably between the pinnacle and the valley in other arts." Now
by the "power of making images," Kauffmann does not intend
simply—and properly—that film is a primarily visual medium.
Referring to Bazin's essay "The Evolution of Film Language," he
adopts the following definition from the French theorist: "By
'image,' I mean in a general sense anything that can be added to
a depicted object by its being depicted on the screen." What
Bazin means is that the film-maker who believes in the image (as
opposed to the one who believes in reality—Bazin is discussing
two different schools of cinema) "aestheticizes" the raw data of
experience through the expressive use of *mise en scène* and editing. Aside from the fact that Kauffmann seems to have an insufficient grasp of what Bazin is about, nothing he subsequently remarks on the subject of the "image" lends any conviction to his
assertion that in film the disparities between a Bergman and a
"routine director" are less than the disparities between, say, a
Conrad and a "routine novelist." It is worth noting that Kauffmann compares *Citizen Kane* and *Stagecoach* "because, in the
exercise of film technique and film mystique [undefined—though
it is apparent that Kauffmann is attacking the *auteurists* without
naming them], both are proficient." *Stagecoach*, Kauffmann says,
is the work of a "film entertainer"; *Citizen Kane* is the work of a
"film artist." But Ford is hardly a "routine director" and *Stagecoach* is more than pure entertainment; so what we have here is a
comparison analogous in the novel form between a *Lord Jim* and
a *The Grapes of Wrath*, not between a *Lord Jim* and a *This Gun
for Hire*. As Kauffmann's later comments indicate, his standards
for judging the differences between a great film and a near great
one, or even between film art and pure film entertainment, can

also be used to evaluate novels (or plays): "intent in the use of technique, and the quality of the materials, the *content*" (italics in original).

(In "The Film Generation," the essay which concludes *A World on Film*, Kauffmann asserts: "In any film except those with fantastic settings, whether the director's aim is naturalistic or romantic or symbolic or anything else, the streets and stairways and cigarette lighters are present, the girl's room is at least as real as the girl—often it bolsters her defective reality. Emphasized or not, invited or not, the physical world through the intensifications of photography never stops insisting on its presence and relevance." According to Kauffmann, this surface reproduction of the world "gives a discrete verity to many mediocre films and gives great vitality to a film by a good artist." The influence of Kracauer is manifest here. Observe, however, that according to Kauffmann the "depicted object" ["the physical world"] plus "the intensifications of photography" [that which is "added to a depicted object by its being depicted on the screen"] makes its impression on the viewer. That *plus* is important: for it refutes Kauffmann's contention that film is somehow unique in that the disparities between art and entertainment are less noticeable than in other arts. Truffaut has remarked of *MASH*: "Robert Altman never once, throughout the entire picture, put the camera in the right place" [quoted by Guy Flatley in *The New York Times*, September 27, 1970]. A world on film is never *the* world.)

Kauffmann believes that some critics "confuse style, a term inseparably weighted with moral resonance, with sheer technique." Technique, he rightly declares, is not an absolute; there must be "commitment" on the part of the film-maker. The *auteurists*, of course, concur. But, whereas an *auteurist* would claim (as Sarris does in "Directors, How Personal Can You Get?" *Confessions of a Cultist*) "a preference for small subjects over large" and "westerns over working-class allegories," Kauffmann writes: "It is a commonplace that style transforms material: *Macbeth* in lesser hands would be a melodrama. But style cannot easily make the trivial into the serious. What is more relevant, style applied to good material produces better results than style applied to inferior material. There is an old adage in sports: A good big man is better than a good little man. Style applied to serious content is better than style applied to trivia." When the *auteurists* first arrived on the scene, they maintained that social-minded critics had been giving high grades to stylistically poor films with strong humanist themes (in their opinion, for example, to films like *The Bicycle Thief*). If social-minded critics had elevated content over style, the *auteurists* then proceeded to elevate style over content. But Kauffmann holds to the traditional notion that style and content cannot be separated, that in the best films style and content are commensurate.

2

"What is truth?" Kauffmann asks in his review of *Salesman*, a *cinéma verité* film by Albert and David Maysles. "A modern Pilate might say that it's not the monopoly of either fact or fiction film, that life is at least as much of a liar as art, and that if the life is being observed and recorded and rearranged, the line can get fuzzy." As Kauffmann sees it, *Salesman* exposes a paradox: "direct cinema does not cut below facts to truth unless the techniques of fiction are applied." Life—in short—is not art (a point which Kauffmann himself, as we have seen, can overlook in other contexts). Further in the same volume (*Figures of Light*), Kauffmann argues that *Tell Them Willie Boy Is Here* is defective because life has been copied too faithfully; if Abraham Polonsky's characters actually said and did what the writer-director has them say and do, such facts still have no "artistic justification."

"The seduction of the camera," Kauffmann writes in his review of De Sica's *The Roof* (*A World of Film*), "lies in making us think that because it can state a thing forcefully, it necessarily states it meaningfully. We have all seen salon photographs of dewdrops on petals, of brick walls and sand dunes that seem to have been made simply because it was possible to make them. But the camera speaks so emphatically that it is only after the initial impact of the utterance that we realize that little has been said." It is not enough for a film-maker to simply present pictures without meaning. "Let us define 'meaning' . . . as the belief about an aspect of life that strikes us as basic or residual in a work of art after the initial emotions and sensations it arouses have passed," Kauffmann remarks in the same book. "In this sense, *Last Year at Marienbad* has no fundamental meaning. . . . I believe that this kind of film is self-limiting and eventually futile. This is not because of accepted definitions of art. The fallacy in this style is that if it is followed absolutely rigorously, it leads not to art but to madness. . . . Art that tries to set down everything, and to set it down as it occurs, must end like a man trying to pick up too much and dropping what he has. Every honest artist who ever lived has known that he told partial lies, that he had to settle for less than he could see or know in order to tell *something*, and has, therefore, compromised with some kind of abstraction or arrangement." Kauffmann's negative evaluation of *The Connection* is also based on his belief that, unlike the work of the "good naturalist," the film made from Jack Gelber's play fails to transform the surface details of life into artistic symbols— that is to say, into *meaning*.

In a review of Sontag's *Duet for Cannibals* (*Figures of Light*), Kauffmann writes: "as with Sontag's novels, she simply does not convince us of the need for the work to exist. After we have added up the totals of aesthetic apparatus, there is still no affective center in the work. It has no *result* in us (save tedium)." In his judgment that *Duet for Cannibals* is a failure, Kauffmann implicitly draws upon three conceptions of art. Adopting terms from M. H. Abrams's *The Mirror and the Lamp: Romantic Theory and the Critical Tradition*, we can say that Kauffmann is appealing to the "objective theory" (the view of a film as a self-contained entity: *Duet for Cannibals* has no organizing principle, no "center," to unify its various elements); to the "expressive theory" (the view of a film as an "utterance" of the film-maker: that "center" which is lacking in *Duet for Cannibals* is an "affective" one: the film has no inner motive drawn from its creator and objectified as a formal organizing quality endowed with the potency to move the viewer); and to the "pragmatic theory" (the view of a film in terms of its effect on the spectator: *Duet for Cannibals* produces "no *result*" in Kauffmann, except "tedium"). In his piece on Sontag's film, Kauffmann enunciates normative judgments with barely a stab at analysis or interpretation (perhaps he felt that the latter omission was justified, however, since Sontag is the author of "Against Interpretation").

The three foregoing theories of art, with varying degrees of emphases, show up often in Kauffmann's evaluations. So does a fourth, which Abrams calls the "mimetic theory": the view of art primarily in terms of the world, of what is imitated. (This should not be surprising. As Abrams points out, these four theories exhaust the ways in which critics can discourse about their subject, for the mimetic, objective, expressive, and pragmatic orientations comprehensively embrace the world, the work, the artist, and the audience.) Here is Kauffmann on Welles: "he lacks the controlling artistic intelligence of an Antonioni or Kurosawa. Which means, ineluctably, that he has no view of life that he wants deeply to state, no vision to convey, no relation with his world of which his films are an expression" (review of *The Trial* in *A World on Film*). Here he is on the movie version of John Osborne's play, *The Entertainer*: "As an index to postwar Britain, the Rice family is relatively useless. The same shabby theatrical story would have been true fifty years before and could be true fifty years hence in any society that Osborne desires. Does he think success will come to all performers in a perfect world? Will there be no self-deception and drink and frantic fornication to keep off the shadows? And if this is to take his story literally, it is his fault for not having made his people larger. They represent little more than themselves" (*A World on Film*).

Kauffmann's theory of adaptation is incontrovertible. Whereas Sarris and the *auteurists* are forced to defend adaptations because so many Hollywood directors have turned out photographed stage plays and wooden film treatments of novels, Kauffmann the pluralist is free to condemn this aesthetically barbarous practice.

"Form and content cannot be easily peeled apart in good works and neatly reassembled," Kauffmann writes in his review of *The Prime of Miss Jean Brodie* (*Figures of Light*). "A rule of thumb can be induced," he remarks in his earlier book. "If we exclude trash, then the further down the scale from greatness toward competence that our original novel [or play] lies, the more likely it is to be successfully adapted for the screen; for it is less likely to be dependent on its original form for its effect" (review of *Sons and Lovers*). If trash is adapted to the screen, the original need not be considered in an evaluation of the screen treatment; however, if a great play or novel is put before the cameras, "reference to the original is unavoidable" (review of *The Sound and the Fury* in *A World on Film*).

In his assessment of *Sons and Lovers*, Kauffmann observes: "The book [or play] must be anatomized and reassembled so as to produce the same effect in a different medium; to the degree that this second life is achieved, the adaptation is successful. But for whom is it done? Those who care for the novel [or play] can rarely be fully satisfied." Where the novel is concerned, the problem of time must be considered: "it would take many hours to get on the screen the full range of even an average-length novel. And to those who don't know or care about the book, the film is frequently unsatisfactory in a different way; for the screenwriters are to some degree hobbled by the book and cannot follow their best cinematic instincts." If a great play *must* be adapted, then it is futile to attempt a substitution of pictures for words, since words *are* the play: "Now language is, if not the enemy, at least the burden of the motion picture," Kauffmann writes in his review of *The Doctor's Dilemma*. "In good pictures the words are good, but the picture does not rely on them in the way that Shaw or Shakespeare or Marlowe relied on them. Admittedly, in plays as well as films, one wants not a single word more than necessary; but language is central to the classical theater, and to the film it is supplementary." Consequently, if a Shaw play is brought to the screen, the words must remain, even if that means an uncinematic film: "you must set out boldly to break the movie world's rules; you must make a filmed play, not a film, or you will end up with little of either. You cannot adapt a great dramatist's work to another form because if he was truly great, he has built the work into the form and vice versa" (*A World on Film*).

Most of the time, Kauffmann writes intelligently on specific adaptations. Now and then, however, he nods. For example, see his review of Mary Ellen Bute's film, *Passages from James Joyce's*

Finnegans Wake, in *Figures of Light*. Tossing his theoretical articulations to the wind, Kauffmann declares: "Bute has coped with [Joyce] sympathetically and impressively. The proof is not in any checking that can be done—one opinion is as good as another—but that, by and large, the film achieves the innermost effect of the great dream novel." To which one is compelled to respond: Nonsense!

3

On occasion, Kauffmann approaches a film in terms of its genre. "If a tragic climax, a purification through death and horrors, is to take us and move us," he begins one of his more neo-Aristotelian passages, "two elements, I think, are essential in a work: Its tonality must be consistently spacious, large; and, related to this, there must be no sense of manipulation to distract us from a conviction of fate" (review of *The Pawnbroker* in *A World on Film*). In the same book, he observes: "Comedy is, in one sense, a matter of selection; you can include comic elements in tragedy but not vice versa" (review of *The Elusive Corporal*).

The Hanging Tree and *These Thousand Hills* prompt Kauffmann to expatiate upon the Western, a genre which he has devoted more space to than any other: "Plenty has been written about Westerns in terms of cultural analysis, but less has been said about them as an artistic form. . . . The Western thrives, I believe, because it is one of the few survivals of pure melodrama, and melodrama satisfies old tribal hungers. The moral issues are clear, the external motions are large, and it is the only current fictional form in which you can be pretty sure that, at the end, the villain is going to be dead: not merely spurned in love or failed in a business deal but good and dead. It is a lovely uncivilized feeling." Kauffmann agrees with Bernard De Voto that Westerns contain much material at variance with historical truth, that Westerns take place in a period "situated not exactly anywhere"; but De Voto "failed to reckon with the superior aesthetic power of romance over fact." Although Kauffmann does not contend that all Westerns are of the same artistic stature, he does argue that even the best of the genre—*The Gunfighter, High Noon, Shane, Cowboy*—are of a "low quality." Melodrama and farce are valid forms of art, however, and Westerns remain ideal cinematic subjects (*A World on Film*).

In *Figures of Light*, Kauffmann returns to the Western as a genre in his review of Sam Peckinpah's *The Wild Bunch*. "The Western, until quite recently, was especially valuable as a mythic preserve: a form in which Good and Evil could be easily identified and in which Good could triumph," he writes. "Lately it is becoming an arena for exultation in gore with perhaps a fade-out nod to virtue—a Theater of Cruelty on the cheap." In earlier Westerns, Kaufmann contends, the Bad Man was a Wallace Beery figure, "a lovable bandit who reformed or gave his life gladly at the end in expiation. Now we get killers as heroes, and everything we learn about them is intended to make them acceptable *as killers*, not to explain how they went astray and might have been good ranchers or bank tellers if fate had been kinder." Not only does Kauffmann seem to vacillate in his evaluation of *The Wild Bunch* but he is also unable to adopt a consistent tone in his description of changes in the Western (the pointless reference to Artaudian theater underlines his uncertainty), though he does not fall into Warshow's simplistic error of calling new Westerns "anti-Westerns" because they differ in some respect from older versions of the genre.

The Wild Bunch is the best Western, in Kauffmann's opinion, since *One-Eyed Jacks*. Although there are "sentimentalities" in the picture, there remains a truthfulness, "a passion for accurate and revealing Americana," that supplies "what has been missing from the laundered Westerns of the past." Something "beautiful" shines forth from Peckinpah's work: a "kinetic beauty in the very violence that his film lives and revels in." The violence is (apparently) justified "because the violence *is* the film"; but Kauffmann finds the frequently used slow-motion technique to depict that violence "irritating." At the same time, he praises the director's expressive means: "Peckinpah likes killing, and he does it very well. His art makes it so generic, so tribal, that we can't even go through the usual self-flagellation, American style, about our

American violence. That would be too easy, Peckinpah seems to say."

Later in *Figures of Light*, Kauffmann begins a review of Peckinpah's *The Ballad of Cable Hogue* as follows: "*The Wild Bunch* was a Western that transcended the form: that is, at its best it pierced right to the forces in us that had originally called the form into being." Normally, when a critic says that such and such a film or novel or play has transcended its genre, he means that it is more than just a Western or a detective story or a revenge tragedy, that it is in a sense unique and deserving of being ranked with the very best films or novels or plays, regardless of kind. Does *The Wild Bunch* fit this description? Furthermore, does Kauffmann say anything in his review of the film to justify its being ranked with *Grand Illusion* or *La Strada*? He praises the "kinetic beauty" of Peckinpah's images; but in *The Cosmos Reader* he argues that "style cannot easily make the trivial into the serious." Can a film by a man who, according to Kauffmann, takes pleasure in showing people getting killed be worth much as art? What has happened to the humanistic side of the critic's pluralistic approach? Nor does Kauffmann argue that *The Wild Bunch* transcends the Western form because it transcends melodrama; that at least would be an aesthetic judgment. But how can a Western be said to transcend its form by appealing to the viewer's lust for violence—when it is also said that this same lust for violence created the form in the first place?

4

Most film critics ignore acting, but not Kauffmann. "In the brief history of the film, the predominant emphases in production have been on the mythic qualities of stardom per se and on direction," Kauffmann writes in his review of *The Chapman Report* (*A World on Film*). "Because of the delights of the former, irrelevant to art, and the accomplishments of the latter, film audiences—even less than theater audiences—are little concerned with the nature and quality of acting." Film acting is not "a diluted form of stage acting"; the two kinds of acting have "almost as many dissimilarities as mutualities, and although stage acting came first, they are not arbitrarily to be ranked One and Two because of this fact any more than the contemporary theater and contemporary film can be thus ranked. We all know that there are untalented stars whose careers depend on their personalities and the kindness of technicians, but we also know from experience that, although genuine film acting perhaps ought theoretically not to exist, it demonstrably does." Some claim that real acting is "impossible without a live audience"; but ex-actor Kauffmann argues: that "belief has at least as much basis in nostalgic sentiment and actors' vanity as it has in art. (If it were really valid, why would it not apply equally to musicians when recording?)"

In his book reviews, Kauffmann has criticized his colleagues for what he sees as their ignorance on the subject of film acting. Warshow's comments on the art, for example, are called "impoverished"; yet Kauffmann does nothing more than exchange opinions with Warshow. Whereas the author of *The Immediate Experience* considers Fredric March "a more commonplace actor" than Lee J. Cobb, Kauffmann asserts that March is far from "commonplace," especially in relation to Cobb ("of all actors!" he adds). Kael's *I Lost It at the Movies* evokes this observation from Kauffmann: "Her opinions on acting are the dogmatic yet hollow assertions of the person, otherwise cultivated, who knows little of the art." He offers—without comment—one example from Kael: "Deborah Kerr's performance [in *The Innocents*] is in the grand manner—as modulated and controlled, and yet as flamboyant, as almost anything you'll see on the stage." Here is one example from Kauffmann on Simone Signoret in *Room at the Top*: "Signoret is so heartbreakingly effective in the role that it is now inconceivable without her" (*A World on Film*).

In his review of *Agee on Film: Reviews and Comments* in *The New Republic* (December 1, 1958), Kauffmann says that Agee, for him, "is a deficient critic" because of their "large basic disagreement" on the subject of acting. Agee, Kauffmann believes, has "little regard for or understanding of" acting; he seems to prefer "well-directed non-professionals as against actors." Kauffmann notes that this strikes him as puzzling in a man of Agee's imagination. Though some movie faces can only be accepted as idol-image movie stars, this is the fault not of the art of acting but of the specific actor. "The fact that fine directors like De Sica have made memorable films with non-actors doesn't really prove Agee's theory. *Umberto D.*, moving as it is, would have been infinitely better with a good actor in the title role." Agee's observations on actors, in Kauffmann's judgment, are "unperceptive"; for example, Agee does not "recognize the vocal shortcomings of Olivier (a not invariably excellent actor) in *Henry V.*" Kauffmann's argument for professional actors over nonprofessional ones appears sound. (As I tried to show earlier in this book, Agee had an aesthetic problem on the score of "nature" versus "artifice.") But Kauffmann is not entirely fair in criticism of Agee, as the reader can judge for himself by studying the latter's evaluation of Olivier's overall performance in *Henry V*.

Kauffmann's two collections of criticism contain perceptive generalizations on acting and sharp comments on individual performers. "Casting 'against type' is refreshing," he notes in his review of *A Taste of Honey*, "but there has to be a fundamental affinity that makes the surface disconnection not only unimportant but paradoxically helfpul" (*A World on Film*). In a review of *The Odd Couple* he notes that film stars can be divided into those we would love to be like and those who represent us realistically. "The first are impossibly attractive, and they embody the beauty inside us that the world never sees—from Valentino and Garbo and Dietrich to both Hepburns (Katharine and Audrey), Peter O'Toole, and Cary Grant. The second embody the good humor, honesty, and warm humanity that, we are all sure, are our hallmarks to the world—Mary Pickford, Jean Arthur, Shirley MacLaine, Jean Gabin, James Cagney, Julie Andrews, Spencer Tracy for a random sample. There are also hybrids, combining glamour looks and earthiness—Fredric March, Sophia Loren, Tony Curtis, Lucille Ball are a few—but it is the consciousness of the two original elements in them that makes the compound effective" (*Figures of Light*).

"What is the difference between a comic performer and a comic actor?" Kauffmann asks in his review of *I'm All Right, Jack*. And he replies: "a performer is a person who does things to make you laugh; an actor creates a character at whose actions and utterances you laugh." Peter Ustinov and Peter Sellers are comic performers; Alec Guinness and Jack Lemmon are comic actors. What is the difference between an entertainer and an actor? Entertainers like Bing Crosby and Frank Sinatra prove "that complete self-confidence and an acute sense of timing will see an experienced performer through a tailor-made part and will give him the gloss of having acted . . . [T]he emotion displayed by Sinatra, one feels, is always Sinatra's emotion, not the character's. . . . If it were possible to see Sinatra in Brando's role in *On the Waterfront*, it would clarify the difference between mere simulation and creative acting" (review of *Some Came Running* in *A World on Film*).

Compare what Kauffmann says of Piper Laurie's performance in *The Hustler* with what he says about Wendy Hiller in *Toys in the Attic*. "Laurie's powers are all interior-directed. She embodies Method views of Stanislavsky, Freud, and Sociology 22 (Mon., Wed., Fri.—1:30–3 P.M.). This is not to mock her; all these qualities suit her part here. . . . But, at present, acting consists for her of taking lines and emotions apart in public. As soon as the audience becomes more important to her than acting 'problems,' as soon as continuous projection becomes her chief aim, she may be a good actress indeed." Like Piper Laurie, Geraldine Page is devoted to the Method; but next to Wendy Hiller—Page's co-star in *Toys in the Attic*—the Method actresses seem artificial: "One can see how [Page] has delved into 'life logic,' examined motives, summoned sense memory—all to some good. The very intensity of her devotion to the Method, of her preparations, has some effect despite her mouth-twistings, despite her 'relating' to objects (halting a line and changing its inflection as she picks up a shopping bag or a loving cup)." But Hiller has a "radiance that in itself gives her beauty and a voice that only has to be heard to compel"; she "acts with a simplicity of technique, a nonexaltation of it, a closeness to her subject that allows no cracks to gleam between her and the character. . . . [Her] acting is a perfect infusion of the character with the appropriate elements of her own voice, personality, being. . . . Page wants you to admire Page playing Carrie with emotional truth. Hiller wants you to be moved by Anna; then, if you care to realize who made the magic, she would be pleased" (*A World on Film*).

Burl Ives and Jackie Gleason are manikins; and Gregory Peck "embodies Gordon Craig's ideal of an actor: an *Übermarionette*, wooden to the core." The imaginative actors receive the most consistent praise from Kauffmann: Paul Newman, Toshiro Mifune, Marcello Mastroianni, Peter O'Toole, and—of course— Marlon Brando, who "is overwhelmingly the outstanding creative artist among contemporary film actors." Brando, says Kauffmann, "begins with a good actor's instrument—his body. . . . [H]e seems to carry in him a silently humming dynamo of energy, bridled and instantly ready. Whenever he moves, something seems to impend. There is in acting, indisputably, an element that is often called star quality; partly it is this constant hint of possible lightning." Blessed with an expressive face, Brando also has a good voice; and he tries "to use himself in playing other people rather than to bring those people to himself . . . Yet, with that paradox which is part of the fascination of acting, he is also always unmistakably Brando, not some flavorless hack with wig and putty nose and laboriously disguised voice. . . . Volcanic emotion, reliable technique, imaginative versatility, slashing personality. With all of these, where will Brando go?" (*A World on Film*).

The reader might profitably compare Kauffmann on Brando with Kael on Brando. Like Kauffmann, Kael calls Brando "the most exciting American actor on the screen" ("Marlon Brando: An American Hero," *Kiss Kiss Bang Bang*). Throughout her books, Kael has written perceptively and enthusiastically about the famous actor, at much greater length in fact than has Kauffmann himself. Although Kael contradicts herself at times on the subject of performance (but then, she wouldn't be Kael if she didn't contradict herself on most subjects, would she?), she nevertheless remains—Kauffmann's disparaging remarks about her notwithstanding—one of the two American film critics who understands the importance of screen acting and who can teach the reader something about it. The other critic, of course, is Kauffmann himself.

5

"Taste is a matter of instances, not precepts," Kauffmann writes in "The Film Generation." "One forms an idea of another's taste—or of one's own—from the perspective of many instances of judgment and preference, and even then, general deductions must be drawn delicately." Let us, therefore, examine Kauffmann's taste by seeing what he has had to say over the years about our leading contemporary film-makers.

No other director has received such consistently high praise from Kauffmann as Antonioni. "I have now seen *La Notte* three times and I speak carefully when I say that I think he is making a new art form," he writes in *A World on Film*. Antonioni is seen as forging a new language relevant to a changed world. Though the Aristotelian concepts of drama suited a society theistically based and teleologically organized, and though films of quality can still proceed from that inheritance, "Antonioni has seen the dwindling force of this inheritance and is finding means to supplement it. He is achieving what many contemporary artists in his and other fields are seeking and not often with his success: renewal of his art rather than repetition." In his review of *L'Avventura*, Kauffmann emphasizes that Antonioni "is more interested in personality, mood, and the physical world than in drama," that he "is trying to exploit the unique powers of the film as distinct from the theater." Antonioni's films are "intensely personal in viewpoint and style"; yet *La Notte* "is so perfectly congruent with our concerns, so piercingly honest, that it is close to a personal experience." Instead of character conflict, Antonioni is giving us "immersion in character." "He is reshaping time itself in his films, taking it out of its customary synoptic form, wringing intensity out of its distention, daring to ask us to 'live through' experiences with less distillation, deriving his drama from the very texture of such experiences and their juxtaposition." Kauffmann finds *L'Eclisse* "as consistently interesting" as *L'Avventura* and *La Notte* but "not nearly as moving," because Vittoria (Monica Vitti) "is more a symbol than a person—almost a pageant figure, the Spirit of the Modern Girl."

The color in Antonioni's *Red Desert* is beautiful in itself; it catches the tones of our "new world"; it makes the "environment a character in the drama"; and it functions subjectively in terms of viewpoint. The "primary meaning and effect" of the picture lies in its symbolic language." In *Red Desert*, Antonioni is not only uninterested in story or the "drama of well-made scenes" but he is also uninterested in emotion or character: his aim is "to fascinate us into reading the hieroglyphics he has unearthed." Stylistically, "there is small trace in [*Red Desert*] of the distention of time that was germane to the trilogy"; and thematically, whereas the trilogy "was concerned with differing aspects of love as the medium of hope in our world," *Red Desert* "is stripped to naked essence—hope or nonhope unadorned: the prospect of human life in the midst of whirling changes." Kauffmann concludes his review as follows: "There are a few living directors who can be compared with [Antonioni] in level of achievement; there is none who is his peer in shaping the film form itself to the needs of contemporary men."

In *Figures of Light*, Kauffmann remarks: "to say that I like *Blow-Up* the least of [Antonioni's] films since *L'Avventura* is a purely relative statement. I would be content to see one film a year as good as *Blow-Up*—from Antonioni or anyone else—for the rest of my life." As in his review of *Red Desert*, Kauffmann is at pains to insist that *Blow-Up* shows Antoninoi developing his art further. "For instance," he writes, "the justly celebrated sequence in which the hero suspects and then finds the murder in the photograph is quite unlike anything Antonioni has done before, in its accelerations and retards within a cumulative pattern. And the theme, too, seems to me an extension, a fresh inquiry, within Antonioni's field of interest. Here his basic interest seems to be in the swamping of consciousness by the conduits of technology." Aside from noting the "exquisite" use of color and giving one example of same, Kauffmann concentrates on the thematic complexity of *Blow-Up*. (He was a little more specific about the visual approach and the function of sound in his television program. See "Selections from Stanley Kauffmann's National Educational Television Review" in *Film as Film*, edited by Joy Gould

Boyum and Adrienne Scott.) Kauffmann's negative criticisms of *Blow-Up* are negligible.

Zabriskie Point, however, is considered a failure. "The fundamental trouble with the film is the script . . . [which] seems the outcome of a poll, taken among all the collaborators, as to what would represent youthful dissent and revolution in America today," Kauffmann writes. "The result is like a checklist, accurate enough, but it could be almost anyone's checklist. And the story rests on tenets of revolution which may or may not be valid but which here are rather grossly assumed, not dramatized." Although *Blow-Up* was Antonioni's first picture made outside Italy, the result was relatively successful because the perspective embodied therein belonged to Antonioni. "*Zabriskie Point* is not just lesser than his best work, as *Blow-Up* is lesser than *L'Avventura*," Kauffmann explains; "it is hardly recognizable as his work, or as a development from it." Kauffmann thinks that Antonioni in his first—and, it is to be hoped, last—American film was attempting "to exorcise a guilt for having been politically quiescent in his recent work, just as the whole film may be an attempt to exorcise a guilt about being middle-aged. Assuming that these guilts exist, I suggest that the first one is irrelevant in an artist of his depth, and the second is a kind of senility in reverse, a contradiction of his own genuine and appropriate vigor." Kauffmann wants Antonioni to make Italian films again, films which are expressive of his own personality. "In the career of this superlative artist," he concludes, "*Zabriskie Point* can only be the occasion for gravest concern and affectionate hope."

Kauffmann has written with balanced judgment—if also with lamentable brevity—of De Sica's and Kurosawa's pictures. Although he has great admiration for the work of both directors, he does not evaluate either one with the quickened pulse occasioned by his essays on Antonioni. Compare, for example, his favorable but rather dull assessment of *Ikiru*—certainly a masterpiece—with his energetic review of *Blow-Up*, a picture which at the time of its release he liked less than any of Antonioni's efforts since *L'Avventura*.

The New Wave, Kauffmann believes, was "rather disappointing" in spite of "several good films" which emerged from that movement. For a time, the critic seemed to think that Philippe de Broca was more important than Truffaut, Godard, and Resnais. Originally, for example, he gave less than a page to *The 400 Blows*. According to Kauffmann, Truffaut's gem ends "before its close" with a mere "photographic trick"; the tone throughout is "slavishly veristic"; and there is nothing in it to stir the emotions. A postscript to the original review, however, takes up two and a half pages. Now—though *The 400 Blows* is still not moving enough for Kauffmann, and though Truffaut's shifting from "the subjective" to "a blunt Zolaesque report" still troubles him—the execution has improved. Indeed, the picture's "incisiveness, its unsentimentality, its sense of urgency and elision are extraordinary in a first full-length work." Yet Kauffmann continues to be disturbed by Truffaut's alternations of mood in *Shoot the Piano Player* and *Jules and Jim*; he finds the structure of both films disjointed, the stories encumbered by what he takes to be irrelevant material. Although he praises the visual quality of *Jules and Jim*, he immediately adds that "there is no controlling sense of style or pertinence." All the same, we are informed—in another postscript—that *Jules and Jim*, in "its execution, is one of the brilliant achievements of the postwar film era"! *The Soft Skin* is pronounced a failure, however. In *Figures of Light*, Kauffmann observes: "*Fahrenheit 451* reminded me in reverse of Disney's hippo trying to be a ballerina: Truffaut was a ballerina trying to be a weight lifter. *The Bride Wore Black* was an arted-up, not-quite-slick thriller." *Stolen Kisses* is called "a very entertaining romance . . . a skillful boulevard comedy" and *Mississippi Mermaid* is dubbed "a commonplace, overextended thriller." Truffaut —whose *The Wild Child, Two English Girls* and *Day for Night* were yet to come—is written off by Kauffmann as a director who no longer has anything to say.

In *A World on Film*, Kauffmann judges Godard's *Breathless* to be "a film that is new aesthetically and morally: Style and subject are perfectly matched." *My Life to Live*, however, "is empty and pretentious"; *A Woman Is a Woman* remains "torpid and clumsy . . . If Phillippe de Broca had directed this very same material, he could have made it tolerable"; *Contempt* has only Brigitte Bardot in the nude to recommend it; but *The Married Woman* succeeds because Godard "has used his armory of experiment, trick, imaginative innovation for a perceptible and communicated purpose." In *Figures of Light*, Kauffmann calls *La Chinoise* "trifling," an exercise in "juvenility." Godard "plays" too much—with the camera, with art and literature, with suicide and murder, with politics; furthermore, *La Chinoise* has no story. *Les Carabiniers* is better—it "has shape and commitment"—and *Weekend*, though it "goes on too long," has much of Godard's "keenest conception and best execution." Kauffmann finds *Pierrot le Fou*, however, unamusing and unenlightening: Godard is again "deliberately fracturing story logic, using narrative only as a scaffolding for acrobatics, cinematic and metaphysical." *Sympathy for the Devil* and *See You at Mao* both left Kauffmann "intermittently quite bored." Yet *Two or Three Things I Know About Her* "turns out to be one of Godard's best" . . . Which really isn't saying much, considering Kauffmann's opinion of Godard's "best."

In *Last Year at Marienbad*, Resnais rejects the "contrivances and arrangements of art," Kauffmann writes: "But far from being a move of liberation, this is, in fact, the most slavish realism. It tries to reproduce actual inner life instead of distilling it, as even the most Zolaesque naturalism does." Kauffmann concludes that he finds infinitely more rewarding films such as those of Antonioni, who replaces tired formulas with appropriate new abstractions, "with new art, rather than with figurative mental tape recorders." Unlike Resnais in *Last Year at Marienbad*, Antonioni is interested in character and can therefore involve us to a degree "that disembodied reproduction of inner processes can never reach. Strictly speaking, Antonioni rearranges and distorts certain realities as Resnais tries not to do; but Resnais's efforts lead only to duplication of experience, and Antonioni's freshly seen artistic order results in illumination of experience. After *Last Year at Marienbad* I knew more about Resnais and Resnais's search for reality; but after *La Notte* and *L'Avventura* I knew more about myself." *Hiroshima Mon Amour*, says Kauffmann, "is a film that diminishes gravely in retrospect and on further viewing." As for *Muriel*, it is a failure distinguished by "extraneous symbolism" and "inexplicable inserts."

Fellini also suffers—according to Kauffmann—by comparison with Antonioni. *L'Avventura* "deals with some of the same matters" as *La Dolce Vita*; but Antonioni's "method . . . is quite different and much more effective. It is not survey, but penetration, not to collect samples but to explore a few people; and it is a scheme always posed against abandonments and possibilities. But what has Marcello [the central character in *La Dolce Vita*] abandoned? Parties where ladies recite poetry and sing folk songs instead of stripping and shimmying." *La Dolce Vita* has "no dramatic cumulation"; and Marcello "is no more corrupt at the end than at the beginning; he is only more successful." Like *La Dolce Vita*, 8½ is brilliantly executed; however, like the first picture, the second one is "superficial" in concept. Fellini doesn't have much to "say." Kauffmann believes that the director is "justly celebrated for *La Strada, The Nights of Cabiria* and *I Vitelloni*"—he likes the latter film "best"—because in the early work "there had been a generally consistent welding of method and meaning." Now Fellini is using theme "as opportunity rather than concern"; in other words, Fellini is merely indulging himself in displays of virtuosity. *Juliet of the Spirits* is even less to Kauffmann's liking than *La Dolce Vita* and 8½; it seems that Fellini is now only "capable of . . . delightful frippery." We do not even get that, though, in *Fellini Satyricon*, which Kauffmann describes as "joyless," lacking either characters or "cumulative story, let alone drama."

Bergman, too, prompts Kauffmann into making comparisons with Antonioni. At the end of his review of *L'Avventura*, Kauffmann writes: "The fountainhead of Bergman's films is mysticism: is the God-man relation still viable? Antonioni seems to have answered that question in the negative; thinks men have to learn self-reliance or crumble; is hoping for the possibility of hope." In his review of *La Notte*, Kauffmann calls Bergman a "more conventional artist" than Antonioni. "Bergman feels present spiritual hungers as keenly as anyone," he remarks, "but his films so far,

for all their superb qualities, exemplify Mulligan's line to Dedalus: 'You have the cursed jesuit strain in you, only it's injected the
wrong way.'" (In *Figures of Light*, we are also told that Buñuel
has the "'cursed jesuit strain' injected the wrong way.") *The
Seventh Seal* is "pretentious," "symbolically opaque and allegori-
cally illogical"; *Smiles of a Summer Night* "is worried by an un-
Gallic laboring of points and an obvious load of philosophical
baggage." *Wild Strawberries* comes nearer the mark, but it still
only "teeters on the edge of complete realization." The film "does
not satisfy" because the structure is made up of "separate jewels,
not architectural blocks." There is no growth; hence "the picture
does not fulfill a fundamental requirement of drama: the protagonist is unchanged at the end. We are *told* he is different, he
utters a few lines to that effect, but they seem appended, not a
convincing development. At best, the immense symbolic apparatus of the picture has produced a very small result."

The Magician reveals conclusively that Bergman is a "Divine
Amateur: enormously gifted, often technically dazzling, essentially undisciplined . . . a flawed artist." *The Virgin Spring* fails
even "more seriously" than *Wild Strawberries*. It "is a religious-
moral charade . . . rarified and abstract. We are left with the
sense that a lesson has been spelled out—in huge, cloudy symbols
of a high romance with God." Bergman's pictures "have become
essentially arenas of spiritual wrestling for the author through his
characters, rather than disciplined artistic experiences whose
prime purpose is emotional involvement of the audience."
Through a Glass Darkly also fails: "Unlike some other postwar
directors who have turned their backs on traditional dramatic
structure, Bergman gives us the feeling that he seeks a relatively
traditional structure and in some measure fumbles it"; *Through a
Glass Darkly* lacks "the unity and cumulation it leads us to expect." And yes, *Winter Light* is still another failure. Like
Through a Glass Darkly, Winter Light is uncinematic; neither
work is a film "per se"; both are "literary." According to Kauffmann, the "spiritual problem" in *Winter Light* has merely been
stated: "it has not been vitalized and freshened to hurt us as it
ought to." Kauffmann also finds *A Lesson in Love, The Devil's
Eye, The Silence, All These Women, Hour of the Wolf,* and

Shame very much wanting. He offers no judgment in his review of *Secrets of Women*; and in his review of *The Passion of Anna*, it is difficult to locate an evaluation, though he again seems to be disappointed (he calls the film a "chapter," which suggests his familiar criticism that Bergman fails to create finished works of art).

Only *Persona*, in Kauffmann's opinion, succeeds artistically. And why? Because "its action and its symbols are more than recognizable, they are disturbing."

Kauffmann writes with commendable verve, insight, and generosity about Antonioni's films, sometimes unduly minimizing defects and glossing over problems, but as a rule being both fair and illuminating on the *how* and the *what*. He is much less rewarding to study, as I have tried to indicate, on the remaining major directors. No other American film critic is harder to please. Kauffmann's taste, however, seems rather narrow; and his criteria of evaluation appear to shift markedly in accordance with his subject.

The comparative method can be a valuable instrument of criticism. Contrasts between the style of two film-makers of genius, for instance, can call attention to the unique features of each. However, Kauffmann exalts one master director at the expense of other, equally masterful directors. In *L'Avventura*, we are told, Antonioni wants the action to unfold "in something more like real time than theatrical time," and that "a difference of ten seconds in a scene is a tremendous step toward veristic reproduction rather than theatrical abstraction." Of course, there is no confusion of art and life in *L'Avventura*; Antonioni's masterpiece is not in question. But why is the Italian director's "step toward veristic reproduction" sympathetically understood, whereas Resnais's experiment with time in *Last Year at Marienbad* is referred to as "slavish realism" and Truffaut's style in *The 400 Blows* is dismissed as "slavishly veristic"? Similarly, *La Dolce Vita* is called bad because there is "no dramatic cumulation"; and *Fellini Satyricon* is considered faulty because it has "no cumulative story, let alone drama."

Yet Kauffmann praises *L'Avventura*, *La Notte*, and *L'Eclisse*, though he himself says that these films show no drama, no "cumulative pattern" or "cumulative dramatic sequence." And although there is "small trace" in *Red Desert* "of the distention of time that was germane to the trilogy," Kauffmann concedes that Antonioni reveals minimal concern in this picture with either story or drama. On the one hand, Kauffmann commends Antonioni for scrapping Aristotelian dramatic concepts; on the other hand, he reacts like a dull-witted classicist to the mixture of genres, or to changes of tone, in Truffaut's and Godard's films. And what aesthetic principle makes Antonioni's concentration on a few people in *L'Avventura* superior to Fellini's more panoramic method in *La Dolce Vita*? The standard used to evaluate the work of these various directors remains obscure. And to speak of the final shot in *The 400 Blows*—one of the most memorable events in the history of cinema—as a "photographic trick" is unpardonable.

In *La Dolce Vita*, Marcello has lost what the characters in *L'Avventura* have lost: the Judeo-Christian and humanistic culture of the past which had previously given meaning to life. One finds the same problem expressed in Bergman's films. Kauffmann prefers Antonioni's approach, however, because Fellini and Bergman regret the loss of spiritual values more keenly than Antonioni. A critic has a right to prize one artist's view of life over that of another; he has no right to invent artistic defects in order to justify his thematic preferences. Would Kauffmann like Bergman's and Buñuel's pictures better if the alleged "cursed jesuit strain" in them was injected the *right* way?

One sometimes gets the impression that when Kauffmann doesn't approve of what a film "says," he dismisses it as "empty" or "juvenile," or else he claims that the film-maker has not communicated his meaning. For example, in his review of Bresson's *Pickpocket* in *A World on Film*, he remarks: "Bresson much too often opens a scene with a shot of the setting into which the characters walk or holds the camera on the setting after the characters leave; it makes for recurrent stasis." Without directly referring to Kauffmann, Sarris replies to this silly criticism in his review of *The Trial of Joan of Arc*: "Bresson has been criticized on at least one occasion for showing a place a beat or two after the people have departed, thus fading out on geography rather

than humanity. Far from being a flaw, this Bressonian mannerism expresses an attitude of man's place in the universe. For
Bresson, place precedes and transcends person, since the world
was here before we came and will be here long after we are
gone. This is hardly the sign of a humanistic temperament, but
no one has ever accused Bresson of being a humanist" (*Confessions of a Cultist*). And isn't it unfair for a critic who has praised
the slow-paced films of Antonioni to charge Bresson's pictures
with "recurrent stasis"? As a matter of fact, Antonioni has been
known to open or close a scene in the Bressonian manner. When
Claudia and Sandro drive off from the deserted town in *L'Avventura*, Antonioni holds his camera on the empty scene for a long
time after they are gone in order to suggest the sterility of modern life and the lack of feeling in people. Clearly, Kauffmann
judges Antonioni by different criteria than he uses with other directors. He rebukes Sarris—though not by name—for calling
Lola Montes "the greatest film of all time," because the movie
medium is only an infant. Yet later in the same book, Kauffmann
begins his review of *Zabriskie Point* by announcing that Antonioni remains "one of the finest artists in film history."

For Kauffmann to give two pages of mostly negative criticism
to *Winter Light* and ten pages of chiefly effusive praise to *The
Graduate*, tells us more than we want to know about his taste. To
declare that *Wild Strawberries* lacks progressive and structural
unity suggests either critical ineptitude or willful blindness. Isak
Borg *is* changed; we are not told—we *see* (if we have eyes to
see) the alteration in his behavior. And how can a responsible
critic seriously maintain that *The Seventh Seal, Wild Strawberries, The Virgin Spring, Through a Glass Darkly*, and *Winter
Light* are not "disciplined artistic experiences"? Of course, there
are some imperfections in these works; but that is true of most
great films—including those made by Antonioni. Kauffmann remarks that Bergman "has always relied substantially on dialogue"; like other critics who have registered this complaint,
however, he fails to support his assertion with evidence. Normally, according to Kauffmann, Bergman is uncinematic, merely
"literary"—and that's bad. But in his review of *Red Desert*, Kauffmann writes: Antonioni "has often been accused of being liter-

ary; if that is an indictment, he has perhaps been guilty, but here he is more purely cinematic than ever." In his review of *Persona*, Kauffmann says: "All of Bergman's mature films are miracles of technique, but the recent ones have seemed picture exhibitions of familiar concepts of our era, neatly stated." How can Bergman's films be "miracles of technique" and at the same time be uncinematic? Kauffmann gives an "A" to Antonioni for his filmic innovations; yet in his review of *Persona*, he informs us that the breaking of fresh ground is "hardly a requisite of art."

Although Kauffmann is excellent at describing the visual and structural side of certain films, he does not invariably give proper emphasis to either element. In general, his reviews contain a short and helpful summary of the action, which he delivers in a clear, serviceable prose, free of jargon and ostentation. He is especially good at interpreting films which are intellectually complex. *Red Desert*, he informs the reader, "is susceptible of considerable textural and thematic analysis"—and he backs up that statement with evidence. He is often unhelpful, however, where the art is simple, or where the art lies in concealing art. Ivan Passer's delightful Czech film *Intimate Lighting*—which Kauffmann rather liked—is allotted less than two hundred words. Complexity and coherence are aesthetic values; but they are not the *only* values. A film isn't necessarily great in proportion to the amount of explication it demands. As Joseph Wood Krutch once observed: "The sweetest nuts are not necessarily those hardest to crack." For the same reason, Kauffmann is poor at conveying the simple charm of silent comedy; see, for instance, his essay on Chaplin's *The Circus* in *Figures of Light*, and how he strains—fruitlessly—to sound lively and appreciative. (Compare this piece with Agee's "Comedy's Greatest Era.")

Kauffmann remains one of our better film critics. Even when one disagrees with his judgment, one generally derives profit from him. He is an intelligent, sensitive man with a wide knowledge of film history, theory, and criticism. It should also be noted that Kauffmann's sense of his own dignity, as well as his sense of perspective, generally prevents him from engaging in those internecine critical battles which Simon and Kael find so bracing. For Kauffmann, the film's the thing . . .

6

Or, at any rate, "the film's the thing" has been Kauffmann's position until recently. Criticism is always in danger of being transformed into something else: psychology, sociology, philosophy, religion. Kracauer regarded modern society as "ideologically shelterless" and ascribed to film a redemptive function. The mistake is an old one. Back in the last century Matthew Arnold expected poetry to take the place of a waning religious faith, to act as a surrogate for Christianity. Of late, Kauffmann himself has become rather skeptical about aesthetic values—a bad sign in a critic's work.

"There are many theories of the movies—who would not wish to be the Aristotle of a new art form?" Thus spoke Warshow. In his introduction to Vachel Lindsay's book, however, Kauffmann remarks: "All the eminent writers on film aesthetics from Lindsay and Bela Balázs to the present have contrasted the appetite for film with the absence of any reliable body of aesthetics—any canon from which one can at least depart. In my view, no film aesthetician has filled the gap nor—for reasons too complex to discuss here—is likely to fill it: I foresee no Aristotle of the film; but Lindsay at least took the first strong step toward analysis." Waiting for an Aristotle can be like waiting for a Lefty or a Godot. Don't we really need *more* Lindsays? Shouldn't the pluralist welcome a multitude of theoretical studies instead of secretly hankering for a would-be Aristotle? How many people today believe that the great Greek philosopher said the last word on literary principles, anyway? Because no Aristotle of the celluloid is likely to appear, does that mean we must give up evaluating films by standards appropriate to an art form? Yet Kauffmann seems to be edging now towards that conclusion.

Throughout *A World on Film* and *Figures of Light*, Kauffmann constantly appeals to artistic criteria, even though that criteria in his hands is not invoked impartially. Still, at the conclusion of his second volume, in a brief essay entitled "The Necessary Film," Kauffmann—although he does not exactly contra-

dict what he has said previously—does suggest that in his next
collection of reviews there might be an important change in emphasis. He observes that through the ages "two factors have
formed men's taste in any art—knowledge of that art and knowledge of life—and obviously this is still true, but the function of
taste seems to be altering. As formalist aesthetic canons seem less
and less tenable [To whom? And which canons that Kauffmann
has made use of in his reviews are now passé? And why?], standards in art and life become more and more congruent [How?!],
and the function of taste seems increasingly to be the selection
and appraisal of the works that are most valuable—most necessary—to the individual's *existence*. [Italics in original. There is
more than a hint here of that Sartrean criticism which opposes
"art for art's sake" and which loftily dismisses those "effete" questions perennially the subject of criticism, preferring instead to
focus on "existential problems."] So our means for evaluating
films become more and more involved with our means for evaluating experience: not identical with our standards in life but
certainly related—and, one hopes, somewhat braver."

The relationship between art and life is a subject which Kauffmann touches on repeatedly in his reviews. Yet it remains a
problem which, apparently, he is reluctant to treat at length. In
"The Necessary Film," he is still asserting the distinction between
film and life, and the separateness of standards in aesthetics and
standards outside the movie theater. At the same time, he is also
plainly gazing back in the direction of that quondam social-
minded criticism which placed more stress on subject matter
than style. One can imagine what will happen to criticism when
films are judged by the degree to which they prove "most valuable—most necessary—to the individual's *existence*." Doesn't this
approach suggest the crudest form of pragmatic criticism? If a
specific film does not address itself to some pressing "existential"
question—it may be the "absurd" one day, revolution the next,
and the biological struggle for survival after that—should it be
rejected out of hand as a waste of time? Is such an approach
essentially different from that Marxist criticism which evaluates

films on the basis of how accurately they mirror the class struggle and how bravely they point the masses toward the barricades?

Thus far, Kauffmann's pluralistic approach, unlike Kael's, has remained—however tenuously in theory—aesthetic . . . But for how long?

CHAPTER EIGHT

Vernon Young, Ethnological-Aesthetic Critic

All art is a game played with ethnic rules.
—VERNON YOUNG

1

Vernon Young was born in London, took up residence in America as a youth, and in 1949 became associated with *The Hudson Review*—first as a critic of fiction, then as a film critic. Experienced as a novelist, theater director, and as a "sometime actor in film," Young has also written extensively on art and architecture. He has published two books of film criticism: *Cinema Borealis: Ingmar Bergman and the Swedish Ethos* (1971); and *On Film: Unpopular Essays on a Popular Art* (1972). The latter—nominated for a National Book Award—is made up of pieces which originally appeared in *The Hudson Review, Accent, Art Film Publications, Arts Magazine, Perspectives on the Arts, Film Quarterly, Industria Annual,* and *Southwest Review,* reprinted (as Young puts it in his preface) "from twenty years of divided but feverish attention to a provocative subject." In 1957 Young returned to Europe to live.

In his standard biography of Ibsen, Halvdan Koht quotes the playwright as follows: "he who would know me fully, must know Norway. The grand but austere nature with which people are surrounded in the North, the lonely, isolated life—their homes often lie many miles apart—compel them to be indifferent to other people, and to care only about their own concerns; therefore, they become ruminative and serious-minded; they ponder and doubt; and they often despair. With us every other man is a philosopher! Then there are the long, dark winters, with the thick fog about the houses—Oh, they long for the sun!" Although Young does not refer to these remarks by Ibsen in either of his film books, he would agree with the dramatist's contention that in order to fully understand an artist's work one must know the artist's country. In *Cinema Borealis*, he writes: "It is a commonplace to observe that the Swede is the way he is because of the physical climate in which for centuries he has dwelled. That climate shapes the man is axiomatic, if inadequately tested. As a correlation broadly considered it is superficially obvious. Anyone visiting Sweden in the winter quickly observes the grim, set, pulled-down-at-the corner mouths, the neutral eyes, the contained, wrapped-tight body movements, all conditioned by the severity of the weather, which is merciless, incessant, protracted. In October the sun sets at four in the afternoon in Central Sweden, in December at two o'clock. Farther north, the situation is too scandalous to be the subject of discussion. Darkness at noon is more than a figure of speech."

As Young points out in his preface to *On Film*, the "leading subject" of his criticism is "film as a cultural phenomenon," or the relation of "film art to its cultural sources." The phrase "film art" needs to be emphasized. Unlike the pure sociological critic, Young avoids reductionism; he does not pursue a neat one-for-one correspondence between outside data and artistic pattern. Because his basic orientation is aesthetic, Young respects the integrity of a film: his ethnological approach is pressed into the service of critical analysis, interpretation, and evaluation, not into some form of pseudo-science. Of course, in one way the sociological method overlaps the ethnological approach of Young. First-hand knowledge of how movies are put together, Young observes in his preface, showed him "how radically the motion picture (more than any art because it is in a sense impure, it is contingent, it tells a story in a social context, and social context is behavior)—how radically it can be misinterpreted by the 'foreign' observer, who is necessarily seeing the particular film with assumptions alien to those on which it was made." The sociological critic would concur. However, aside from the fact that Young stresses the climatic features of a specific country, whereas the sociological critic normally restricts his attention to film in its social, political, and economic aspects, the two approaches differ radically on theoretical grounds. "Sociological film criticism is forever mistaken," Young writes in "*Umberto D.*: Vittorio De Sica's 'Super'-Naturalism" (*The Hudson Review*, Winter 1956), "because it is forever misled—on humanitarian principles or by self-righteousness or from color-blindness—into confusing ends with means. Asserting that importance lies in subject matter, it fails to recognize that no subject is important until awakened by art; assuming (to give charity the benefit of the doubt) that love is greater than art, it fails to acknowledge that the art *is* the love. . . . To praise [*Umberto D.*] for its human appeal is as needless and as miserly as to praise a beautiful woman for her conspicuous virtue." In spite of his aesthetic orientation, and in spite of his last remark, Young often includes praise of a film's "human appeal" in his essays.

Oversimplification is rarely Young's style. "Climate, in itself, can never be the sole shaping factor in a people's destiny," he declares in his Bergman book. "No generalization about a country can or should hope to catch the inhabitants without exception like helpless fish in a net," he adds elsewhere in that study. "Logically, there are events and individuals of the Swedish scene exempt from the character I have sketched, but I have not been writing a personal memoir in which I might select only what delighted me or pleased my friends. I have been trying to present the dominant motifs in Swedish society in order to emphasize, with those in mind, the nature and difficulty in such a milieu of the creative effort and, too, of the social effort. On certain days in Sweden, you feel you should note in a diary that Someone smiled."

The relationship between an artist and his culture is a complicated one. According to Young, "the scope of a country's subject matter is determined by the character of its social environment and its cultural saturation. And the quality of whatever experience an artist finds in that environment or recalls from a cultural memory will, of necessity, be distorted creatively by the imposition of his personality and the resources of his medium. Art arises authentically when experience is transfigured as, from the flash of observation, the artist creates a style" (*Cinema Borealis*). Repeatedly, Young refers to those cultural assumptions and traditions which form the matrix of the film-maker's creative act. "Set it down in the good book: everything else being equal (an economic foundation and a visual tradition), countries with the higher proportion of cultural lag make the most vivid films," he writes in "Films from the Perimeter"; and he adds: "Japan, for instance—where timeless occupations linger in fact and where atrocious historical codes survive as subjects for art because their kinetic power is irresistible." In his discussion of a scene of hari-kiri in a film by Masaki Kobayashi, he observes: "Among unexpected consequences of my seeing this film, I found that it reduced to virtual nonsense a favorite aphorism from the late Aldous Huxley: 'One culture gives us the pyramids, another the Escorial, a third, Forest Lawn. But the act of dying remains always and everywhere identical.' If Mr. Huxley now inhabits a world where time is more plastic than even he supposed, he may be in a position to submit this conclusion to a number of fellow shades. And somewhere there must be a samurai who died trying to gouge his insides out with a bamboo sword because he had sold his own more effective weapon."

Young's ethnological method represents a new—and welcome —approach in American film criticism.

3

"Culture I understand as the gratuitous expression of a people," Young writes in *Cinema Borealis*, "in other words the customs and arts, of no earthly use, without which man is a boor." The key essay in *On Film* is the opening one entitled "Our Local Idioms," which Young in his preface calls "a statement of my premises" (the "statement" remains implicit, however). In that piece, Young briefly attempts to suggest the indigenous character of movies from various countries, offering numerous examples in support of his generalizations.

He begins with Italy, a land which he obviously loves, and a country which has given the world a body of films second to none in artistry and humanity. As Young sees it, the Italian is rooted to the family, so much so that "society is simply *famiglia*, writ large." Italian films are "based on a conception of total community; the subject involves an outrage to that community or a defection from it. The object is to restore the broken balance, expel the intruder, mollify the prodigal son, mourn the outcast." Witness *The Bicycle Thief, Bitter Rice, I Vitelloni, La Dolce Vita, Rocco and His Brothers, The Bandits of Orgosolo*, and *Seduced and Abandoned*. Not surprisingly, the theme of loneliness or alienation is frequently presented with more emotional depth in Italian pictures than in those from other nations. Young cites *La Strada, The Children Are Watching, Umberto D., Time Stood Still, Il Posto*, and *L'Avventura*. "No Italian could have conceived *Last Year at Marienbad*, for Italians have a health that forbids the reduction of people to equations," Young writes. "No doubt Italians are less sophisticated than the French: also it is true that they can't be bothered to play such abstract games." (But doesn't Antonioni, in *L'Avventura* and other films, aim for a high degree of abstraction in his treatment of characters in order to show the absence of feeling and the death of love in people? The apparent contradiction can be resolved; however, one would appreciate a little help from the critic in resolving it . . .)

The French as a people are more difficult to classify than the Italians because the "more complex a country's intellectual heritage, the harder it is to account for the polarities of attitude and disposition we find there." Tentatively, Young suggests that "intellect and intuition are, in the French, less separable than in other peoples"; hence the Gallic "film-maker is likely to be a poet apparently using prose for his immediate purpose. The infusion of these delicate properties we call *wit*, the single word that perhaps explains the French film artist's genius for endowing any subject with a tone peculiar to it, yet keeping his distance from it, as it were." The French artist knows how to make every subject both general and particular in application, and he always does so with exquisite style.

Style also remains pertinent to a discussion of the Japanese.

"Heroism is Kurosawa's subject; things as they miserably are in constricted middle-class circles was Ozu's; blank disbelief is Teshigahara's. But in common their eye for stylistic interpretation is never blurred." Precision—that's the hallmark of Japanese style. The landscape in Teshigahara's *The Case* remains "as clean as a pebble garden or a print by Hiroshige." *Woman of the Dunes* "is visually pure and edited with analytical severity. The result is somewhat antiseptic; it has the attraction of a nude you might appreciate without desiring." Japan is a country which has always lived by order; but since the Second World War, the individual Japanese has seen "the vitiation of every authority and ego fortification maintained for centuries: his social pyramid— family to shogun—his traditional ethos, his ceremonious exchanges, and his domestic integrity." The Japanese film-maker's emphasis on style is bound up, then, with his culture. And in the postwar period, Nipponese artists have responded to the dissolution of old cultural forms by "an overanxious attention to surface clarity."

Empiricism, in Young's judgment, is the philosophical bias of British film-makers. "Since the English distrust ideas, no harrassed schoolmaster in an English film could have become an archetype in an expressionist world, like Professor Rath in *The Blue Angel*; instead, the British made *The Browning Version* and *Term of Trial*." The empirical British filmmaker eschews symbolism and universality: he attends to his own "scaled society, each class or vocation in possession of its own manners, its own aims, its special avenues of escape, its exclusive absurdities." *Los Olvidados, Rashomon, La Strada*—these pictures "embody a generalization powerful enough to be called great"; but English directors make *Brief Encounter, Tom Jones, Billy Liar*—films that are "socially aware, even-tempered, genial under pressure." Evidently, Young believes that film-makers from France, Spain, Italy, and Japan can transcend their "local idioms" and create movies with universal themes, whereas directors from England are prevented from doing so by their restrictive culture.

In Young's judgment, pragmatism is the distinctive "local idiom" which appears in American films, even though he believes that life in the United States is more various than our movies suggest. Documentaries, he claims, express "the most authentic American experience"; he offers *The River, The Plow That Broke the Plains, The Battle of San Pietro, The Quiet One,* and *Time Out of War* as examples. As Young points out, these films were not produced in Hollywood, a place which has merely given the world "hints of the real thing—moments or sequences, rarely the whole, rich but disconnected scenes in a few Westerns, a high degree of zest and some rhetorical cynicism in the Hecht-Mac-Arthur films made on Long Island in the early '40s [sic] (*Crime Without Passion, The Scoundrel, Angels over Broadway*) and, a little later, Hollywood's life-is-a-jungle films about battered detectives and twisted lives: *Murder My Sweet, The Blue Dahlia,* and Nicholas Ray's *They Live by Night.*"

Even though America has not turned out as many film classics as have some foreign countries, Young's list of "authentic" Hollywood movies seems a quirky one, oddly truncated. The popular fare mentioned above project, according to Young, "a soured dry form of social accusation without crusading fervor, sometimes a neo-Elizabethan relish for life lived sub-socially or beyond the fences." He asks: "But where in these films is there any conception of man as more than a merely instrumental animal? . . . Where, in short, is consciousness?" He then goes on to praise the "visual poetry" of Huston's *Reflections in a Golden Eye* (a picture which almost no other critic has liked) because, in his view, it "helps locate what has been missing"—namely, "an atmosphere of spiritual infirmity and moral caprice quite as present in the American scene as the robust virtues favored by the extroverts of American expression."

"Critical judgment," Young remarks in "Long Voyage Home with John Ford," "is nothing if not comparative." Throughout his essays, Young makes striking distinctions between the art of one film-maker and that of another, frequently in terms of their different ethnological backgrounds. For example, he contends that the New Wave could not be exported because "you can't transplant a cultural assumption. . . . As a Frenchman, the film-maker of today, like his elder contemporaries, sees life as logical, which is not to say he doesn't (therefore) see it as terrible, just as the Italian feels life as lyrical, which isn't to say he doesn't experience

it also as a nightmare (8½ is here the consummate expression).
The poverty of most Anglo-American films is (among other factors) the result of there being behind them no implicit life-feeling (which informs a rhythm as well as a philosophy). . . . The
short way of saying this is to declare that our films are not made
by poets" ("Some Obiter Dicta on Recent French Films"). To
Young's way of thinking, neither empiricism nor pragmatism has
inspired the greatest films; compared to Italian and French pictures, English and American movies are superficial. "They never
express, with any artistry, an inborn collective principle that goes
deeper than the subject of the hour-and-a-half; their viewpoint,
when you can isolate one, is always and only social—at a cate-
gorical level." Of the two, the American film, according to Young,
is poorer than the English.

"Our films—the exceptions barely justify the courtesy of a concession—are worse than incompetent and lower than juvenile;
they are meretricious where they're not massively vulgar; they
serve beauty or use as little as any popular art in the history of
mankind," Young writes in "Love, Death, and the 'Foreign' Film
—1957." "Every shallow Hollywood film is shallow precisely because it travesties an existing cultural shallowness: the tacit belief
that it's both desirable and possible to legislate passion and death
from the scheme of things, and that social security alone can
bring the good life into existence. Every good imported film is
not merely technically better [a point which many critics of
course would dispute], it's in another world of art. It *is* art.
Especially when it deals potently and in cinematic terms, as it
does often, with those irreconcilables which our population at
large is too terrified by to confront: the co-extension of life and
death, of attraction and revulsion, love shaped from the shock of
death, material sacrifice for the peace of personal dignity."

Kauffmann, as we have seen, believes that style plus "serious
content" results in better films than style plus "trivia." Probably
Kauffmann, and most other theorists, would agree with Young in
giving more points to a film with a universal theme (*La Strada*)
—other things being equal—than a picture with merely a local
theme (*Brief Encounter*). But Young also believes that "serious
content" is "determined" by the ethos of the film-maker's native

land. If one follows this argument to its logical conclusion, one is bound to declare that the American film is doomed, by and large, to second-class artistic status unless the prevailing "local idiom" undergoes a profound change. Few critics would deny that much of what is wrong with American films simply mirrors what is wrong with American life. Nevertheless, if Sarris seems too indulgent toward our native product, Young appears much too severe. Furthermore, if American novelists have created a body of work equal in merit with that of any other nation in this century, why can't American film-makers do likewise? The problem would seem to depend less on the American ethos than on the conditions of film production in this country. In other words, American directors will create better films when they have more artistic freedom.

3

Although Young has had much to say on the ethnological approach, he has not been overly concerned with articulating his views on criticism in general. Here and there, one comes across a brief quotable remark—such as "Criticism is a method of rationally explaining the emotional experience one has already had" or "Criticism carries the obligation of interpreting as far as possible what is demonstrable; it is not your dream of the film you made while watching the one made by Bergman" (*Cinema Borealis*). In "Some Obiter Dicta on Recent French Films," Young refers briefly to his "belief that among the critic's obligations is the salvaging of neglected films before they go softly into that dark night . . ." But on the whole, the rest is silence.

For whom does the critic write?—that, however, is an important question to which Young addresses himself in the Preface to *On Film*. The critic, he observes, is a "man talking to other men; else he is a voice in the wind. Presumably he is talking to those who share something of his education, of his beliefs and, as strongly, his disbeliefs, and to a degree his disposition. I have never, or rarely, known for whom I was writing. It was made pretty clear to me for whom I was not writing—among others, most 'film people' who never read opinions expressed outside the film publications or the columns of the wide-circulation press."

Since Young published most of his work in *The Hudson Review*, he had some idea of his average reader. "He was very likely affiliated with a college, either as a student or as a teacher; he was closely interested in the arts; he was worldly by inclination; he was not the sort you talk down to, and he would welcome a minority voice (otherwise he would not be reading that magazine)." All the same, Young worried about how knowledgeable his audience remained on technical and historical matters. "I was never sure to what extent I should be explicit and footnotey or, on the other hand, how casual I could be with my side references to the field. I have an unholy fear of insulting a reader's intelligence." This worried him until he realized that the anxiety threatened his ability to communicate. Next, he began to discover that film criticism was often read by people who seldom went to a movie! "They simply liked to read about movies if they found the critic's point of view interesting and the content vividly re-created. I felt better after that."

As might be expected, Young's ethnological approach to film makes him somewhat impatient with what he regards as the insular attitudes of American critics. In "Films from Hungary and Brazil," he criticizes his "should-I-say colleagues" for not sufficiently appreciating South American movie fare. ("You think I like film critics any better than Bergman does?" he asks parenthetically.) Too many critics, he remarks, "*never* discover anyone before being clued in by the French"; and he adds: "The Catholic ethos . . . is not a proclivity of your typical Anglo-American film critic who, when he's not Jewish, is Protestant or sniffily secular." In "Some American Films: A Modest Proposal," Young writes: "Critics are . . . in no position to judge the authenticity of a Western, as far as I can make out. . . . In New York you have perhaps a score, can I say, of 'influential' movie critics, who are bounded geographically and in social attitude by Times Square, the Village, Madison Avenue, and the MMA. They wouldn't know an Apache from a Snake, or a Two Grey Hills from a hole in the ground (maybe—if they saw them both together)."

Young rarely mentions the name of another critic, either in

commendation or condemnation. In "Our Local Idioms," however, he chides Agee in passing for "too soon" declaring Huston "great." This is unfair, since Agee concludes his essay on the director by looking forward to the day when Huston "might become" a "consistently great artist." (True, that 'consistently' is ambiguous; but Agee makes plain that Huston's "work as a whole is not on the level with the finest and most deeply imaginative work that has been done in movies.") Young recommends Kracauer's *From Caligari to Hitler*, but wisely adds that the reader should have "reservations demanded by certain ironies and contradictions of history that qualify many of the simplifications therein" ("Program Notes for Two Classics"). The Marxist stance of John Howard Lawson is scored in "I've Been Reading These Film Critics" (an essay on, for the most part, various contenders for the critical flyweight title); Susan Sontag, in that piece, is also upbraided for asking us to "experience art and life without approval or disapproval." In "The Brave American," Young takes issue with Kauffmann's judgment that Welles has "no relation with his world of which his films are an expression. He is a scene and sequence maker, not a film-maker." Young remarks: "As a Judgment Day verdict this is probably defensible, but I should personally recommend clemency. I believe that Welles's total contribution (to our enjoyment—hang the history of the medium!) is richer than the sum of its parts." And in *Cinema Borealis*, he observes: "I have always felt it a pity that Stanley Kauffmann's criticism of Bergman's more fruitful films was ungenerous but on the subject of such fruitless ones as [*All These Women*] he has my support."

4

When Young came to *The Hudson Review*, one year after its founding, that magazine was very much under the influence of the New Criticism in literary studies. Young's general aesthetic would seem to owe something to the formalist approaches of T. S. Eliot—who is referred to frequently in *Cinema Borealis*—and R. P. Blackmur—who is quoted (from "A Burden for Critics") at the head of "Film Chronicle: Notes on the Compulsive Revolution" in *On Film*. (Blackmur—though a formalist—is not always classified as a New Critic.) Over the years, the emphasis of *The Hudson Review* has changed, so that today the criticism appearing in its pages reflects the new mood of eclecticism or pluralism. Young's strength as a critic resides, I believe, in his ability to fuse the formalist and ethnological approaches to film.

"Art may comprise a degree of intellectual activity, but it is not a synonym for intellectual activity," Young writes in his introduction to *Cinema Borealis*. "Art is the formal embodiment of the imagination." Like the New Critics, Young believes that art is not a substitute for philosophy: it has its own purpose and *raison d'être*. Nor does he hold with the theory that art should be evaluated on pragmatic grounds: "art," he writes in "European Film Notebook," "never solves anything." In discussing *The Passion of Anna* in his book on Bergman he informs us that a chief aim of art "is to arouse emotion." "I have never been convinced that the greatness of any work of art is proportional to its assumed intellectual complexity," he writes in "Nostalgia of the Infinite"; and in his introduction to *Cinema Borealis*, he observes: "Complexity is one of many modes attained by the artist in his attempt to express more than meets the eye. Art is forever complex because the creative prescience of the artist reveals a world of implication which the subject in itself cannot wholly contain. And art is forever classically simple because in any instance—here I speak of narrative and poetic art—the essential subject is normally reducible to a gnomic text, a general statement that satisfies our need to explain the moral power which the work of art exercises over us."

The worth of a film does not lie in its "gnomic text" per se, for that text could no doubt be found in dozens of other pictures. Young suggests that it is the "texture" (to borrow a term from John Crowe Ransom), not the paraphrasable statement, argument, or theme (what Ransom calls "structure") that gives importance to a film. A picture is valuable not because it tells us that life is beautiful or tragic, but because it involves us emotionally in a series of experiences which makes us *feel* the beauty or tragedy. And much more. For as Young remarks, a "film may be about a lot of other things, closer to the director's heart" than the "gnomic text."

As noted, Young believes that a work of art exercises a "moral power" over us. This does not mean, however, that he seeks uplift from the screen. "I don't expect a movie-maker to console me. I expect him to be authentic," he explains in his analysis of *The Naked Night*. Furthermore, as he points out at the end of "International Film," the genuine movie artist also challenges *us* "to live authentically." Now, since the grave is an end from which none of us can escape, "All the memorable films are ultimately about death" ("'A Sad Tale's Best for Winter': On Re-Seeing *The Third Man*").

Young's concern with moral truth in art leads him to reject pornography and sentimentality, both of which he sees as the "polar consequences of impotence." Pornography is "the forked radish thing-in-itself, devoid of any ideal development to distinguish it from the coupling of rabbits." He refers to *I Am Curious* as *I Am Spurious*, calling the Sjöman film "the sewer toward which Swedish film, in certain hands, has been heading for some time. Taken together with *Elvira Madigan*"—which Young describes as a sentimental film, that is, as a film which is "all ideal extension without human contingency"—"it suggests the plight of a society deficient in the culture that would alone dignify its isolation, steadily substituting non-commitment for authentic living, at every level. Sex, goes the rumor, is its sole resource; logically enough, a failing one" ("Poetry, Politics, and Pornography").

Referring to Stephen Dedalus's cry: "History is a nightmare from which I am trying to awake," Young asks: "What do we do when we awaken, *without history*—which is to say, with a view of it as nightmare, merely—and with a present condition in which we find no more vital diversion than pornography, as unconsoling a game as war?" ("War Games: Work in Progress"). A number of critics—among them Tyler, Simon, and Kauffmann—defended *I Am Curious* for Grove Press in court, contending that the picture was a "serious work of art." Only Kauffmann was sophisticated enough to declare that the phrase "a serious work of art" is "not much of an aesthetic recommendation." Although

Kauffmann manifestly refuses to consider Sjöman's film pornographic, he does call it "mediocre" and argues that human beings
need "areas of privacy in sexual matters" (*Figures of Light*).
Young makes the same point in *Cinema Borealis*. After quoting
with approval a passage from George Steiner's "Night Words" in
Language and Silence, in which the author asserts: "There may
be deeper affinities than we yet understand between the 'total
freedom' of the uncensored erotic imagination and the total freedom of the sadist. . . . Both are exercised at the expense of
someone else's humanity, of someone else's most precious right—
the right to a private life of feeling," Young adds that, ironically,
it was Bergman's "tragedy of violation, *The Virgin Spring*,
[which] opened the way for the violation of everybody by
everybody else."

It has been said that pornography is merely prudery turned
inside out. Young opposes both tendencies. In his review of *The
Priest and the Girl*, he writes: "Helena Igney is the most persua-
sive rebuke to celibacy I've seen for nigh twenty years, palpably
bewitching, with her young amplitude, heavy eyelids, earthy
hands, and long Raphaelesque neck. (I am dedicating my next
bull to her.) There is one particularly impressive piece of cinema,
probably suggested by *Woman of the Dunes*, when she sits stark
maddeningly naked in the desert. The camera frames her face
and shoulders, *primo piano*, tendrils of corn-silk hair blowing
into the lens. After which, a curve of shoulder and naked back—
pure draftsmanship. The priest, in profile, kisses her arm; past
reason haunted, he drops to his feast; the camera remains above
it all, just focusing the melody of her face. Beautifully done:
nothing Swedish here." *Beautifully done* . . . Which apparently
means: Done with artistry, imagination; done with respect for
human sexuality, without either false modesty or crude animality
—no impotence here.

Similarly, although Young scorns sentimentality, he defends
sentiment, or honest feeling and emotion. (How could he fail to
do so, considering his appreciation for Italian films?) He writes:
"Most people fail to make distinctions; if they are touched at all
by an experience they call it sentimental, whereas I am inclined
to believe that sentimentality arises from aesthetic ignorance (ei-

ther in the artist or the viewer), the exploitation of a feeling for its own sake, with scant regard for its context" ("My First Love"). Although Young might begin an essay with a discussion of morality or culture or sex, he normally, as the foregoing suggests, concludes with aesthetic analysis and evaluation.

In "The Sound of Silence," Young observes that "the secret doctrine of the film artist" is: "watch the outside, listen to the inside—and *camera placement, camera placement, camera placement!*" Film is basically a visual art. In "Fugue of Faces: A Danish Film and Some Photographs," an essay on Dreyer's *The Passion of Joan of Arc* (which was originally published in 1955, and which remains one of Young's most perceptive and beautifully written essays), he remarks: "If [a critic] is honest, he will admit that instances of a film, in its own aesthetic terms, supplying the spectator with an experience equal in serious definition and in style to the arts with which it is contemporary, are distressingly rare." However, Dreyer's masterpiece "forces our consent to the proposition that *to see* is as fruitful as *to know*, when the object of our seeing has been invested with the form that inspires knowledge. Knowledge of the poetic order, let us say."

Young points out that like painting the cinema is not a substitute for verbal revelation. An "illiterate" art, film constitutes a world of feeling which sharpens our senses and stimulates our minds even as does great plastic art or the ideas of a critic or novelist. "The relative immediacy of even an exceptional motion picture is deceptive. Easy enough, in many cases, to follow the visual story line, but extraordinarily difficult for most people to recognize the selective and complex means by which a sequence of photographs, moving forward in time as variously as water or as music, has become the instrument of a moral imagination."

It is important to point out that Young is not an "unqualified believer in a Golden Age of the Silents" ("One Man's Film Festival"). His judgment of Griffith, for instance, in "Footnote to a Cinematic Primer" is harsh. And eleven years after the piece on Dreyer was written, Young could look back over the period between 1957 and 1964, and observe: "no *revenant* with a lapsed party-membership card, a volume of Paul Rotha at his beck, and a picture of Garbo next to his mother over the bed can persuade us that there was only one Golden Age (in a mere fifty years of film-making) or that it had more to offer the mature mind and the exacting eye." Young believes that no other period in film history can boast of more accomplished works than the one beginning in the fifties. Whether he also believes that the best of Fellini, Bergman, Antonioni, Truffaut, and Kurosawa equal the best by artists in other disciplines, he does not say (though few, if any, critics of the arts would argue the contrary). (See "The Verge and After: Film by 1966".)

One of Young's best known essays is "The Witness Point," published in *New World Writing, Fourth Mentor Selection* (1953). Young opens his piece by underlining the basic differences between film and drama, and between film and the novel. The "movie begins with *the art of photographed motion*"; it is this mobility which distinguishes film from theater. If the screen tries, in the manner of the stage, to "debate ideas" the result is "relative stasis." The form of a play must be violated in an adaptation, otherwise "the movie's integrity will be sacrificed for that of the play." Because Shakespeare's structure is open, his plays are an exception to the rule of "incompatibility of genre." (Nowhere does Young indicate how Shakespeare's plays succeed artistically on the screen. In "London Film Chronicle," he calls Welles's *Othello* "supreme film art"! The same essay includes a panegyric for *A Man for All Seasons* ["riches for the eye and ear"], and sarcasm for "purists" who don't agree with Young's judgment.) The chief difference between the page and the screen is the greater literalness of film. "The spectator's private mind is made up for him. . . . There is substituted instead this particular image or sequence, dictatorially composed: not any street lined with poplars, vanishing to a distant sky of one's own impalpable painting but this street, these poplars here, this housefront so."

Young then takes up the subject of film technique. "Snobbery toward 'mere technique,'" he remarks, "is untenable. Every inch of a movie *is* technique, under, over, and above all felicities of paraphrasable content and of personality." (Compare with Mark Schorer's well-known formalist essay "Technique as Discovery," which appeared in the first number of *The Hudson Review*.

"When we speak of technique," Schorer declares, "we speak of nearly everything.") "Just as a poem is, by Mallarmé's sane correction, 'written not with ideas but with words,'" Young notes, "so a movie's totality is made up of concrete syntax, built from experience with the medium, a syntax primarily visual, or today *audio-visual*." (Now, which is it? To say that film is in equal measure an audio-visual medium hardly squares with the emphasis Young places on *the art of photographed motion*," or what he argues in *On Film*. If sound has become just as important as the image, then why can't the film-maker "debate ideas" —thus "imitating the relative stasis of theater"?) Briefly, Young proceeds to discuss two standard filmic devices: the close-up and the dissolve, but without saying anything noteworthy about either one.

The term "the witness point" is first introduced at about the three-quarter mark in the essay. By "the witness point," Young intends: "the camera's coign of vantage not simply within the action of the scene but throughout the entire film. *Whose eye* is the camera, at any moment, intended to represent? Is the strategy to be omnivisual, like Tolstoy's in *War and Peace*, so that the point of view is ricocheted from one participant to another? Is one actor to be concentrated on to the exclusion of others and always seen through another's eyes or is the angle of vision to proceed *from* him?" Young discusses *The Lady in the Lake*, where all the action is seen from the viewpoint of one narrator, and the "deployable view" of *Rashomon*, in which the main event is seen from different angles of observation ("multiple dramatization"). Where Young speaks of "the witness point," other film critics use the expression "point of view." ("Point of view" is, of course, also a term used in criticism of fiction and occasionally of the drama.) It could be argued that "the witness point" is preferable to "point of view," since the latter is an ambiguous term. Ask the average student, "What is the point of view in *Citizen Kane*?" and you will be given an answer having to do with Welles's theme, not with his technical strategy for revealing that theme. Young's "the witness point" would appear to avoid such confusion.

Young concludes "The Witness Point" (that title is really a

misnomer!) by commenting on sound, structure, and the finished whole, or work of art. "The subtle uncertainty which belies critical conviction on the subject of what constitutes form is one reason for my having avoided the 'final' questions in favor of the less exalted matter of the craft. For I think we are in a safer position to raise the old dilemma of content determining form or form determining content *after* we have acknowledged that movie appreciation should begin with understanding the idiosyncratic contributions of the form, and not by passing judgment, derived from extrinsic standards, on the paraphrasable content." Perhaps Young decided not to include "The Witness Point" in *On Film* because he felt—and rightly, I would say—that much of it now seems commonplace for what Kauffmann has called The Film Generation. Yet in view of some persistently obtuse attitudes on the part of many film critics (amply documented—sadly enough—in the present study), Young's concluding remarks still seem relevant.

5

Of the silent film directors—or of those directors who began work in that period—Dreyer has received the most praise from Young. I have already referred to his excellent analysis of the visual approach in *The Passion of Joan of Arc*. In a footnote to the Bergman, Young presents a concise appraisal of Dreyer's career, pointing out "three fundamentally separate cinematic styles" in the late director's work: "*The Master of the House* was . . . an eloquent achievement of domestic tension, confined to a single bourgeois setting, in which Dreyer cut from half-length and close-up shots to objects in the home, building drama from an unspoken dialogue between people and their things. He distilled this method for *The Passion of Joan of Arc* . . . so that two-thirds of the film consists only of close-up faces (or even backs of heads) in a fantastic crescendo of speaking power (silent, of course). *Vampyr*, allegedly a commercial job, was nonetheless a brilliant synthesis of styles from Germany and perhaps from Jean Epstein." Young points out that in the latter film Dreyer took full advantage of the camera's ability to place the spectator in the witness point. However, after *Day of Wrath*, Dreyer "lost his life-rhythm," and was increasingly inclined—"in *Ordet* fatally"—to slow "long shots of characters grouped as on a stage; we watched them cross the room for no dramatic or cinematic reason." In Young's judgment, Dreyer's later pictures are "cinematically dead."

Observe the point made by Young that in *Day of Wrath* and after Dreyer "lost his life-rhythm." As noted earlier, the emptiness of "most Anglo-American films" can be traced in part, according to Young, to their lack of an "implicit life-feeling (which informs a rhythm as well as a philosophy)." These terms—"life-feeling," "life-rhythm"—are far from being self-evident in meaning. In "The Witness Point," Young remarks that in *Day of Wrath* Dreyer did not "fuse" the "elements": "It is my opinion that this film could have been radically improved by correction of certain faults in the montage. . . . The conceptual values would not have been disturbed; in fact, they would have been enhanced." Such remarks are maddeningly vague. *Day of Wrath* and subsequent Dreyer pictures are supposed to be uncinematic because they do not move. Yet as Young points out in his essay on *The Passion of Joan of Arc*, Dreyer's "concentration" in that masterpiece "on a single cinematic element"—namely, the close-up—made that picture "appear relatively static." By Young's own account, then, it would seem that Dreyer's "life-rhythm" was never exactly jazzy.

The early Chaplin is said to have been "a master of cutting and timing." From *Modern Times* on, however, the great comic should have "placed his idiosyncratic genius for pantomime and his occasionally seminal ideas at the disposal of a sympathetic director who might have created a context in which they were neither dissipated nor overdeployed." *Limelight* represents a "creative cinematic imagination gone to seed. . . . It is everything, most of the time, a movie *shouldn't* be: overwritten, underdirected, slowly paced, monotonously photographed, fumblingly cut—and oh so *dreary*, far beyond any justification from the milieu, a penury of the soul" ("Adventures in Film Watching"). Griffith and Eisenstein are both, in Young's view, limited film-

makers. *Intolerance* is a *"motion picture,* which is to say a product wherein the relationship of paced visual images not only tells
a story but creates thereby an aesthetic intrinsic to its mechanis-
tic means." Nevertheless, Griffith is just a "Hollywood Faustus":
a director with "no philosophy and no ideas, with bad taste and a
middle-class apprehension of history" ("Footnote to a Cinematic
Primer"). In the same essay, a typical Eisenstein film is defined as
a "thesis saga"; and it is said that Griffith and Eisenstein "very
nearly eliminated all cerebral interest from the motion picture."
("I have never been convinced that the greatness of any work of
art is proportional to its assumed intellectual complexity"—
Vernon Young, "Nostalgia of the Infinite.") In his essay on
Olympiad, Young scornfully refers to Griffith, Eisenstein, and
Flaherty as the Holy Trinity; in his long piece on Edward Tisse
—Eisenstein's cameraman—he praises some of the Russian director's technical effects but again calls him a propagandist. Not
even Eisenstein's famous Odessa Steps sequence in *Potemkin* es-
capes without criticism: the close-ups in that classic example of
montage strike Young as being "overprolonged" ("The Witness
Point").

As for Hitchcock—from whom the English film "received its
essentially empirical approach"—he is dubbed in various essays a
"full-time ghoul"; a "corpulent bourgeois"; " 'Tubby' . . . who
became cinematic lard ages ago"; and "that deck steward among
the diabolists." In *Cinema Borealis,* Hitchcock's technique is said
to be "commonly dedicated" to "shallow issues." According to
Young, Hitchcock's one bid for fame (mentioned in "Our Local
Idioms" and "The Witness Point") is his use of "the camera as
protagonist, the incorporation of no more in a scene than the
principle observer, at a given moment, is likely to see." When
Hitchcock came to America, he changed his technique and "subsequently saw too much!" And that is all Young can find to say
about the director of *Notorious, Strangers on a Train, Rear Window, Vertigo, Psycho,* and *The Birds.*

"If a director is great who has made two great movies (give
him three, I'll not argue too hotly), Buñuel is a great director,"
writes Young in "Thoughts After Attending Another Film Society
Buñuel Series." "He is not a master, for this title implies that the

artist so named is in perfect control of his medium even when he is doing a commercial chore or is not too taken with his immediate subject. This is simply not true of Buñuel; he has made bad movies and he has made many just average ones, flavored by 'Buñuel moments,' some of them silly." *Los Olvidados* is "among the great movies"; *L'Age d'Or* "was a furiously inventive response to the fractional existence of modern man"; and *Viridiana* remains "a mordantly beautiful" film. But *Robinson Crusoe* "is perhaps the test by which [Buñuel] most seriously failed, or which at least defined very clearly the substance of his bias—that he finds it easier to sneer than to think." *The Destroying Angel* is "tedious"; and *Belle de Jour* is "merely nasty-minded[,] . . . shoddy stuff." Buñuel suffers from an illusion—to wit, "that if you accumulate enough evidence of men's depravity you will have thereby defined man as depraved. . . . I don't know whether idealism or timidity inspires Buñuel's compulsive talent for depicting cruelty, but I suspect there is little genuine compassion involved." Buñuel has no insight into normal life: he "would be rattled by the arrival of Utopia; he would be compelled to renounce it, for its advent would put him out of business."

Young writes with the most fervent appreciation of Japanese and Italian films. In "The Witness Point," he remarks that (as of 1953) *Rashomon* "is perhaps closer to the perfect union [of parts] than any film yet produced." And in "The Japanese Film: Inquiries and Inferences," he praises the body of movies from Japan, because that work has "touched—above all, in *Rashomon*—the deepest and most implacable concerns of man, with cinematic values unmatched by any present body of film-makers." Kurosawa is a master of the witness point, editing, and the wide screen. "All the evidence we have defines [him] as perhaps the most physical director in the history of the movies" (*"The Hidden Fortress*: Kurosawa's Comic Mode"). Kurosawa "confines himself in many films to the surface of things, but his touch on that surface is always incisive and resounding—and one can usually hear the clanking reminder of mortality behind the flapping banners or beyond the sound of thudding arrows" ("Three Film-Makers Revisit Themselves").

On one occasion, in his review of *Red Beard*, Young is so

overpowered by Kurosawa that he remains unable "to observe the proprieties of criticism. To analyze *Red Beard* with a view to impressing the academic filmgoer (thematic parallels, shot relationships, distribution of close-ups, and the like) or those who must be appealed to on sociological grounds (exposure of medieval conditions in a Tokugawa-period clinic) is in either direction to fall short of the mark. Kurosawa's art is principally the sum of his conviction. By now we can take for granted that he knows how to achieve the intensity at which he is aiming—aesthetic distance is not his ideal—and where he hopes to place the viewer whom he hopes to subjugate." Young confesses to being "subjugated": he is still—after two months—unable to render a "detached appraisal" of *Red Beard* (though he remains aware that the film has *some* defects). Lavish praise is also heaped on *The Hidden Fortress*; but *High and Low* is an "exciting failure"; *The Seven Samurai*—albeit cinematically accomplished—"has no heart"; and *Ikiru* (generally considered one of Kurosawa's greatest films) is cluttered and suffers from anticlimax.

Kurosawa's only rival for "sheer velocity and virtuosity" is Fellini, "the supreme epic mannerist" ("The Verge and After: Film by 1966"). *The White Sheik* is "the most artful Italian comedy short of *Miracle in Milan*"; *La Strada* is a masterpiece; *Il Bidone*, though not equal to *La Strada* in "human and evocative appeal," shows Fellini "at his cinematic best"; *La Dolce Vita* is a "great film" which "could supply Italy's film-makers with ideas for the next decade"; and 8½ remains one of the best pictures of the contemporary period. *Juliet of the Spirits*, however, is "tawdry" and "tasteless." Even Fellini's script for *The Miracle* qualifies as a "short masterpiece." It comes as a shock then to hear Young speak late in the day about "the best and the worst," the "delights, no less than the tediums" of Fellini's pictures, since until the review of *Juliet of the Spirits* he has had nothing but praise for the Italian master. It would seem that Young had made up his mind about *Juliet of the Spirits* before he even saw it: at one point he refers to the picture as *Juliet 9½*, and adds that he is "trembling at every advance report." In *Cinema Borealis*, Young says that Bergman "shares with Fellini and Jean-Luc Godard the dubious distinction of having transferred the most public of the arts into a confessional lined with mirrors." Yet 8½—certainly a "confessional" film—is ranked by Young, as noted, among the outstanding pictures of our time, and it is so ranked in the same essay wherein he sneeringly refers to *Juliet* 9½ ("The Verge and After: Film by 1966").

"What distinguishes Antonioni among his contemporaries in cinema is the degree to which, by a flawless and quite personal feeling for the *internal* (not only the meticulous duration and pacing of shots in a sequence, but also the spatial tensions within the shot), he infuses his films with steadily mounting suspense," observes Young in "Nostalgia of the Infinite." "And although the movement of life in his films seems to share at times that random and unwilled progress by which our own daily lives proceed, it has a rhythmic beat calculated with extraordinary finesse. . . . The cinema of Antonioni is *essential* cinema. . . . [He] penetrates the naturalistic surface and sustains a driving undertone of dread." The trilogy—*L'Avventura, La Notte,* and *L'Eclisse*—represent a "masterly comment": *L'Avventura* and *La Notte* appear on the same list of landmark films as 8½, *La Notte* being judged as an "almost perfect film" ("Of Night, Fire, and Water"); *L'Eclisse,* although disappointing after the first two pictures in the trilogy, would be "impressive" if it had not followed them ("Films to Confirm the Poets"). *Red Desert,* however, is a "damned silly movie." According to Young, Antonioni "perfected a formalistic style which he was unable to rescue from mannerism, principally because he couldn't infuse it with creative variations of his single theme" ("The Verge and After: Film by 1966"). As for *Blow-Up,* "it's all texture, no core." Antonioni "treats with fashion-photo affection the phenomena in which he once found cause for tears. *Blow-Up* is like the latest copy of *Vogue.* It commandeth the eye but sticketh not in the memory" ("International Film"). As in the case of Fellini, Young's harsh strictures on Antonioni's later films seem to have altered his judgment of the earlier ones. For example, there is nothing in his review of *L'Eclisse* (to say nothing of his remarks on *L'Avventura* or *La Notte*) to prepare us for the negative retrospective commentary occasioned by *Red Desert.*

Like Kauffmann, and unlike the *auteurists*, Young holds De Sica in high esteem. The Italian director is a "great cinematic spirit" ("International Film Scene"), whose "generalization is absorbed in the particular" ("The Moral Cinema: Notes on Some Recent Italian Films"). In "The Brave American," Welles is praised because he is one of the few directors "who realizes that De Sica has a kind of nobility." De Sica's art, however, presents a challenge to the critic because his pictures seem to lack style; "for style is the integration of an artist's temperament in the form of his art, and the De Sica film is one in which as far as possible the eye behind the camera betrays no consciousness of itself." And Young adds: "Which is why De Sica baffles the aesthetic analyst: he directs one's eye not toward art but toward life, thereby making pronouncements on the art nearly superfluous. We know it *isn't* life we're watching, but the cinematic subtleties it's our function and pleasure to elucidate have been predigested in the conception of the film, leaving the critic little to say of specifically cinematic import until De Sica commits an error of judgment. This is an extremely rare occurrence" ("The Moral Cinema").

Yet, as Young would no doubt concede, it is one of the tasks of criticism (as I noted in my discussion of Kauffmann) to explain that art which seems artless. Aesthetically, it remains much easier to show the greatness of a *Citizen Kane*, say, than of an *Umberto D.* Nevertheless, the De Sica film *is* art, and the critic's job *is* "to elucidate" art.

Perhaps Young's pessimism about demonstrating the visual "subtleties" of a De Sica picture, however, stems from his unhappy experience in writing "*Umberto D.*: Vittorio De Sica's 'Super'-Naturalism." (Which might also explain why he did not include that essay in *On Film*.) In "*Umberto D.*," Young ably underlines De Sica's use of sound, and his analysis of character and theme remains perceptive; but he fails to do justice to the pictorial quality of the film. "De Sica's compositions rarely startle one by their ingenuity. *What* he focuses on at a given point is more significant than the *way* he focuses," Young writes. "The way is never neglected, it simply isn't exploited; for it is to De Sica's purpose to move with un-elliptical life as closely as he dares

without vitiating motion-picture technique altogether. To subordinate the essentially cinematic as he does is itself a technique
of ineffable skill; and to efface his signature as a director from
the style of a film argues a modest purity of aim."

Hasn't Young made his task a bit too easy? To say that *what*
De Sica shows is more important than the *way* that he shows it,
is to say that De Sica's content is more significant than his form.
Yet as Young points out in the beginning of his article, the error
of sociological criticism is that it places the primary stress on
subject matter, failing "to recognize that no subject is important
until awakened by art." If the "essentially cinematic" means "*the
art of photographed motion*," and if De Sica subordinates this
art, then what "technique" is he using—what "ineffable skill" is
he displaying as an *artist in film*? If "style is the integration of an
artist's temperament in the form of his art," and if De Sica is
prone "to efface his signature as a director from the style of a
film," then the result is not a "modest purity of aim" but an
uncinematic slice-of-life. It is precisely this alleged lack of a
filmic style in De Sica (together with other alleged defects) which
has prompted the *auteurists* to banish him from their sundry
pantheons.

Young comes to praise De Sica but instead buries him.

This is unfortunate because, at his best, Young can make the
reader "see" a film better than any other living American critic. I
don't mean to suggest that "*Umberto D.*: Vittorio De Sica's
'Super'-Naturalism" is entirely devoid of Young's ability to expli-
cate a movie's visual progression. At one point he explains how
De Sica's camera, "with flat-lighted neutrality," reveals the vul-
garly furnished house wherein the protagonist drags out his im-
pecunious existence; and he catalogs for the reader numerous
items which bring out the shabby nature of Umberto D.'s sur-
roundings. At another point, Young refers to some important
visual symbolism in the picture. And in his discussion of the
scene in which Maria is shown rising in the morning, he observes: "There is little in it that could not be performed on a
stage, but in its brief duration and its breathing nearness, in the
particular placing of the camera for each view of the pregnant
girl struggling to experience joy which gives way to fear and then

to a daydream indifference, it is a marvel of movie timing and perspective." But in general, the essay on *Umberto D.* is a disappointment.

However, when Young is at the top of his form—such as in his essays on *Olympiad, The Passion of Joan of Arc,* and *Forbidden Games*—his ability to see, together with his passion for searching out the aesthetic and cultural and moral significance of what he sees, makes him one of the very best American film critics.

6

In an article on Bergman's *The Lie* (the Swedish director's first television script to be shown in this country), John Simon calls *Cinema Borealis* an "erratic but fascinating book" (*New York Times,* April 22, 1973). Simon is right. Although it is only fair to add that Young's study *is* a book—which is more than can be said of *Ingmar Bergman Directs,* with its plot summaries of four pictures, thirty-page interview with the film-maker, and more pictures that can be found in a film distributor's catalog.

It does not require profound intelligence to discern what is "erratic" about *Cinema Borealis.* Ironically, Young turns out to be nearly as "ungenerous" towards Bergman as Kauffmann! Of the thirty-one pictures directed by the Swedish giant, Young allows passing grades to a mere six. And even of those six, he has a few strong reservations. *Summer With Monica*—"perhaps the least identifiably personal film Bergman has made"—is praised. (Can it be, in part, that Young is overreacting to *auteur* criticism?) Likewise, *The Naked Night* and *The Seventh Seal* are commended. Although Young respects *Winter Light* and *The Silence,* he doesn't really like them. *The Virgin Spring*—"Bergman's least personal work"—is the masterpiece. However, *Wild Strawberries, Through a Glass Darkly,* and *Persona*—along with the twenty-two other films—are considered failures.

As early as 1961, Young noted that Bergman "has now passed the cape where his art can enlarge our perceptions" ("European Film Notebook"). It therefore comes as no surprise when, in the concluding portion of *Cinema Borealis,* he writes: "After *The*

Virgin Spring . . . I feel exposed for the most part to a doctrine of existence that repels me." Young is impatient with what he calls "the pre-renaissance temper" of Bergman's "fanaticism." He explains: "I believe in the power of the mind, provisionally at least, to make choices and to exercise discriminations." Bergman strikes Young, too frequently, as an anti-intellectual: "Bergman is impressed by man's sinfulness; I am depressed by his ignorance." Young rejects not only the *what* of Bergman's films after *The Virgin Spring* but also the *how*. With the exception of *Winter Light*, he finds the later films, as he puts it in his section on *Through a Glass Darkly*, lacking in a "sufficient degree of expressiveness to ratify the economy of setting and the paucity of action." The subject matter of Bergman's pictures after *The Virgin Spring* is arid, according to Young, and so is the artistry.

The evaluative side of *Cinema Borealis* is poor because Young tends to give the reader too little analysis to justify his judgments. One would expect that a critic with Young's keen eye for the visual dimension of motion pictures could put to rest forever the fatuous assertion that Bergman is not really "cinematic." Yet Young has no more to tell us about Bergman's visual imagination than Simon. As noted, Young exempts *Winter Light* from his generalizations about the later films in his discussion of *Through a Glass Darkly*; however, in his section on *Winter Light*, he contradicts himself and declares that the film is "far too little cinematic, in my feeling for that term." Criticism begins with feeling ("Any critic who pretends that his initial reception of a work of art is not principally subjective is deceiving himself," Young writes. "If you do not feel the power and truth of a film such as [*The Virgin Spring*], no argument can persuade you"); but criticism doesn't—or at least *shouldn't*—rest on feeling ("Criticism is a method of rationally explaining the emotional experience one has already had"; "Criticism carries the obligation of interpreting as far as possible what is demonstrable"). Similarly, Young has almost nothing to say about either structure or sound in Bergman's films. As for "the witness point," it is barely referred to and not invariably in an illuminating way. For instance, Young briefly remarks that in *Wild Strawberries* "the witness point" is "as often as possible that of old Borg." Now, aside from the fact that sundry pages could be written on the subject of viewpoint in this complex and beautiful picture, there is this to be noted. In one sense, the entire film is from Borg's point of view, since *Wild Strawberries* is a first-person narrative; however, in terms of the visual projection of the action, there are relatively *few* subjective shots from Borg's "witness point."

Bergman has been blessed with perhaps the finest acting company any film director has ever had. Yet surprisingly, Young has nothing to say on the score of acting. In "Adventures in Film Watching," he writes: "Film criticism can usually afford to disregard actors in a film's total effect, unless they are grossly bad or overwhelmingly good." This is a dubious proposition. Even assuming that it were true, however, it reflects negatively upon Young as a critic, since many performances in Bergman's pictures *are* first-rate.

One is forced to speculate on whether Young chose the right subject for a full-length study. Although he concludes that where Bergman's "art represents decisively 'the emotional equivalent of thought,' it is preeminent . . . in film history," he does not on the whole write as sympathetically about the Swede as he does about De Sica or Kurosawa. Young's ethnological approach in *Cinema Borealis*, as we shall see, is of great value; the fact remains, though, that he does not like Sweden—any more than he likes much of the subject matter or expressive means of Bergman himself. Sometimes Young sounds uncomfortably like a neo-classical critic as he raps Bergman's knuckles for being too "personal," or for his religious "fanaticism"; at other times, he sounds like a romantic critic as he chastises Bergman for being *too* restrained, *too* austere. ("Austerity is one thing," Young testily remarks, "but aridity is something *more* disagreeable." The italics are mine.) In "Thoughts After Attending Another Film Society Buñuel Series," Young writes: "I am sometimes led to believe that ninety-five out of every hundred 'film people' lost their daddies (if not their mummies) when very young. Once they have discovered a director who has made two or three films with which they are *d'accord*, they adopt him as their liege lord; their life occupation then becomes a jealous defense of every celluloid foot he has absent-mindedly exposed (pun intended)." Young makes much the same point in *Cinema Borealis*, when he accuses Bergman of wanting critics to praise *all* his pictures, even the bad ones. To do so, Young rightly suggests, would be an abdication of critical responsibility. Nevertheless, Young has not given the body of Bergman's work its due. And his failure is precisely in that area where he is, it seems to me, generally at his strongest —namely, in his ability to fuse the ethnological approach with an equally enlightening aesthetic evaluation based on close attention to expressive detail, especially visual detail.

What is "fascinating" about *Cinema Borealis*, however, are the various "extrinsic" approaches Young takes toward the whole body of Bergman's work. In the preface to *On Film*, the critic correctly—though jokingly—refers to *Cinema Borealis* as a "solid historical study." Since biographical information remains one of the primary kinds of material used by the historical critic, *Cinema Borealis* includes data on Bergman's life. Nonetheless, Young introduces this mode of inquiry, so often abused in the past, with the following notice: "I should prefer to discuss Bergman's films without touching his personal life at all, but not only do the films more often than not make this a difficult discipline, Bergman himself vitiates one's sense of discretion by the provocative egoism he has so often displayed. Beyond the more obvious connections, however, without which his films can only academically be analyzed, I shall make an effort to be diffident. His marriages, for instance, are in my opinion completely forbidden territory for the critic."

In terms of the biographical approach, Young's principle of selection is based on an interpretive criterion: Bergman's parents, his upbringing, his schooling, and the like, are relevant to *Cinema Borealis* only to the extent that such sources of knowledge illuminate the reader's understanding of Bergman the artist. Although Young notes that the director's films represent an unsurpassable opportunity for the Freudian critic, he passes up the chance to psychoanalyze either Bergman or his artistic progeny in depth. All the same, the critic does not shut his eyes to the obvious relationship between Bergman's ambivalent attitude towards his father and the various motifs open to inspection in the work. In Bergman's early films, Young observes, "seemingly unrelated to the God-is-absent [theme], there is a distinct note of sexual hostility toward the older men depicted." The "God-is-absent" theme is also related to Bergman's feelings about his father, who was a clergyman, and who would not speak to little Ingmar as punishment for "breaches of conduct." As every freshman knows, Freud believed that the child fashions his picture of God on the model of his father. "When a man, seriously dedicated, writes his first books or makes his first films he is the sum of all the forces which have made him, but these forces are not consciously available to him in expressive forms," Young explains. "In short, his art suffers because he doesn't himself know who he really is; it suffers just as much if he too strenuously makes this a primary question, with a blind eye for all those other mortals and toward a world in which he is of no more account than a blade of grass. This was certainly Bergman's case: an overweening preoccupation with his own pains and an overwhelming innocence of their real source. If it may be said that his total production has been a nagging adventure in self-revelation, the earlier films . . . scarcely transcend that definition, whereas the later films ["later" here meaning, no doubt, *Summer With Monica* and after] are often works of art." As can be seen, Young's biographical approach is performed with admirable tact.

Young also considers the influence of other artists on Bergman's development. Here again, Young does not merely cite the historical fact of influence—he translates the fact into interpretive terms. For instance, he points out the enormous authority of Strindberg in any attempt to understand Bergman's cinema. Both artists rebelled against an oppressive Swedish Lutheranism; both reveal ambivalence toward God and women in their work; and both these temperamental titans use their art as "an instrument of the ego"—a circumstance which, as I have previously suggested, Young does not find to his taste. (Like T. S. Eliot, Young favors "impersonal" art.) Young makes an interesting case for the influence of Hitchcock on Bergman, too. *It Can't Happen Here* "is a political melodrama unabashedly modeled on the work of Alfred Hitchcock. . . . [Almost] every shot, chase, switch, and audio-visual irony is referable to earlier Hitchcock. There are reflections of a pursuer on the beveled surface of a headlight, the beating of

a traitor behind a movie screen onto which is being projected a
Donald Duck cartoon, and church bells tolling as Natas [the
protagonist] finds his escape route cut off." In Simon's interview
with Bergman, conducted after *Cinema Borealis* appeared, the
director admits to having been influenced technically by Hitchcock, thus verifying Young's thesis.

At the beginning of this chapter, I quoted some of Young's
observations on Sweden to illustrate his ethnological approach to
film. More specifically, Young attempts to relate Bergman's work
to the *Fyrtiota-lists* or Forty-ists. "Normally," Young writes, "the
movies represent but a shadow, or a popularization, a shadow of
a shadow, of a country's guiding beliefs." During the forties there
were some poets in Sweden who experienced guilt feelings over
their country's neutrality in the Second World War; they responded to their crisis of conscience by espousing neutrality in *all*
things, including "metaphysical neutrality, with no quarter given,
one infers, to political imperatives or the implications of history
and with no consolation forthcoming from nature, philosophy,
art, religion, or their friends." The philosophy of the *Fyrtiotalists*
was merely an intensification of an already existing Swedish cultural trait.

As Young sees it, Bergman was a "belated" *Fyrtiotalist*, or one
who believes that to live is "to choose between the indifferent
and the impossible." Young is quick to add, though, that the
Fyrtiotalists only account in part for the anguished subject matter of Bergman's early pictures. "The real sources of Ingmar
Bergman's films were in himself, but what is a self? An accumula-
tion of temperament around the living cell of a culture? The
sources of the Bergman films were in his local Swedish inheritance, with all that implies of external conditioning and personal
reaction. The matter of the films, whatever else came to be included, represents the strategies with which he met the consequences of his inheritance."

An important part of *Cinema Borealis* is Young's attempt to
counter the conventional picture of Bergman's country as sexu-
ally joyous with a view of it as essentially puritanical and pro-
hibitive, a society where the figures on sex murder and rape are

steadily rising. Underneath the surface image of Sweden exported by publicists resides, Young believes, "the desire of a stodgy people to protest that in actuality it has a nostalgia for chaos, since chaos at least implies a collision of forces, a condition of disorganized vitality." Young buttresses his argument with data compiled from Herbert Hendin's *Suicide and Scandinavia*, a psychiatric study, and Jack D. Douglas's *The Social Meanings of Suicide*, a sociological inquiry. For a self-proclaimed utopian nation, Sweden has an astonishingly high suicide rate. Young accepts Hendin's thesis that "the Swedish would-be suicide is brought to his pass by the failure of rigid performance expectations, accompanied by a strong self-hatred for that failure." Bergman is a genius, hence he is not a typical Swede; yet not even a genius "can wholly transcend his culture." In the "first thirteen film scripts Bergman wrote and/or directed there were six suicides or suicide attempts; in four films a girl was seduced by a much older man; one wife died from the alleged neglect by her husband; three children perished, one murdered at birth; three wives and one sexual rival were murdered in fantasy; there were three abortions, apart from those referred to in *Port of Call*, and of the young men represented as heroes two were crippled, one a homicidal maniac and a number certainly infirm of character."

With nice discrimination, Young throughout his book weaves together biographical, attributive, and ethnological approaches to Bergman's pictures, revealing much first-hand knowledge of Sweden and considerable scholarship in secondary sources. (Young's long hours in front of the movie screen have not kept him from reading broadly and deeply, as a glance at his notes will testify.)

In spite of its "erratic" features, then, *Cinema Borealis* is an important book—a challenge to future critics. If Young could bring together the aesthetic, ethnological, and other approaches he has mixed so well in some of his essays in a book on a worthy director for whom he has a genuine liking, he might give us that exemplary work of American film criticism which we sorely need. Even in its imperfect state, however, *Cinema Borealis* stands head and shoulders above almost everything else being published on motion pictures today. It tells us much about the state of film criticism in America when both *Cinema Borealis* and *On Film* (the latter's nomination for a National Book Award notwithstanding) are virtually ignored and books like *Confessions of a Cultist* and *Deeper Into Movies* are extravagantly praised.

CHAPTER NINE

Dwight Macdonald,
"Congenital Critic"

It comes down, ultimately, to value judgments ("taste," "opinion") which can never be settled as conclusively as the freshness of an egg. Which is not to say that one man's opinion is as good as the next one's. Before the ultimate is reached a critic goes through a process of defining, describing, reasoning, and persuading which is drawn from his own special experience and knowledge and which may or may not persuade his readers that his judgment is more accurate—"true" or "right" would be claiming too much—than other judgments, according to their experience and knowledge. Readers have their own ideas, too, if they're worth writing for.

—Dwight Macdonald

1

When Dwight Macdonald stepped down as film critic for *Esquire* magazine in 1966, he closed out—or appeared to close out—over forty years of intermittent criticism of screen art. In the early twenties, Macdonald attended Philips Exeter Academy, and through an English teacher there he later made the acquaintance of the younger James Agee; the two men found that their more passionate mutual interest, however, involved not literature but film. After graduating from Yale, Macdonald and three other cineasts put out *The Miscellany*—a "little 'little magazine'" (600 circulation)—which lasted from 1929 to 1931. Mac-donald has been an associate editor of *Fortune* (1929–1936), an editor of *Partisan Review* (1938–1943), the editor and publisher of *Politics* (1944–1949), and an advisory editor of *Encounter* (1956–1957), in addition to being movie critic on *Esquire* (1960–1966). For many years Macdonald was also a staff writer for *The New Yorker*. During the thirties, forties, and fifties he published occasional film criticism, but only his work on *Esquire* had regularly to do with the movies. In 1966, Macdonald taught History and Criticism of Cinema at the University of Texas; he lectured on the same material three years later at the Santa Cruz campus of the University of California. Editor of *Parodies* (1960), he has also written six books, including studies of Henry Wallace and the Ford Foundation, *Memoirs of a Revolutionist* (1957), and *Against the American Grain* (1962), which leads off with his well-known essay "Masscult & Midcult" and is followed by a section in which there is a discussion of Agee.

Anyone unfamiliar with Macdonald's film criticism might jus-tifiably assume from his background that the sociological ap-proach would best define his method. Once a Marxist, then a Trotskyite in the thirties ("I have long ago," he remarks, "shed my illusions about Marx and Trotsky"), Macdonald has always been a politically conscious, social activist. As a guest reviewer for *The New York Times* (June 7, 1970), he soundly thrashed *Getting Straight*, which prompted the film's director and writer to make a reply (July 12, 1970) wherein they accused him of not being involved in today's world. In his reply to their reply (same date), Macdonald pointed out that he was one of the founders of Resist in 1965, an organization whose purpose was to help draft resisters, and that he had aided Students for a Democratic Soci-ety and had publicly supported the strikers at Columbia Univer-sity in 1968. "My problem is too much involvement: too many Pentagon marches, Sheep Meadow demonstrations, draft-board picketings; too many years, decades, centuries of exposing the moral absurdities of American society (it is wearying when your five-year campaign to dump Johnson succeeds and you get—Nixon); too many committees joined, petitions signed, speeches made, checks contributed. But what can you do?" Macdonald adds. "It's necessary, like film criticism, critical criticism that is, the destructive kind Hollywood needs rather than the constructive kind it wants."

A familiar charge made against Macdonald is that he "hates movies"—a mindless criticism often directed at anyone who fails to applaud every shoddy picture that comes out of Hollywood (or what passes for "Hollywood" today). Only a man badly in need of a straightjacket would devote forty years to writing about a subject which he loathed. Of his work for *The Miscellany*, Macdonald says that it exemplifies "that innocent missionary enthusiasm in which we early cineasts lived and had our critical being—so little yet written! so many yet to be converted!" Macdonald's criticism makes it abundantly clear that he loves movies: not in the way of the unthinking buff or the toady of the industry, but as one who wishes to see the film realize itself as an art form. As early as 1929, Macdonald wrote: "Historically, it is to be expected that the movies should give us our highest type of aesthetic expression. Long ago the other arts reached, and passed, their climaxes in respect to technique." Over the years, Macdonald has attempted to uphold standards against the tawdriness of mass culture, or *kitsch*, in a way reminiscent of Matthew Arnold's struggle against the Philistines in the last century.

Still, as I have tried to suggest, neither Macdonald's sociocultural interests nor his moral fervor have distorted his critical perspective: aesthetic concerns come first, sociological and moral approaches come second in this critic's theory and practice. In 1969 *Dwight Macdonald on Movies* was published. It remains the writer's one book of film criticism and it contains selections dating from the twenties to the sixties, drawn from *Esquire, Film Heritage, Partisan Review, The Symposium, Encounter, Politics, Problems of Communism*, and *The Miscellany*. The volume is poorly organized (even more poorly than the average collection of film criticism). Macdonald begins with essays which he evidently believes to be among his more interesting efforts (on Agee, 8½, and Antonioni, for example); then he moves on to "Revivals" ("Our Elizabethan Movies," written in 1929, and "Notes on Hollywood Directors," as of 1933); then forward to "American Themes" ("The Doris Day Syndrome," and the like);

then backward to Eisenstein, Pudovkin, and the classic Russian cinema, ending with reviews of some post-Stalin films; followed by sections devoted to other national cinemas, including our own once again; followed in turn by a section on a genre, namely, "The Biblical Spectacular"; and then, finally, he concludes with "Trims and Clips" (his "favorite section"!), an accurately described "grabbag" of snippings from articles, film reviews, and book reviews. Yet in spite of its hodgepodge construction, *Dwight Macdonald on Movies* represents American film criticism of the highest order. Macdonald's priorities are correct (in that he attempts to do justice to both art and reality, in that order), and his writing is intelligent, readable, and witty; he is constantly examining his applied criticism in the light of his theory of film and his general evaluative criteria.

2

In his "Forenotes" to the book, however, Macdonald modestly disparages his ability to theorize. "I know something about cinema after forty years, and being a congenital critic, I know what I like and why. But I can't explain the *why* except in terms of the specific work under consideration, on which I'm copious enough. The general theory, and the larger view, the gestalt—these have always eluded me." At times one suspects a typical American distrust of theory on Macdonald's part, such as when he remarks: "No one can reach more inane conclusions than a thoroughgoing theorist" ("Advanced Bird-Watching"), or when he refers to himself as a "pragmatic" thinker and humorously boasts that only once in his life had he ever adhered to a general principle for any length of time ("Forenotes"). All the same, Macdonald is one of our better theorists, his generalizations on film art and film criticism taking up a larger proportion of space in his critiques than in that of most other critics in this country.

"Art," Macdonald defines in one place, is "something all of a piece and consistent with its own assumptions" (*"Last Year at Marienbad"*). In his essay on 8½, he observes: "I could never understand why 'art for art's sake' is usually sneered at—for what better sake?" Macdonald is a bit facetious here; neither elsewhere in his theoretical observations nor in his practical criticism does he hold with that extreme form of aesthetic criticism which concentrates on beauty alone, minimizing or totally ignoring meaning and morality. What he appears to be stressing, however, is the need to give first consideration to the artistic properties of a movie.

He archly accounts for his initial overestimation of *Last Year at Marienbad* in terms of "a secret craving, a prurient itch for a low sensual experience of visual imagery"; he subsequently came to think less of the film—though not less of its pictorial quality—because "what *was* the whole, expressed with such disciplined virtuosity?" Macdonald defends beauty against anti-art film criticism ("When a modern critic hears the word 'beauty,' he releases the safety catch on his fountain pen"); but, since he also believes that beauty is not enough, he argues for content against the *auteurists*. The "form," he notes, "*is* the content, while the content is so profoundly affected by the form in which it is expressed as not to be separable from it. One-sided judgments result from the Sarris approach. . . . The Russian 'socialist-realist' critics reach absurdity by considering only literary-political content, Sarris achieves it by overemphasizing visual form" ("Film Criticism: A Note on Method"). Later, in "Trims and Clips," Macdonald returns to this subject: "There's something in this emphasis on technique, which is at least more sensible than the opposite view that was held over here in the thirties when the proletarian novel, the 'committed' artist, and other absurdities of primitive Marxism were taken seriously. . . . But I wonder whether filmmakers shouldn't begin to pay more attention to subject matter." He suggests that films—foreign and American—neglect the working life of modern man. "Most of us spend half our life at work . . . but this is the dark side of the moon as far as movies go; it is only our off-duty hours that are recorded on the silver screen."

Macdonald views form and content in a work of art in respect to the personality of the artist, the film as film, and the viewing audience. The great film-maker, Macdonald writes, imparts to his work "a certain individual quality" ("Notes on Hollywood Directors"); however, because he confesses to "a reactionary prejudice in favor of communication" (*"Shadows"*), Macdonald also declares: "Art has often been created from the artist's neuroses, but only when he has been able to break through from *his* world to *the* world, from the personal to the public" ("Kazanistan, Ingeland, and Williams, Tenn."). A "work of art is impersonal fabrication as well as personal expression. If the latter is too prominent, the universal element—the form—is destroyed and the audience is involved only insofar as it is interested in the personality of the artist. . . . The romantic movement, with its exaltation of the subjective over the objective, the artist over the work, has a lot to answer for" (*"The Trial"*). Eisenstein's *The General Line* (*Old and New*) and Dovzhenko's *Soil* (*Earth*), though both films are brilliant, reflect a "split between form and content"; at times, Eisenstein seems bored with his theme and indulges in "technical fireworks" ("Soviet Cinema"). On the other hand, Chaplin neglects form in favor of content in *Monsieur Verdoux*; "to call a badly flawed movie great because of its theme and its creator's intentions is like saying an orator is eloquent but inarticulate" ("The Case of M. Verdoux").

If an artist is to create, Macdonald declares, "he must believe in something—realism, romanticism, communism, his own importance, it doesn't matter what. He must have standards of some sort, and feel a certain pride in maintaining them. He may let himself be bent by outside pressure to a greater or lesser extent, depending on his temperament, but his sense of integrity must draw the line somewhere" ("Notes on Hollywood Directors"). Are the films of Eisenstein and Pudovkin "propaganda"? To this question, Macdonald replies: "art is often aimed at the glorification of some social class. That the artists of the renaissance glorified the aristocracy and that the Soviet artists glorify the proletariat is not a very important distinction." According to Macdonald, the artist accepts the prevailing beliefs of his time— or challenges them—but whatever his stand, his main order of business is his art. The artist might take dictation on theology or politics, but he will not allow himself to be told how he is to shape that material artistically ("Eisenstein and Pudovkin in the Twenties").

The foregoing essay was written in 1931; in 1969, Macdonald expressed some doubts—not spelled out, unfortunately—about his discussion of art and propaganda nearly forty years ago. However, in 1939 he distinguished the early Soviet film from the Stalinist variety as follows: "In the twenties, 'propaganda' meant that Soviet directors made films expressing certain basic social values with which they were in ardent sympathy. The word, 'sympathy,' in fact, implies a detachment which was not the case: they were part of the society founded on those values, and this self-identification was a potent inspiration to them. In the thirties, they must become political hacks, lending their talents to whatever maneuver the Kremlin has put on the order of the day, obediently and fearfully treading the official line" ("Soviet Cinema"). By 1957, Macdonald was defining "propaganda" as a "one-sided view" of life; hence *The Birth of a Nation* and *Ten Days That Shook the World* "are propaganda, with negroes as the villains and southerners the heroes in one as against the same relationship between bourgeois and workers in the other" ("D. W. Griffith"). Yet in "Forenotes," Macdonald praises *The Birth of a Nation*, calling it the work of a cinematic "genius."

If form and content are inseparable, how can Macdonald argue that the artist will permit his content to be determined by external pressure but not his form? Can "art" also be "propaganda"? Does a "one-sided view" of life necessarily imply "propaganda"? On the one hand, some aestheticians argue that inclusiveness is a mark of great art; on the other hand, some believe that every artist has a strong personal—that is, idiosyncratic, "one-sided"—viewpoint which he wishes to convey. Is a film "propaganda" only when a viewer, or a ruling class, or even a whole society, rejects its theme? Perhaps the word "propaganda" points to material in a work of art which seeks some practical effect, such as the liberation of women or world revolution? If so, how is the critic to decide where artistic "conviction" or "belief" ends (with all that such terms imply in respect to the filmmaker's desire to impress upon the viewer his way of looking at life) and "propaganda" begins? If we accept the notion that art has the power to change our lives, then on what basis—aesthetically speaking—do we draw the line between "art" and "propaganda"? If Macdonald has not satisfactorily answered such questions, he has at least inspired them . . . And of how many other American film critics can that be said?

In "Cosa Nostra," Macdonald remarks: "I have nothing against pornography when it's good, clean sex." "Pornography," however, "cannot be art: because the view of life is too restricted, the aim too narrowly utilitarian . . . [T]he combinations and permutations of physical lust are severely limited by the not-at-all infinite capacities of the human body" (*"The Pumpkin Eater"*). In other words, "pornography," like "propaganda," represents a "one-sided" viewpoint. Although Macdonald believes that even the best films neglect too many important areas of life in favor of sex, he does not therefore advocate a ban on sexual themes. Indeed, he favors "more nudity in films; also more eroticism and sensuality" ("Cosa Nostra"). What he opposes is perversion and prudery. At times, "one thinks that the only way to get real sex past the censors is to combine it with sadism; rape seems less objectionable to them than seduction, perhaps because it is less enjoyable" (*"Lolita"*). What Macdonald asks for from American movies with erotic content is *wholeness*. In the finest European pictures sex is not isolated but treated "as a natural part of everyday human existence—sometimes tragic, sometimes poignant, sometimes funny" ("Trims and Clips").

"I like to be entertained," Macdonald writes, "and I think that a movie that is not entertaining cannot be considered art" (*"Tom Jones"*). Film is an art which appeals "to the eye and the ear at least as much as to the mind" (review of *I Lost It at the Movies*). To a critic's statement that 8½ "is really a visual experience, its only profundity resting there," Macdonald replies: "And what better resting place?" He praises Mervyn Le Roy because his films are never dull: "Whatever his movies fail to do, they always *move*" ("Notes on Hollywood Directors").

In "Trims and Clips," Macdonald describes a scene in *The Birth of a Nation* in which a black man asks Lillian Gish to marry him. Griffith's title reads: "The Black's Mad Proposal." Macdonald explains: "The scene simply illustrates this title. Extraordinarily crude. Yet here, *in petto*, is the basic aesthetic of the cinema. (Or *an* aesthetic, anyway.)" Macdonald's substitution of "an" for "the" shows prudence—though he immediately adds: "A movie is, or should be, a series of such illustrations, each of them demonstrating some idea or situation."

Some readers will rightly view this statement as attributing a too rhetorical, or at least a too rationalistic function for cinematic images. Like Descartes, the film-maker has a clear and distinct idea; then he illustrates this idea with a picture. Now, in spite of what purists might say, some important film artists probably often do work this way. Many, however, do not. They create intuitively: they think in images. And the meaning issues from the images—it doesn't exist beforehand, in the sense of a theme waiting to be demonstrated visually.

In his piece on 8½, Macdonald complains that " 'serious' critics have by now become habituated to profound, difficult films that must be 'interpreted' from the language of art (what's on the screen) into the language of philosophy (what what's on the screen 'really means')." But can't this failing of "serious" critics be traced, in part, to their belief that every film is constructed— "or should be"—to illustrate a series of "ideas"? In "Forenotes," Macdonald himself writes: "Cinema . . . is mute when it comes to expressing ideas. . . . But there are too many ideas around in this specialized age, and not enough sensory perception of what's right in front of our noses or eyes (as against our brains). That's one reason I like movies."

Macdonald's evaluative approach involves two basic questions about a film: "Did it change the way you look at things?"; and, "Did you find more (or less) in it the second, third, nth time? (Also, how did it stand up over the years, after one or more 'periods' of cinematic history?)." *The Birth of a Nation, Grand Illusion,* and *Children of Paradise* are pictures which altered Macdonald's view of reality. *Citizen Kane* and 8½ remain fresh for him after repeated screenings; but *The Wedding March, The Case of Lena Smith, Blood of a Poet, I Vitelloni, Breathless,* and *Hiroshima Mon Amour* do not. He concludes: "A masterpiece delights first by its originality and then by its familiarity" ("Forenotes").

Throughout his book, however, Macdonald goes beyond asking these two questions in his judgments of movies. "Any person who is truly observed is interesting, if only because he is unique. What makes Hollywood's characters dull is that they are conventional types who are conventionally observed. . . . One mark of a bad movie . . . is that the characters exist only as functions of the plot, which means they have lots of Big Moments, but no small ones" ("Kazanistan, Ingeland, and Williams, Tenn."). "How seldom does one see human beings on the screen, each behaving according to his personality, each being always unexpected—and presenting their [traits] without rhetorical emphasis and without explanation. Things are not 'built up' any more than they are in real life; scenes are not resolved, they just stop, sometimes abruptly, sometimes ebbing away. Often nothing 'happens' at all" ("Trims and Clips"). Yet art is not life. "Dissonance can be a kind of harmony, as the destruction of form can be a kind of form, but only if it is deliberate. . . . An artist is an ascetic; he omits and simplifies, passing up chances for effects if they don't suit his purpose" (*"Saturday Night and Sunday Morning"*). Macdonald has high praise for *The Lady with a Dog*, except for its final scene when "the lovers analyze their situation instead of existing within it. Exposition is the enemy of art."

A criticism which recurs often in Macdonald's reviews is one involving the mixture of genres, or modes. As he sees it, *Monsieur Verdoux* "is really two films, one a sentimental melodrama, the other a comedy in the old Chaplin style that burlesques the melodrama. What makes it confusing is that Chaplin shifts gears between the two without apparently knowing he is doing so." Macdonald observes that in *Shoot the Piano Player*, Truffaut deliberately mixed up "three genres which are usually kept apart: crime melodrama, romance, and slapstick comedy. I thought the mixture didn't jell, but it was an exhilarating try" (*"Jules and Jim"*). In *I Lost It at the Movies*, Kael writes: "What I think is exhilarating in *Shoot the Piano Player* is that it *doesn't* 'jell' and that the different elements keep *us* in a state of suspension—we react far more than we do to works that 'jell.'" She also correctly points out that film-makers mix genres much more frequently than Macdonald allows.

No doubt, Macdonald would argue that if a film doesn't "jell," it fails as art. (In "Trims and Clips," Macdonald says of *Children*

of Paradise: "it is all of a piece and every piece of it is of the best
workmanship. A rough definition of a masterpiece.") It is important to remember that Macdonald's formalistic approach does
not include a neo-classical resistance to the mixture of genres in
itself. "I don't say that discordant genres cannot be controlled so
as to make a whole," he remarks, "merely that [Karel] Reisz [in
Morgan!] hasn't done it." Similarly, he says of *Getting Straight*
that the problem "is how to shift gears between incompatible
modes: comedy and pathos, realism and fantasy, satire and feeling. It can be done successfully but it takes a sure hand and a
sensitive touch"—two gifts which the makers of *Getting Straight*,
he believes, lack.

3

A film critic writes for audiences and other critics, Macdonald
maintains, not for film-makers. "The critic's job doesn't include
second-guessing the director by giving him helpful suggestions as
to how he might have made a better film. . . . I wouldn't want to
see a movie by a director who had to learn to make movies from
my reviews. They say it's easy enough to be critical, or negative,
or destructive, but it isn't really. To stick to serious, negative,
unconstructive criticism takes a lot of thought and effort" ("Forenotes").
If the critic doesn't also write for film-makers, why does Macdonald remark in his reply to the creators of *Getting Straight* that
Hollywood needs destructive rather than constructive criticism?
Furthermore, Macdonald's choice of "constructive" and "destructive" as modes of criticism is not a happy one, nor is his use of
these terms altogether consistent. Most readers would interpret
"constructive" criticism to mean one which attempts through patient discussion of specific films to bring about improvements in
the art—an aim which, in spite of what Macdonald says, remains
evident in much of his own applied criticism. Such an approach
obviously does not preclude negative judgments. "Constructive"
and "destructive" are words which should properly indicate degrees of emphasis within a single critical approach rather than

mutually exclusive critical methods. "Destructive" criticism suggests the mere exercise of spite; that is to say, Simonism. The term scarcely does justice to Macdonald's own practice; even when he is at his most devastating—such as when tearing apart one of Hollywood's pretentious farragoes—he clearly presents a rational case, replete with critical evidence, in support of his negative evaluation. Finally, as Macdonald uses "constructive" in his discussion of *Getting Straight*, the word implies simple puffery; but in "Forenotes," although this meaning is again suggested, "constructive" is also equated with "helpful suggestions as to how [the film-maker] might have made a better film." Traditionally, the latter practice has been considered one of the critic's primary obligations.

At the theoretical level, there appears to be some confusion in Macdonald's mind about what the act of criticism entails. In his introduction to Simon's *Acid Test*, he distinguishes two functions of criticism: one, passing judgment—especially negative—or the evaluative function; and two—by way of Matthew Arnold—the "disinterested endeavor to learn and propagate the best that is known or thought in the world." As Macdonald points out, the first use does not rule out the second. However, aside from the fact that Macdonald hardly begins to define the critic's job of work here, it needs to be observed that there is a tendency in his theoretical pronouncements and in his reviews of film books to define criticism exclusively in terms of *evaluation*.

"Praise is agreeable always and to the most dedicated artist," Macdonald writes, "but I should think it would be more helpful if it were informed, that is, cut by the tartness of criticism, even the acid of rejection" ("The End"). Note Macdonald's use of the word "helpful." The main point I wish to make, however, is that Macdonald believes that praise isn't part of the critic's function but that disapproval is. Now, if criticism involves the weighing of good and bad in a film prior to making a judgment, why should commendation be barred but not condemnation? In his review of *I Lost It at the Movies*, Macdonald writes: "The trouble with most film criticism today is that it isn't criticism. It is, rather, appreciation, celebration, information, and it is written by intellectuals who have come to be 'insiders' in the sense that they are

able to discourse learnedly about almost any movie without thinking much about whether it's any good."

What does Macdonald intend by "appreciation"? Generally,
the word implies the critical judgment to see value in a work of
art, and to enjoy it; if one appreciates a film, then, one ipso facto
renders a verdict on it. However, as Macdonald uses the term, it
seems to mean "a lack of negative evaluation" or "an absence of
any evaluation." He says of John Russell Taylor—unfairly—that
he "is better at appreciating films than at criticizing them"; and
he finds *I Lost It at the Movies* (in spite of its shortcomings)
superior to Taylor's *Cinema Eye, Cinema Ear*: Kael's book "is
sharp, direct, angular, *disrespectful*, and often *acidulous*"; Taylor's "is smooth, urbane, *reverential*, often evasive, and always
mellifluous." The italics are mine.

Macdonald comes much closer to defining the critic's job—and
to describing his own practice—when, in his review of the Kael,
he lists three tasks for criticism: "1) to judge the quality of the
film; 2) to state precisely, with examples, just why one thinks it
good, bad, or indifferent; and 3) to relate it to other films and the
history of the art." Even here, however, Macdonald suggests that
of the three functions, the first—rendering a verdict—is the most
important. There are nitwits on the scene who insist that evaluation has nothing to do with criticism, and perhaps Macdonald is
overreacting to them. Whatever the reason, he puts too much
stress on the judicial function.

If the critic describes, analyzes, and interprets a film as objec-
tively as possible, the reader will need little help in arriving at
an estimate of the picture's worth. The critic's evaluation, that
is, should be woven throughout his presentation; if at the end
of his review or essay he wishes to make his judgment explicit,
no harm is done. But it would seem only proper that
evaluation follow analysis, not the other way around. The latter
procedure tends to get the cart before the horse. Contrary to
what critics might like to think in their more vainglorious moments, the serious reader is more interested in understanding a
film than in hearing the critic's judgment of it. To be sure, the
reader normally also welcomes the judgment; but in the process
of getting it, he doesn't want to be treated like a fool. Which is

how he might feel if, at the start, the critic raps out a verdict and then proceeds to explain why the poor dunce of a reader should agree with him. The implicit judgment, and the judgment which follows the presentation of evidence, leave the reader feeling that he has arrived at the evaluation himself, or that he has at least been persuaded in a reasonable manner. It is a question of emphasis, strategy. My quarrel with Macdonald on procedural matters, however, is not of crucial significance. Provided the critic *does* "state precisely, with examples, just why [he] thinks [a film] good, bad, or indifferent," he has done his job, or a large part of it. And if, in addition, he relates the picture "to other films and the history of the art," so much the better.

What a critic says of other critics often reveals much about his own approach to films, a point which has already been suggested in my commentary regarding Macdonald's assessments of Kael and Taylor. Not surprisingly, Macdonald writes most warmly about his friend, Agee. The latter's strengths as a critic, Macdonald contends, are a love of the medium, "intellectual power," "a broad cultural background," "moral independence," and a knack for writing. Macdonald's criticism possesses these same qualities. Take, for example, the matter of style. Macdonald is not only right up there as a writer with Agee, Kael, and Young, but he is also the wittiest of American film critics. Even if one doesn't agree with his opinion of *Morgan!*, for example, one must still admire his treatment of that film's ending:

> But stay! What is this vision materializing, in extreme close-up? I vow 'tis Vanessa Redgrave, no more his wife, true, yet pregnant and smiling. Our hero looks up from his occupationally therapeutic gardening at this vision of well-groomed, well-to-do beauty and asks, "Mine?" and she smiles, she smiles, she smiles, and after a while he gets it—'e's not tha quickest lad, oor Morgan—and he smiles, they both smile and Morgan is a man again and the camera pulls back and up and we see that the flower bed he's been working on is a huge hammer and sickle and its a jolly cute ending which nobody can deny.

As much as Mcdonald admires Agee's criticism, he thinks that the latter's love for the movies occasionally gets the better of him, with the result that false meanings are read into a picture or improper evaluations rendered. "A lover sees many aspects, mostly interesting ones, of his beloved that more objective observers miss," Macdonald observes, "but he also sees many aspects, mostly interesting ones, that aren't there." One need not agree with Macdonald's censure of Agee to observe that, although he also loves movies, Macdonald has an ability to maintain a critical objectivity which keeps that love within proper limits. He reports that Agee "always looked at the parts [of a film], I always at the whole" ("Agee and the Movies"). In his essay on *Monsieur Verdoux*, Macdonald argues that Agee praised Chaplin's film not because of its cinematic artistry—which according to Macdonald, the film lacks—but because of its content. Ironically, Kael has made the same charge against Macdonald himself. "The liberal audience," she writes in *Kiss Kiss Bang Bang*, "may be so touched by a film on a contemporary political subject or a contemporary experience of any kind that some may be willing to overlook the nature and quality of the contact, like Dwight Macdonald when he hailed *To Die in Madrid* as a masterpiece. It's a simple mistake in the arts to assume that anything that moves us must be a masterpiece."

The merits Macdonald finds in Kael's criticism—"wit, clarity, and precision," knowledge of her subject, a "sensible" approach, and the ability to both generalize and particularize—are qualities evident in his own work. Furthermore, the weaknesses he finds in her method—"she seems to me stronger on the intellectual than on the aesthetic side," and "she is obsessed with other critics, using their opinions too often as a springboard for her own performance and almost always quoting them adversely, and often unfairly"—are equally revealing. Although Macdonald is fully respectful of a film's intellectual aspect, he approaches cinema as a primarily aesthetic experience. Except when addressing himself to the work of a particular critic, as in a book review, Macdonald ordinarily keeps his mind on the film instead of attacking other critics (his reviews of *8½*, *Monsieur Verdoux*, *The Cardinal*, and *The Birds* are exceptions). When Macdonald does discuss other critics, he is almost invariably fair (his treatment of Taylor is again an exception). One might disagree with Macdonald's judgment but one rarely has the feeling—as one has so often with Kael—that he is deliberately lifting a knee to another critic's groin.

Macdonald clearly distinguishes his own method from that of Warshow in his review of *Monsieur Verdoux*: "Warshow writes [of Chaplin's film] almost entirely in psychological and sociological terms, as was his custom. (Anyone interested in movies or popular culture will find *The Immediate Experience* brilliant and original, but he mustn't expect much aesthetic criticism, or much interest in it.)" Kracauer's sociological approach, in Macdonald's judgment, also does not seem overly pertinent to film art. *From Caligari to Hitler* is in one review called a "good but limited" work; elsewhere it is referred to as "an interesting over-demonstration" of a political thesis.

According to Macdonald in his introduction to *Acid Test*, Simon is a "good critic"—a combination balloon-pricker and Matthew Arnold. In addition, Simon is "fair-minded" and "tolerant of and generous to other critics." The essay is not, unfortunately, one of Macdonald's more perceptive ventures into criticism of criticism; however, the article does throw light on Macdonald, if little on Simon. At one point, Macdonald refers to his colleague's weakness for puns and admits to having the same weakness himself. He does not see, though, that the abilities credited to the author of *Acid Test* are largely projections of his own talents into the work of another. A critic's "loyalty is not to friends, ideologies, or movements," Macdonald argues, "but only to the quality of the specific work he is considering." He proves this statement in his later essay on 8½ by taking Simon to task for "finding nothing to praise" in Fellini's "obvious masterpiece." In Macdonald's judgment, Simon has a polemical ax to grind. After analyzing one of the latter's sentences directed against 8½, Macdonald concludes that it is "about as obtuse or perverse or both as you could get in eighteen words."

It is always reassuring to see reason come out on top.

4

One can discern Macdonald's various critical approaches at
work in "The Biblical Spectacular," reviews of *Ben-Hur, King of
Kings, The Greatest Story Ever Told,* and *The Gospel According
to St. Matthew.*

Because *Ben-Hur* is a "spectacle," Macdonald writes, many
critics assume it "must be judged by modest aesthetic standards."
Noting parenthetically that *The Birth of a Nation, Intolerance,*
and *Potemkin* are likewise "spectacles," he proceeds to attack
William Wyler's film precisely where it is supposed to be at its
best. "The big spectacular moments—the seafight, the Roman
triumph, the chariot race—failed because Wyler doesn't know
how to handle crowds nor how to get a culminating rhythm by
cutting," Macdonald explains. "He tries to make up for this lack
by huge sets and thousands of extras, but a Griffith can make a
hundred into a crowd while a Wyler can reduce a thousand to a
confused cocktail party." The sets and props look fake; and the
color is "the glaring kind that makes people stand out like wax-
works, with no relation to the background." Although there is
little sex in the film, there's plenty of sadism: devoid of either a
sense of awe or tragedy, the crucifixion remains, quite simply, a
brutal event. The story is static, the characters flat, the acting
wooden. *Ben-Hur* is "bloody in every way—bloody bloody and
bloody boring."

Nicholas Ray's *King of Kings* is only a slight improvement over
Ben-Hur, as the beauty of the Gospel story again gives way to
sensation, sadism, and sentimentality. Once more, the characters
are stereotypes and the acting is almost uniformly bad; and once
more, the *mise en scène* appears false. The Last Supper, for
example, resembles a "suburban cookout with picnic tables and
bowls of tossed salad." According to Macdonald, the "genre is
hopeless. . . . On the evidence of such films, we are neither a
Christian nor an artistic nation." Then, clearly demarcating
analytical or formalistic criticism from nonartistic commentary,
Macdonald raises two further points. He observes that "1) only
those miracles are shown which can be explained naturally, post-

Freud: the healing of the blind man and of the paralytic; 2) the responsibility for the crucifixion is again displaced from the Jews to the Romans, who are again made the fall goys." Macdonald (who describes himself as "a WASP by upbringing" and "a lapsed Presbyterian") concludes once more that neither the film-makers nor their audience are truly devout.

After his review of *Ben-Hur*, Macdonald received many angry letters from Jews accusing him of "bigotry." Macdonald concedes that the Gospel account might be in error in depicting the Jews as responsible for Christ's death; perhaps the Romans were more guilty than the records suggest. All the same, he refuses to be tagged as an anti-Semite. No racial group, he argues, is "sacro-sanct"; if one declares that a group of Jews twenty centuries ago contrived in the death of Christ, one should not necessarily be open to the charge of branding today's Jews as "Christ killers." At the present time, if a critic pans a black film actor, he receives letters reviling him for being "anti-negro." Says Macdonald: "I daresay that if one referred to what Sitting Bull did to General Custer, some Indian Protective league would jump into action." As a reviewer, Macdonald reserves the right to state matters as he sees them, "free to joke, praise, or criticize" any human group. "Myself, I should consider it humiliating to be exempted, like a child or a lunatic, from the ordinary give and take of discussion, and I think the common 'liberal' attitude today of so exempting Jews and negroes is patronizing."

The Greatest Story Ever Told is still another failure. Little authentic sense of history emerges from George Stevens's mish-mash; for example, once again a nonJewish actor (here Max Von Sydow) plays Christ. Also, with the exception of Judas, most of the disciples are not Jewish. Too many well-known actors appear in "cameo" parts. Macdonald describes the Woman of No Name "who pushes through the crowd as Jesus is healing the sick and, after he has grappled with her, cries out in purest Bronx, 'Oi'm cured! Oi'm cured!' and turns around to run toward the camera with arms waving in triumph—and damned if it isn't Shelley Winters. A shock like that can suspend belief for quite a while." Pictorially, the film is a Hallmark greeting card; the music is "more Wagnerian than Christian"; the Lord's Prayer "gets lost" in the Ultra Panavision 70 scenery; and the content is "theologically circumspect." ("The Romans are the bad goys again—though Pilate looks Jewish for some reason—and the Jews couldn't be more friendly to the founder of Christianity.")

Although Macdonald, as noted, claims that a film critic should not write for film-makers and should not offer directors advice on how to fashion better pictures, he does exactly that in his review of *The Greatest Story Ever Told*. On the evidence of Hollywood's biblical spectacular, he submits five rules for future success: 1) use the Bible alone as source material (avoid the Fulton Ourslers); 2) cast unknown actors; 3) aim for authenticity—make the past seem as alive as the present; 4) "Keep it small. In spirit: no dramatics, sparing use of emphatic close-ups and photography, no underlining of a story that still moves us precisely because it is not underlined. . . . Also keep it small literally: no wide screen, no stereophonic sound, no swelling-sobbing mood music (maybe no music at all), no gigantic sets or vast landscapes or thousands of extras milling around"; and 5) tell the greatest story reverently, according to the text but with awareness of the latest historical studies, and regard the feelings of modern groups—Catholic, Jewish, Buddhist, Taoist, or Moslem—irreverently.

Pier Paolo Pasolini's *The Gospel According to St. Matthew* is a better film than its Hollywood predecessors. The Italian remains faithful to the Bible; the past lives again because the treatment is "non-picturesque"; and the landscape and people both seem authentic. During the first half hour, Macdonald felt that perhaps Pasolini had mastered the difficulties of his chosen genre. Later, however, the film began to disappoint him. Pasolini's excessive reliance on the close-up—which at first seemed to bring the characters to artistic life—soon had a deadening effect. Realism vanished, and words like "arty" and "high camp" describe the result. The worst aesthetic offense, in Macdonald's view, is a twenty-minute scene of Christ in a tight close-up, preaching the Sermon on the Mount. Hence the climax of the film—or what should have been its climax—is monotonously presented. "I don't like to be preached at for twenty minutes head-on in a movie even by Jesus Christ, in whose Message I have the liveliest and most respectful interest." Macdonald concludes by questioning Pasolini's fundamental conception of Christ. As presented in *The Gospel According to St. Matthew*, the great spiritual teacher appears "an unsmiling fanatic, a reserved bureaucrat, combining the worst features of Trotsky and Stalin." The Marxist Pasolini has thus replaced sentimentality, Macdonald argues, with an equally unsatisfactory austerity.

As can be seen from Macdonald's essays on "The Biblical Spectacular," he mainly asks of a film that it succeed artistically; but he supplements his basically formalistic approach with probing questions about the historicity of the movie, its moral significance, and its social ramifications. His critiques are presented in an orderly, systematic way, leavened by wit and humor. At his best, Macdonald reviews not only a film but also the temper of an entire culture.

5

Macdonald has a fairly balanced view of film history, finding good and bad works in every period. He defines these periods as follows: 1) The classic silent period (1908–1929); 2) the early, or medieval, sound period (1930–1955); and 3) the later, or renaissance, sound period (1956 to date). American, German, and Russian film-makers dominate the first period: Griffith, Stroheim, Murnau, Lang, Pabst, Eisenstein, Pudovkin, and Dovzhenko. The second period—"which could also be called 'primitive' if the comparison is to the later sound period, or 'decadent' if to the earlier silent period"—witnesses the demise of the German film and the near demise of the Russian film, both destroyed by authoritarian governments. Elsewhere the coming of sound caused a temporary "regression." Nevertheless, some good work was done: Eisenstein's *Ivan the Terrible*, Mark Donskoi's *The Gorky Trilogy*, Vigo's *Zéro de Conduite*, Renoir's *Grand Illusion* and *Rules of the Game*, Carné's *Children of Paradise*, De Sica's *The Bicycle Thief* and *Shoeshine*, Rossellini's *Open City* and *Paisan*, and some pictures by Hawks, Ford, Lubitsch, Welles, and Clair. The third period returns the cinema to the greatness of the silent period. "After the doldrums of the thirties and forties, an aesthetic of the sound film is being developed." Directors like Fellini, Antonioni, Bergman, Buñuel, Kurosawa, Truffaut, and Resnais are making the sound track "a structural element and not just an ornamental gimmick pasted on by the engineers." Ironically, the renaissance of the film has occurred everywhere save in those countries (the United States, Germany, and Russia) that dominated the silent period.

As Philip French has observed, Macdonald is not wholly stable in his judgments of films in the second and third periods. To quote French: Macdonald "writes in 1942 that 'it has been many years now since, anywhere in the world, a film has been made which, aesthetically speaking, is cinema at all,' only to refer a few pages later to *Grand Illusion* and *The Rules of the Game* as masterpieces and to cite *Citizen Kane* everywhere as a great picture." At different times Macdonald has said: "the reissue of *Children of Paradise* has renewed my faith in the cinema, somewhat tried by recent events" (1960); "when one adds *Breathless* to *L'Avventura, Hiroshima Mon Amour*, and *Shadows*, I think it not premature to say that the sound film, after thirty years of fumbling around, is beginning to develop a style of its own" (1961); "the renascence of the sound film that began with Bergman in the mid-Fifties . . ." (1967); "a depressing aspect of the last two years is the falling off of almost all the major directors . . . perhaps the movies will revive in a few decades or years" (1966). French rightly concludes that such inconsistencies are the "product of loose thinking and random collecting of occasional journalism" (*Sight and Sound,* Spring 1970).

Griffith, according to Macdonald, was an "instinctive genius, creating a whole new art form *ex nihilo*" ("The Eisenstein Tragedy"). He anticipated the Russians in both form (montage) and content (epic subjects). Because Griffith *did* work instinctively, however, his films are uneven, oscillating between "emotional power and bathetic sentimentality . . . From any point of view except a cinematic one, his pictures are absurdities" ("D. W. Griffith, or Genius American Style"). Furthermore, Griffith failed to develop: he had no real insight into either the world or himself; his technique became old-fashioned, his moral ideas passé

("Notes on Hollywood Directors"). Yet *The Birth of a Nation* still looks good to Macdonald "after fifty years of imitation" ("Forenotes").

Eisenstein, as opposed to Griffith, was a self-conscious artist, a theoretician who brought to maturity the cinematic language the American director unthinkingly discovered. In "Our Elizabethan Movies," Macdonald compares Eisenstein to Marlowe. "The inhuman brilliance of their technique quite dominates the slight philosophical content of their work," he observes. "Compared to the mature appreciation of human values that marks a Shakespeare, a Chaucer, or a Protozanov, they are gifted barbarians." Macdonald finds the same "vigorous, pulsating rhythm driving without hesitation towards its climax" in the speeches of Tamburlaine and in the sequence portraying the "Potemkin" as it gets ready for battle. For all his limitations, however, Eisenstein remains in 1960 "the greatest talent the cinema has yet known" ("The Eisenstein Tragedy").

Macdonald has little insight, however, into the art of either Dreyer or Hitchcock. *The Passion of Joan of Arc* is a "sterile and monotonous" film, with symbols instead of characters ("Trims and Clips"). Yet Macdonald praises *The Birth of a Nation* wherein the "characters are not individualized, they are more like mythological personages, abstract and simple, than like real people" (*"The Cranes Are Flying"*). As for Hitchcock, he is at best, says Macdonald, a mere craftsman; the critic much prefers the early Hitchcock to the later one. During his English period, Macdonald remarks, the director's work was characterized by "technical brilliance," superficial realism, "economy of means," and "tight, logical plots." In Macdonald's judgment, *Psycho* is "third-rate Hitchcock, a Grand Guignol drama" and *The Birds* is practically all bad. In the latter film, the *mise en scène* seems fake, the characters unreal, and the plot largely devoted to "extraneous matters"—in other words, it isn't "tight" or "logical."

In "Forenotes," Macdonald says that he has seen *Citizen Kane* "seven or eight times, and it's still fresh." It is, in short, a masterpiece. And *The Magnificent Ambersons* is a "near-masterpiece." Welles, says Macdonald, needs a realistic story to keep his filmic imagination under control. "In *Othello* Welles might have had something solid to push against, but he escaped, with a loud hiss, into cinematic camp. In *Mr. Arkadin* and *Touch of Evil* he let himself go, like an overweight matron indulging in desserts, in melodramas which seem to have been whipped up entirely for theatrical effect." Similarly, Welles's adaptation of Kafka (his "style has never been more baroque") remains a failure (*"The Trial"*).

Macdonald is also not overly sympathetic to the body of Bergman's work. He considers *The Naked Night* the Swedish director's best film, closely followed by *Wild Strawberries*; but for the others—well, there just doesn't seem to be that much there, really. Like *The Passion of Joan of Arc*, *The Seventh Seal* has symbols in place of characters. *Through a Glass Darkly* is better than most Bergman films—it's "classically compact"—but there's "too much talk" (this is, according to Macdonald, "a Bergman fault") and "too much heavy dramatics"; as for the theme ("that people should love each other and that much unhappiness is caused by their inability to communicate"), it's a mere exercise in "banality." Bergman's problems fail to interest Macdonald: "I don't feel guilty, I don't believe in God and am not much interested in whether I'm right or not." Perhaps Bergman could arouse Macdonald's concern if he were more cinematically inventive, but—unfortunately—he's not. "Meanwhile, I shall continue to enjoy the secular portions of [Bergman's] movies," the critic sighs. The review takes up all of two paragraphs.

Winter Light gets three paragraphs, though the third is only two sentences long and part of the second constitutes a long quote from the director himself. Not much room here for the critic to back up his evaluative comments with examples. So we are *told* that *Winter Light* is dull, talky, undramatic, and uncinematic. Compared to *Through a Glass Darkly* and *Winter Light*, however, *The Silence* is "rich." Surprisingly—after what we've heard about Bergman's inability to express his vision in cinematic terms—*The Silence* shows that the Swede "has achieved a mastery of technique that makes most other directors seem clumsy and tongue-tied." A remarkable development! Yet before the brief review is over, we learn that Bergman's symbolism is "heavy-handed," and that the well-worn theme of "noncommunication" is not conveyed with "aesthetic consistency." Macdonald concludes: "If this trilogy is Bergman's idea of accepting life, one wonders what he would give us if he rejected it." To which one might add: If *The Silence* is Macdonald's idea of Bergman's technique at its best, one wonders what he thinks of that technique at its worst.

In "Antonioni: A Position Paper," Macdonald isolates four attributes in the work of the Italian director: 1) "His photography is severe and classical"; 2) he is "a master of calculated composition"; 3) he "is also a master of what might be called film choreography, bringing out the emotional meaning of a scene by the interacting lines of motion of the actors"; and 4) he "can explore character with novelistic subtlety." In his review of *L'Avventura*, Macdonald offers intelligent and perceptive comments on the film's structure, sound track, theme, and subtheme. He thinks the island scene too long, however, and the acting of the main parts uneven. *La Notte*—which failed to please Macdonald—retraces the same themes as *L'Avventura*, but this time Antonioni does not succeed. "It occurred to me that the reasons for his characters's unhappiness have progressively become vaguer in Antonioni's films." *La Notte* lacks even the slight story evident in the previous film, so that in the latest work "nothing happens." *L'Eclisse*, unlike *La Notte* (which at least has some great scenes) is a total failure: it is pretentious, filled with bad acting and arty shots; and it has no content "beyond the most gaseous kind of smart philosophizing." *Red Desert* is also disappointing. As Macdonald sees it, Antonioni's subject matter gets thinner, his technique more mannered with each passing film. In a footnote in "Trims and Clips," however, we are told that *Blow-Up* justified the critic's continuing faith in Antonioni. The 1966 film is "a fast, hard, varied entertainment which substitute[s] satire for angst and [is] delightfully lacking in Monica Vitti."

8½ is a masterpiece. Except for that one film, though, Fellini's work does not come up to Macdonald's standards. *The White Sheik* is crude beside Antonioni's *La Signora Senza Camelie; La Strada* leaves a "sentimental aftertaste"; *La Dolce Vita* is "sensationalized, inflated, and cinematically conventional"; and *I Vitteloni* has not worn well. Only *The Nights of Cabiria*, prior to *8½*, comes near satisfying Macdonald's requirements. In 8½ there is a "constant shifting of gears"; however, "you always know what gear you're in." Fellini "has found the objective forms in which to communicate his subjective explorations." The theme is expressed "not in Bergmanesque symbols" but "in episodes that arise naturally out of the drama." Visually, the film is a delight from beginning to end. "I hazard that 8½ is Fellini's masterpiece precisely because it is about the two subjects he knows the most about: himself and the making of movies." But *Juliet of the Spirits*, according to Macdonald, is still another Fellini disaster.

In Macdonald's hands, Kurosawa doesn't fare much better than Bergman or Fellini. *Rashomon* and *They Who Step on the Tiger's Tail* "are the best Kurosawa I've seen, because they are all of a piece." Generally, however, Kurosawa strikes Macdonald as a director "who is unsure of his style," because he has "a tendency to overlabor and repeat"—*Ikiru*, if we are to believe Macdonald, shows this—and to mix-up "incompatible genres." *The Hidden Fortress* is "a potboiler"; *Throne of Blood*, based on *Macbeth*, "omits the poetry, the psychology—and the tragedy. What's left is cops and robbers"; and *Yojimbo* is even worse than *The Hidden Fortress*.

Breathless, in 1961, was praised by Macdonald. By 1966, though, Godard's style "had been imitated so much by others, and by himself, that the originality was less apparent than the new conventions its success had established. The whole film had dimmed, and I was irritated—and bored—by the same artifices that had delighted me when Godard first invented them." *A Woman Is a Woman* Macdonald found "resistible" and *My Life to Live* "tedious." So much for Godard.

The 400 Blows, Macdonald believes, is a "minor classic." I have already commented on his opinion of *Shoot the Piano Player*. *Jules and Jim* remains Truffaut's most important film, as of 1962, although Macdonald still has reservations about the director's fondness for alternating moods. He calls each of Truffaut's first three pictures a "triumph" but brands *The Soft Skin* a failure: we know little more about the characters at the end of the latter film than we knew at the start; in short, the Scribean plot is all. Before leaving Truffaut, Macdonald discusses the director's two main traits: "He takes you right into the kitchen, communicating his delight in the very process of making a movie, the pleasure, sensuous and intellectual, of making statements that couldn't be as well stated in any other medium. And he has a peculiar knack for presenting a *mise en scène* that is neither bigger than life (Welles, Resnais) nor smaller than life (Bresson, Olmi) but exactly life-size."

Initially, *Hiroshima Mon Amour* was called "the most original, exciting, and important movie" Macdonald had seen in years. Like *Breathless*, though, Resnais's film does not encourage repeated viewings, since over the years its innovations have become commonplace. The critic's revised opinion of *Last Year at Marienbad* was referred to earlier. Macdonald has some trenchant remarks to offer on Resnais's *Night and Fog*, a documentary about the Nazi death camps. The film "included much gruesome material—too much for me, I had to close my eyes several times." But Resnais knows "how to resensitize the spectator by a change of pace, by using such material only for the dramatic highlights of a composition that is predominantly muted grays and browns. Some things are too terrible to be looked on without the mediation of art; like wearing smoked glasses to look at the sun." Mainly, Resnais achieves aesthetic distance by switching back and forth from the present to the past, "using color shots of the weed-grown, pastoral ruins of the camps today to contrast with black-and-white shots of the terrible past." Macdonald concludes: "Such devices assimilate these infernos to everyday experience; this doesn't make them less infernal—on the contrary—but it makes it possible to experience them emotionally."

Macdonald is at his best when discussing Griffith, Eisenstein, Antonioni, Truffaut, and Resnais. He is less rewarding to read when dealing with Welles, Bergman, Fellini, Kurosawa, Godard, Hitchcock, and Dreyer. As previously noted, Macdonald's trouble is that he is often too eager to evaluate, especially in a negative way. Truffaut, a former critic, has remarked: "What is worthwhile, yet difficult, is analysis. . . . What is interesting is not pronouncing a film good or bad, but explaining why" (*Film Quarterly*, Fall 1963). In his review of *I Lost It at the Movies*,

Macdonald writes of Kael: "I often disagreed strongly, but since she always gives specific reasons and examples for her opinions, I knew just where and why we parted company; as with any good critic, one learns from her misses as well as from her hits." In general, Macdonald's comments on Kael can with more justice be applied to his own criticism. He does not give the reader enough analysis or explanation or examples when discussing certain Bergman and Fellini and Kurosawa films, but he does so regularly enough in his critiques of other directors to make him very much worth reading.

There are American film critics who seem to think that the tougher they are, the better their criticism. And there are readers —the kind that are easily intimidated—who apparently share in their delusion. Agee, Kauffmann, Young, and Macdonald are our finest movie critics, however, not because they are difficult to please (after all, Simon and Kael are also difficult to please) but because, when they like a film, they tell us more about it than other critics do: they see deeper into it—see the art that is there, and also what that art means in the context of this picture, of other pictures by the same artist, and of the human condition. Film criticism can scarcely do more.

APPENDIX

Film-Makers on Film Critics

"No film-maker likes critics, no matter how nice they are to him. Always, he feels that they didn't say enough about him, or that they didn't say nice things in an interesting way, or that they said too many of their nice things about other directors. Since I was a critic, I am perhaps less hostile to critics than other directors are."

—François Truffaut

.   .   .

"I learn more from critics who honestly criticize my pictures than from those who are devout."

—Ingmar Bergman

.   .   .

"To criticism we owe not excluding one aspect of the cinema in the name of another aspect of the cinema. We owe it also the possibility of making films with more distance and of knowing that if such and such a thing has already been done it is useless to do it again."

—Jean-Luc Godard

.   .   .

"The critic merely by saying, 'I am a critic,' inflates himself and causes himself to see not what exists but what he thinks ought to exist. But things are only what they are. Therefore, the critic is usually mistaken. A truly humble critic would look at things from the inside, not from the outside. If the thing is vital and you look at it from your external point of view, you will never understand but will only project onto it what you think it should be."

—Federico Fellini

.   .   .

"A Danish critic said to me one day, 'I have the impression that there are at least six of your films that are stylistically completely different, one from the other.' This moved me, for that is something I really tried to do."

—CARL DREYER

. . .

"My father was a film critic. I went to screenings with him when I was small, two or three films every day."

—BERNARDO BERTOLUCCI

. . .

"You highbrows writing on movies are nuts! In order to write about movies you must first make them."

—ORSON WELLES

. . .

"Sometimes I pick up a magazine and read a piece of film criticism— to the end only if I like it. I don't like those which are too free with praise because their reasons seem wrong and that annoys me. Critics who attack me do so for such contradictory reasons that they confuse me, and I am afraid that if I am influenced by one, I will sin according to the standards of the other."

—MICHELANGELO ANTONIONI

. . .

"I've never read a critic who didn't put false meanings into my work."

—AKIRA KUROSAWA

. . .

"I am never affected by critics. I don't esteem. I go my own way, mistaken or not. I trust my conscience and my sensibility."

—VITTORIO DE SICA

. . .

"At last you give the finished picture to the audience and along comes a reviewer who has to meet a morning edition deadline. In addition, perhaps his wife is betraying him or maybe he has hemorrhoids or something. In any case, he cannot write an honest review; and, good or bad, favorable or unfavorable, I cannot accept it. That's why I don't give a damn about reviews."

—Fritz Lang

. . .

"With the exception of a number that you could count on one hand, people who write about film are journalists who went into this field because they didn't know what else to do. Instead of helping get an audience for the director, they damage him."

—Ermanno Olmi

. . .

"I am surprised that some critics say that my camera technique is old-fashioned, that I have not kept up with the times. What times? My technique is the outcome of thinking for myself, of my own logic and approach; it is not borrowed from what others are doing. If in art one must keep up with the times, then Rembrandt would be a back number compared to Van Gogh."

—Charlie Chaplin

. . .

"I try to put myself in the place of the critic."

—Jean Renoir

. . .

"I read the *Cahiers du Cinema.* Sometimes I'm very amused at reading these very nice articles about my work . . . And then I read what they think of other gentlemen and I think . . . Well, I don't know what to think. I'm not so sure, then, that their judgment is all that . . . [unfinished]."

—George Cukor

. . .

"You see, when a director has been let down by the critics, when he feels that his work has been passed on too lightly, his only recourse is to seek recognition via the public. Of course, if a film-maker thinks solely in box-office terms, he will wind up doing routine stuff, and that's bad too. It seems to me that the critics are often responsible for this attitude; they drive a man to make only so-called public-acceptance pictures. Because he can always say to himself, 'I don't give a damn about the critics, my films make money.' There is a famous saying here in Hollywood: 'You can't take a review to the bank!' Some magazines deliberately select critics who don't care about films, but are able to write about them in a condescending way that will amuse the readers."

—ALFRED HITCHCOCK

. . .

"The more vicious a critic is in print, the more cowardly in person."

—LINDSAY ANDERSON

. . .

"I think too many critics write about a movie as though it exists alone in time. This is crazy. You have to take every movie not only in the perspective of the other films of that director, but also in the whole context of film history—which isn't very long, so I don't know why it isn't done. The worst thing we have in film writing is a lack of film scholarship and the fact that the first thirty years are virtually lost. A whole school of critics think they like movies, but they don't. They think it's all very nice to like films—within limits. You can't have a passion for them, because after all, it's still a bit juvenile to sit in a movie theater for six hours. . . . However, people who read books for hours are eggheads, geniuses. It's really a kind of Victorian anti-movie theory."

—PETER BOGDANOVICH

. . .

"I am glad when the reviews are good. When they are bad, either it is my fault or the reviewer was in a bad mood. For the most part, I think I've been well treated by critics."

—RENÉ CLAIR

. . .

"The major New York critics are deliberately laying for individual directors. . . . They begin to view film criticism as some form of creative art, with each one performing a specific role. Pauline Kael is 'The Great Debunker'. . . . The height of absurdity was reached in a recent review of the critical work of Parker Tyler. The reviewer started out by saying, 'I don't go to the movies, but I love reading books of film criticism.' The whole situation has become ridiculous. And I think it has a lot to do with career building."

—SIDNEY LUMET

. . .

"I don't care what a critic says about a picture so long as he loves films, so long as he hates the particular example because he loves film in general."

—CAROL REED

. . .

"I think that it would be interesting and basically democratic if there were a forum where producers, directors, actors could face the critic after the criticism, of course in a civilized way, and he would face the creators of the picture and discuss with them his review, give them explanations and be open to criticism himself. Right now it is impossible to criticize the critic. . . . I think that would take criticism one step further into real honest controversy, not a controversy that somebody starts and it stops right there because the other party has no way to answer."

—OTTO PREMINGER

INDEX

Film Titles and Directors